THE CHELSKI REVOLUTION

THE
CHELSKI
REVOLUTION

HARRY HARRIS

JOHN BLAKE

Published by John Blake Publishing Ltd,
3, Bramber Court, 2 Bramber Road,
London W14 9PB, England

www.blake.co.uk

First published in paperback in 2004

ISBN 1 84454 082 0

British Library Cataloguing-in-Publication Data:

A catalogue record for this book is available from the British Library.

Design by www.envydesign.co.uk

Printed in Great Britain by Bookmarque, Croydon

1 3 5 7 9 10 8 6 4 2

Papers used by John Blake Publishing are natural, recyclable products made
from wood grown in sustainable forests. The manufacturing processes
conform to the environmental regulations of the country of origin.

Pictures reproduced by kind permission of Camera Press,
Francis Glibbery and the Daily Express

Every attempt has been made to contact the relevant copyright-holders,
but some were unobtainable. We would be grateful if the appropriate
people could contact us.

To Poppy, a new Junior Blue.

Acknowledgements

For their invaluable contributions and insights, my thanks to Roman Abramovich's PR John Mann; Giancarlo Galavotti of Gazzetta della Sport; Pini Zahavi; Chairman Ken Bates; former Chief Executive Trevor Birch; Keith Harris of Chelsea's financial advisers Seymour Pierce; Mel Goldberg; David Mellor; Vanessa Obagi, the Marketing and PR Manager at Chelsea TV; and for the numerous 'exclusive' interviews.

Special thanks to John Blake for the foresight to launch the book early while other publishers were unable to have the same vision to do so. My gratitude, too, to Adam Parfitt, Editor-in-Chief at Blake Publishing.

CONTENTS

CHELSKI ...
OR CHELSKOV?

*'Roman Abramovich has parked his Russian tanks
on our lawn and is firing £50 notes at us.'*
DAVID DEIN, ARSENAL VICE-CHAIRMAN

ROMAN ABRAMOVICH'S TAKEOVER OF Chelsea turned the football
world upside down with the biggest spending spree in the history
of the game – 11 new players for £110m in seven weeks, which left the rest
of the global game gasping in disbelief. All the established principles of
belt-tightening in a depreciating football economy were instantly
eradicated.

Appropriately, in Monte Carlo, the Russian multi-billionaire parked one
of the world's largest yachts in the marina, and watched the draw for the
Champions League via a satellite link, while Chairman Ken Bates
represented the Chelsea delegation at the ceremony. Europe's élite were
taking notice of the new Chelsea, and the all powerful G-14 group, the
collective of Europe's pre-eminent clubs, invited them aboard.

Arsenal Vice-Chairman David Dein also attended the Champions League
draw in Monaco, and conceded that the Russian revolution at Stamford
Bridge could change the face of English football and clearly threaten the
Gunners' position as London's dominant club for the first time in decades.
Dein said, 'Roman Abramovich has parked his Russian tanks on our lawn
and is firing 50-pound notes at us.'

Was it a joke, an insult, or just jealousy? As Chelsea's summer spending surpassed the magical £100m mark, their London rivals had spent a trifling £1.5m on goalkeeper Jens Lehmann.

Former Inter Milan defensive legend Giacinto Facchetti, now Vice-President of the San Siro side, said, 'In every time there is one president who comes into football and wants to make his club very strong and very important. Abramovich is the one now and he is trying to buy great players for his club to make them big. It's not the first time it has happened. We have had Berlusconi, Moratti and Cragnotti. Now we have Abramovich. You have to take Chelsea seriously. They are suddenly at the same level as Arsenal and Manchester United.'

Though money cannot guarantee landing them the championship, Chelsea's transfer frenzy at the start of the new Roman Empire pushed them instantly to the top of the Premiership wage-bill table at £1.5m a week. The Russian oil billionaire's deep pockets can cope, but the new arrivals in a frenzied orgy of summer spending swelled their annual expenditure on salaries to more than £70m. At a time when other top clubs are reducing their expenditure, particularly on players' salaries, this total exceeds their rivals Manchester United and Arsenal.

Chelsea's wage bill has increased steadily over the past few seasons, reaching £55.9m for 2001/02 – a rise of 11 per cent from the previous year, according to the Deloitte and Touche *Review of Football Finance*. This rose little during the summer of 2002/03, when Chelsea splashed out just £500,000 on transfers, but the world record spree of £110m on 11 new signings transformed a club strapped for cash before the takeover on 2 July into the biggest global spenders in a matter of a week.

Hernan Crespo and Juan Veron arrived as the highest wage-earners. There was, though, some initial difference of opinion within the Chelsea hierarchy about whether Veron was actually worth the £15m fee to Manchester United, as well as wage demands that exceeded £95,000 per week. It was decided that the answer was 'yes', though there is a limit to Chelsea's largesse, because the club were unwilling to meet Christian Vieri's demands for £120,000 a week and Inter's £25m transfer fee for a 30-year-old. Instead, Chelsea purchased Crespo from Inter for £16.8m and then signed Claude Makelele from Real Madrid for £16.8m.

Let's face it ... signing stars from such exalted clubs as Manchester United and Real Madrid would have been simply unthinkable just weeks earlier.

Manager Claudio Ranieri wanted 'champions', as he called them; players who had won titles, Makelele, Veron and Crespo, and they followed

Glen Johnson (£6m from West Ham), Damien Duff (£17m from Blackburn), Geremi (£6.9m from Real Madrid), Wayne Bridge (£7m from Southampton), Joe Cole (£6.6m from West Ham), Neil Sullivan (£500,000 from Spurs), and another spectacular purchase, Adrian Mutu from Parma, to replace Franco Zola.

Chelsea stalwarts John Terry, Eidur Gudjohnsen and William Gallas all received major pay rises when signing contract extensions.

Despite the new-found playing talent, Chelsea remained well behind their rivals in one vital area – training facilities. While Manchester United have the hi-tech Carrington complex and Arsenal have wonderful facilities at London Colney, Chelsea still train in Harlington on pitches owned by Imperial College, next to the M4 near Heathrow Airport. While these may be good by university standards, they pale into insignificance behind most in the Premiership who have custom-built centres. The matter has not escaped Abramovich's attention. Speaking from his base in Chukotka, where he is a governor, he said, 'I met the players once during training and we agree on the necessity of building a new training ground.' Apparently, the £20m or so it would cost is no longer prohibitive!

But it was the spending power in the transfer market and the sheer speed of the transactions that caught the game's imagination throughout the world. Almost single-handedly, Abramovich had reignited a stagnant transfer market in the Premiership. The knock-on effect of his spending spree was that clubs such as West Ham had cash with which to survive after selling Cole and Johnson; Southampton had funds to spend on Kevin Phillips after selling Bridge; and Blackburn were flush with money after the departure of Duff for £17m. Graeme Souness signed £7.5m Barry Ferguson and loan star Dino Baggio and said, 'I'm absolutely delighted with what we've done in the transfer market.' Andy Cole was similarly impressed with Rovers' team-building with new arrivals Ferguson and Baggio. The former England striker said, 'When the manager sold Damien Duff and David Dunn, he told me would be bringing in creative replacements and that's what he has done. The new signings will keep creating chances and I'll try to stick them away.'

'Chelski' and 'Red Rom' were immediately coined by the tabloids, finally able to enjoy a feeding frenzy of transfer speculation when previously there was hardly any news beyond David Beckham, Ronaldino and Harry Kewell.

Abramovich's advisers usefully pointed out that 'ski' is a Polish language construction and Chelsea should correctly be labelled

'Chelskov'! But Chelski stuck, fans had 'Kalinka' as the 'in' mobile phone tune, and expectation levels reached fever pitch.

The Chelski Revolution traces the extraordinary events surrounding the Abramovich takeover, with inside information from within the camp. The book unravels the complexities of the rival bids for Bates's shares, the attempts to buy the Harding Estate share holding on the cheap, the 1920 German Government Bonds, the Colombian connection, the shock move by Celtic's Dermot Desmond, and the talks with the Californian Pension Funds, as well as the intrigue of the David Mellor connection.

And what are the ramifications of Chelsea splashing a world record £110m on 11 new recruits in 62 days at an astonishing £1.75m a day? Will the spending end there? What of the galaxy of players who could be available in the January transfer window or next summer, when another £100m at least will be available for even more stars? David Beckham, Brazil captain Emerson, Ronaldo, Raul, Wayne Rooney, Michael Owen and Steven Gerrard are among them. Can they be bought? Who knows? You wouldn't have thought so pre-Abramovich ... but now anything is possible.

With Abramovich's millions as ammunition, Chelsea are gunning for glory at home and in Europe. While another title contender is welcome, it is worth examining the depth of the envy of rival managers and chairmen, notably Sir Alex Ferguson and Arséne Wenger, whose transfer budget was slashed because of Arsenal's financial burden of a £400m move to Ashburton Grove.

'What's happened at Chelsea is incredible,' says Colin Gordon, one of many football agents wondering where their next transfer commission is coming from. 'I can't think of any parallel anywhere else in football, ever.'

Gordon, whose clients include David James and Shola Ameobi, thought he knew all the sub-plots of this overhyped transfer market. But he happily admits he was wrong. 'The way Chelsea are spending Abramovich's money, and planning to spend even more money, is utterly unique – buying almost an entire team of proven performers in a very short space of time. It's galling even for Manchester United and Arsenal because they can't compete, and I never thought I'd hear myself say that. Chelsea are probably now in a class of one in terms of being able to buy players. The implications could be huge.'

Potentially, the impact of the new order at Chelsea will have massive repercussions, not just for the club and the rest of the Premiership. There is the question of the future of the England Head Coach, with Sven-Goran Eriksson having been widely touted as the man to take over from Claudio

Ranieri. Here, there is an opportunity to examine in detail the infamous meeting between Abramovich and Eriksson four days before the new owner was introduced to Ranieri. Alternatively, having recruited Manchester United chief executive Peter Kenyon, would they eventually like Sir Alex Ferguson to come to the Bridge?

Significantly, Abramovich's arrival may also result in a shift in the balance of power of English football and could even change the culture of the sport.

Senior figures within football are still stunned by the speed and scale of the Russian's revolution in SW6, where the new Chelsea team is quickly coming together.

Stamford Bridge has instantly become the Premiership's new soap opera. Beyond the headlines, though, Abramovich's takeover raises a raft of fascinating and important questions. Will his new Chelsea gel? Will the Premiership be more competitive? Will it send transfer fees and salaries sky high again? Might it force clubs to spend money they do not have? Can all that money buy success anyway? And is there at last a serious new challenger to the total domination that Manchester United and Arsenal have exercised for the past five years?

'Chelsea changing hands has breathed fresh excitement into football. I think it's going to be an amazing Premiership contested by the same four or five teams [as last season], but with added fascination now,' says Paul Elliott, the former Chelsea and Celtic centre-half. 'Abramovich is building a mini Real Madrid in the Premiership. I can see the vision he has long term, to dominate the Premiership with a European style.' Elliott says that it is impossible to evaluate how the creation of 'Chelski' will affect everyone else in the top flight 'because it is a unique deal'.

But that has not stopped the managers, chairmen and chief executives of many of Chelsea's Premiership rivals starting to worry that Abramovich's huge wealth will resurrect two damaging traits in English football – clubs paying over the odds to sign players and big names successfully demanding unreasonably high salaries.

Comparisons are drawn between today's 'new Chelsea' and the Jack Walker-funded Blackburn Rovers team which pipped Manchester United to the Premiership title on the last day of the season in 1995. Kenny Dalglish's squad cost more than £25m to assemble, a fortune in those days. Almost all of Blackburn's money went on British talent, including Alan Shearer and Chris Sutton. Henning Berg was the sole foreigner. But football has become much more cosmopolitan since then. So far, Chelsea – or, to be specific, the kingpin Israeli football agent Pini Zahavi, Abramovich's headhunter-cum-adviser – bought or targeted both Premiership players and foreigners.

There is another important difference. Barring the odd player recruited personally by a chairman, managers in the English league have always had the biggest say over who was bought and sold. Dalglish found or approved all Blackburn's buys. Ranieri, though, was among the last to find out about Johnson's arrival and admitted that he did not know whether the new owner had made an offer for Patrick Kluivert or not. But after the initial teething period, Ranieri was regularly consulted and his targets acted upon. But the new methods unfolding at Stamford Bridge make Chelsea the first big British club to adopt the principle – popular in Italy and Spain – of the owner, or president, or chairman, buying the players.

The lesson from home and abroad is that money does not necessarily bring success. Inter spent tens of millions of pounds without landing the *scudetto* in years. Lazio have won a solitary Serie A title, after Eriksson spent £120m on players, and are currently a mind-boggling £150m in debt. In the past decade, Sir John Hall spent big at Newcastle United, Liverpool broke records for the likes of Stan Collymore during the 'Spice Boys' era, and Chelsea themselves previously tried to buy success through European stars such as Ruud Gullit, Gianluca Vialli and Gianfranco Zola. Yet none of these clubs managed to break Manchester United's and Arsenal's stranglehold on the Premiership trophy.

Abramovich is clearly great news for Chelsea with their new-found clout in the transfer market. They surely have to be considered genuine contenders for the title this season. Opinion is divided, though, as to whether the Premiership – now arguably the least competitive and most predictable of Europe's best leagues – will be more than the usual two-horse race.

'In terms of overall competition, it has only upped the ante for one club, and this league needs to be more competitive in general, not just at the top,' says Jon Holmes, the influential agent to stars such as Beckham, Alan Shearer and Michael Owen, who briefly served as Leicester City's Chairman during their recent takeover by a consortium fronted by Gary Lineker.

'I don't see Abramovich's spending making it a more competitive league,' adds another influential agent, Jon Smith. 'For Portsmouth, the problem is that it makes it a less level playing field. Only the strong will get stronger. It'll make the top echelon of the Premiership more competitive. But if they are taking the best players from the likes of Blackburn and

Southampton, then they consequently become weaker. We won't fully appreciate the significance for a year or so.'

Will Ranieri will be around then? Insiders strongly suspect that Eriksson will eventually take over. Results will ultimately determine Ranieri's future.

Chelsea's pursuit of players the England Head Coach admires or has worked with before – Veron, Crespo, Geremi, Bridge – suggests he had some sort of impact. Eriksson's reputation has undoubtedly been tarnished by his now-notorious rendezvous with Abramovich, with several tabloids openly describing him as 'a traitor'. But his stock within football as a highly respected coach is unchanged. Chelsea now look odds-on to grant him the return to club management he craves, but only if Ranieri fails. That could be bad news for the England team because there is no obvious successor-in-waiting, except possibly Steve McClaren at Middlesbrough.

The takeover of Chelsea is also bad news for Arsenal, London's undisputed top club for the past 15 years. At the end of the 2002/03 season, it seemed that Gallas, possibly the best centre-half in the top flight, might move to Highbury. Now he is staying put. In a huge shift in power, it is now Chelsea who are trying to persuade Arsenal's prize assets to join them.

The Gunners' summer was already shaping up badly with Wenger talking to Real Madrid, uncertainty over Vieira's intentions, financial constraints blocking the arrival of any significant new players and the confusion over their proposed new stadium. It just became a lot worse. The possibility of Vieira or Henry one day crossing the Thames is no longer the laughable prospect it was on 1 July.

Heysel, Hillsborough, Bosman – moments or events that change football for ever are rare. The Russian revolution in SW6 is shaping up to be just as significant. Even Sir Alex Ferguson thinks so. When asked to assess whether the situation at Chelsea would change the Premier League for ever, he replied, 'It's possible, but it depends on how well they do in their first season. That might activate a lot of things.'

Arsenal were one of many Premiership clubs Abramovich looked at before he completed his shock takeover of Chelsea. Old Etonian Chairman Hill-Wood says, 'He may have looked at it but he didn't talk to us about it. And we would not have been very receptive if he had. I think his arrival at Chelsea is a positive move and I don't see it does any harm to us. It's not a position that fills me or the rest of the Board at Highbury with dread. Money isn't everything – it's how you spend it and how you invest it. I don't think he's a fool ... I'm sure he can't be a fool ... but I think it's going to be good for competition. There are people who can compete on a higher financial level than us who haven't actually been more successful. So it's not something that worries me at all. I wish him luck and hope he's successful.'

While examining the end of 21 years of the Bates era, and the sad farewell of Gianfranco Zola, *The Chelski Revolution* primarily focuses on the new and exciting chapter in the history of one of England's most prestigious football clubs, the challenge for Manchester United's title and the quest for glory in the Champions League.

Roman Abramovich has transformed Chelsea. Now fans wear CHEL$K* t-shirts and baseball caps, give the Russian owner a standing ovation at every home game where Cossack music is more popular than Blue is the Colour. Abramovich has also transformed English football.

THE BUILDING OF ROMAN'S EMPIRE

THE FOUNDATION STONE OF Roman Arkadyevich Abramovich's fortune lies in oil. His personal worth is now estimated at around £8.2bn. But Abramovich replies, 'It is very difficult for me, I do not sit with a calculator. I do not sit and calculate how much I am worth.' His share of the aluminium Russian industry only serves to add to his vast wealth. There were no pictures published of this intensely private 'oligarch' until 1999, he rarely gives interviews, and there is scarcely any TV footage until he arrived at the Bridge. But with his acquisition of Chelsea, the sudden emergence in English football of Roman Abramovich has changed the dynamics of the Premiership and has stimualted intense speculation about the man whose headquarters overlook the Kremlin across the Moscow River. He is quietly spoken, has an unassuming appearance and seems perfectly comfortable conducting business in trademark jeans and a dark blue Burberry T-shirt and designer stubble. At the age of 36, he hardly gives the appearance of one of the world's wealthiest individuals.

His interests range from aluminium, trucks and hydroelectricity to meat processing and pharmaceuticals; he owned 26 per cent of Aeroflot, Russia's national airline, but sold his stake in February 2003 to the

National Reserve Bank; he was also a member of a consortium of businessmen who helped start up TVS Television on behalf of a 'homeless' group of independent journalists. It never quite garnered the ratings of the TV6, the channel it replaced, and was in turn replaced on its national frequency by a state-owned all-sport channel, Sport.

Abramovich's oil business, Sibneft, announced the following dividend payments in 2003: $1.09bn (announced in March and approved at the annual shareholders' meeting in May) based on 2002 results; $1.006bn (announced in July, and approved at an extraordinary shareholders' meeting in September) based on six-month 2003 results. On 30 September 2003, it was announced that a November extraordinary shareholders' meeting would be asked to approve Sibneft's final pre-merger dividend, with the amount to be determined based on nine-month results and announced in mid-October. All this adds to the mogul's existing wealth and highlights the fact that his takeover bid for Chelsea was effectively 'loose rubles'. It also underpins his profoundly deep pockets if he needs to buy new players for the club.

Sibneft's shares leapt after the announcement. On the Russian stock market, the shares were up 20.2 per cent, adding to Abramovich's wealth on paper. But despite Sibneft's reputation for paying vast dividends, shareholders and analysts were stunned at the size of the payout. 'This is much better than expected,' said sales trader Olga Avdeyeva. Sibneft's policy is to pay out all net profits, minus what is needed to for capital investments, in dividends. This also benefits minority shareholders.

Abramovich's financial successes seem to know no bounds. He is still buying up more assets, including Stalin's biggest tank factory! Megatranskor Group, controlled by him, is buying Siberian plant Omsktransmash from the Russian Government in a £30m deal. Founded in tsarist times, the tank factory played a key part under Stalin's rule in the allied victory during the Second World War. Abramovich wants to switch the company's major output from tanks to tractors and railway carriages.

Abramovich appears to be selling assets more than acquiring new ones. He sold a fifty per cent stake in Russian Aluminuim for $3bn (£1.8bn) to raise his personal fortune to £8.2bn. His investment vehicle, Millhouse Capital, sold the stake in RussAl to Basic Element, controlled by another Russian tycoon Oleg Derispaska. The recent deal made Abramovich the world's richest man under 40.

For the first time since the late Jack Walker bankrolled Blackburn

Rovers to the title in 1995, there is a new buying power in the league, and it certainly adds up to the biggest shake-up in the British football industry since the creation of the Premier League in 1992. Manchester United no longer have a monopoly on cash. Abramovich and his partners have an asset management company called Millhouse Capital, which oversees their stakes in Sibneft, Russian Aluminium, Omsk Bacon, Planeta Management and others. Through Millhouse, funding was passed on to Chelsea Ltd, the company set up to buy Chelsea Village/Chelsea Football Club.

Whatever the actual size of his investment, he is definitely having fun. Abramovich explains, 'I am realising my dreams of owning a top football club. Some will doubt my motives, some will think I am crazy.'

Roman Abramovich was born on 24 October 1966 in Saratov, a city on the Volga. His parents were of Jewish-Ukrainian extraction from southern Russia, but he had little time to benefit from their love and support – his mother died when he was a few months old, and his father died in a construction accident when he was three.

Roman's mother Irina, known affectionately as Irochka, was a piano teacher. She died tragically at 28 having a termination because she could not afford another child. Her only son Roman was a day short of his first birthday when she was killed by blood poisoning in Komi, one of Russia's most remote regions. Irina's decision was hardly uncommon. Many women chose to have abortions rather than give birth to more than one child during a time of severe housing shortages and poor financial prospects.

Eighteen months later, Abramovich's dad Arkady, known by the family as Arkasha, was killed after a crane collapsed on him. He was 32. Arkady discovered a broken jib on the crane during a site visit and, on an already-delayed project, he tried to fix it himself. But the jib fell, crushing his legs and leaving him trapped. He died in hospital ten days later of post-traumatic shock.

Roman's parents met in Saratov in southern Russia. Arkady was studying at the city's Institute of Construction and Building and worked on a collective farm picking potatoes in the bleak autumns. Irina came from a Ukrainian family.

Soon after marrying, the pair returned to Komi where Arkady got a job in construction. Not exactly bristling with nightlife, Komi had one tiny cinema with a repertoire of Soviet propaganda films. After a spell sharing a tiny flat with his mother Tatyana, they moved into two small adjoining rooms provided by his company in a block of flats, typical accommodation for the time, commonly known as *semeynoe obschezhitie* – a Soviet expression for young family house. Irina and Arkady had a bedroom and a small kitchenette but shared a small bathroom with dozens of other couples in their block, dashing along the freezing corridors in winter when temperatures outside fell to -40°C.

After his father's death, Abramovich's close-knit Jewish family never considered sending him to a state orphanage. Arkady was the youngest of three brothers and, as Abramovich grew into a young man, he learned from his devoted uncles, Leib and Abram. As Arkady was the only brother to have had a son, Roman's future was especially important to the Abramovich name. He was raised by Leib and his wife Ludmilla. The couple also have two daughters, Natalya and Ida.

It was the uncles who saved and paid for the engraved granite stones used to mark the tombs of their brother and his wife. Irina's is decorated with a harp to symbolise her musical talent. Each year, on the anniversary of Arkady's death, the brothers would spend the day saying prayers at his graveside.

Flat 4 of Block 22, Oktyabrskaya Ulitsa in the town of Ukhta, northern Russia, is where Abramovich spent his childhood, believing that his uncle and aunt, Leib and Ludmilla, were his parents and that his older cousins, Natalya and Ida, were his sisters. The apartment block now houses a clinic for sexually-transmitted diseases, and boasts a patchwork of rusting pipes and cracked tiles.

Leib Nakhimovich Abramovich always intended to break the news to his nephew, but the youngster found out on his first day at school by mistake when a teacher let it slip and then had to tell him that his real parents were in the cemetery.

While his cousins, Natasha and Ida, 13 and 10 years his senior, shared the largest bedroom at the back of the flat, Roman had the tiny front bedroom, leaving his uncle and aunt to sleep on the sofa in the sitting room. Leib was Chief of the Supplies Department of the state logging company UkhtaLes, and Ludmilla was head of the trade union. Neighbours remember the polite little boy who kicked a plastic ball, played ice hockey and chalked on the concrete with his pals.

Before his death, Abramovich's father worked as the Chief of the local construction industry. Leib's position meant that, while he wasn't paid much, he had access to a Volga car.

Roman was enrolled in Ukhta City Municipal School Number 2 at the age of six, in September 1973. His name still sits in the old register – he is listed as number 29, Abramovich, Roman, male, born 24 Oct '66, Jewish, enrolled in Form Number 1. It was a short walk to school, along the banks of the Chibyushka river.

At the age of 14, he was sent to Moscow, where he shared a cramped, one-room flat with his grandmother, Tatyana, and enrolled at School Number 232.

At 17, he failed to get into Moscow's prestigious Gubkin Oil and Gas Institute. Without a place, which would have allowed him to postpone his compulsory two-year national service, he was forced to join the Army as a truck driver in the artillery detachment. Aged 20, Abramovich returned to Ukhta and enrolled at the town's Industrial Institute where he studied for two years before successfully applying for a transfer to the Moscow Auto Transport Institute, a prestigious engineering school where he studied for a year.

It was around this time that he met Eugene Shivder who was studiying at the Gubkin Russian State University of Oil and Gas in Moscow. He has remained a close confidant and partner ever since. He started his first company, Ooyut-Comfort, in 1987 while still a student, making plastic toys, dolls and ducks and selling them at the markets springing up around Moscow, as well as dabbling in retreaded tyres. He became extremely rich, extremely fast, by 'exploiting the hybrid law of the Gorbachev–Yeltsin transition which allowed companies to trade on the huge difference between Soviet and Western prices for raw materials'.

In 1999, he was elected to the lower house of the Russian parliament, the State Duma, from the Russian Far East region of Chukotka, where he was invited to run by the local governor. He also founded the charity Pole of Hope and sponsors a Russian ice hockey team, Omsk Avangard, which came second in the Russian premier hockey league last year.

He met his attractive second wife Irina Malandina, a glamorous former Aeroflot air stewardess, on a plane. At the time he was married to Olga, a women three years his senior. Irina would return from some exotic locations with examples of Western goods and Roman copied them in Russia. At the time, Roman lived in a single-room Moscow flat with Olga and step-daughter Anastasia.

Now Roman and Irina and their five children – Anna, 11; Arkady, 10, who is named after Roman's father; Sonya, 8; Arina, 2; and Ilya, 6 months – have several luxury homes. Irina studied for a law degree as she started her family and more recently she enrolled for a doctorate in Fine Arts in Moscow, an affirmation of their growing mutual interest in collecting paintings. He lives in a 99-acre walled estate outside Moscow where they have entertained Vladimir Putin on numerous occasions. They also own a castle in Bavaria, with nearby skiing, one of Roman and Irina's hobbies. Then there is a £10m villa in Nice in the South of France.

One of the Russian's newest luxury homes is the 424-acre estate called Fyning Hill, consisting of secluded woodland in Rogate on the South Downs near Midhurst in West Sussex, once the British bolt-hole for King Hussein of Jordan in his grand design to spend more time in this country. He bought the £12m estate more than two years ago from Kerry Packer, the Australian media magnate. The seven-bedroom house, built in the 1920s, has stabling for 100 horses, two polo pitches, a swimming pool, a tennis court, a clay pigeon shoot, a rifle range, a trout lake, an equestrian centre and a go-kart track. There is a separate house, six cottages, a staff flat and four guest apartments. He has been spotted driving through the village in a red Bentley and arrives on the estate by helicopter. Putin is reputed to have flown in for lunch! The stables are being converted into a massive £2.5m complex, comprising a bowling alley, gym and indoor swimming pool.

Abramovich also owns a plush, multi-million-pound apartment in Lowndes Square, Knightsbridge, and although he plans a more permanent residence in this country, he has said publicly that he does not plan to leave Russia permanently. 'I'm most comfortable in Moscow. I spent most of my life there. I like the seasons.' But his intention was to move his family to Fyning Hill, and place the Knightsbridge flat on the market with estate agents Knight Frank for £5m and find something more suitable for his family in town. Although the two-level flat has four large reception rooms and four grand bedrooms, he is seeking a house with at least four or five more rooms as he is spending more and more time in London, even more so now he has bought Chelsea. 'I like the lifestyle in England. It's multinational and multicultural. There are signs that remain from the Empire, and I like that. People are used to dealing with different people. Everyone can feel comfortable there. This also goes for the United States,' Abramovich observed.

As the football industry wondered how long he would maintain his 'hobby' by pouring money into Chelsea (when asked if he'd be around for at least ten years, he replied, 'It's hard to talk about ten years. Maybe 20 years, 50 years,') it was a breathtaking example of extravagance and decadence that swept through the English game from a 36-year-old man who not only controlled his business empire, but from a separate floor at the top of his nineteenth-century merchant's house, he also runs the governorship of Chukotka, 4,000 miles away in Siberia. There he has invested millions, building homes, improving schools and public buildings for the area's 73,000 population, mostly reindeer herders and fishermen. He provided the region's first international-standard hotels, supermarket, cinema, a restaurant/billiards hall that brews its own beer, a college, a museum and house of culture, an international-standard medical facility, a fish processing plant. The list goes on, and he is treated like a god there. He is also known to contribute to many charitable local causes.

Just as the domestic champions started to pull away from their rivals on the back of a profitable £140m-a-year business, a Russian billionaire has upset the balance. The directors at Old Trafford should be worried. If a steel industrialist like Walker, worth £330m, could take Blackburn to the top of the Premiership, just think what a man like this could do.

Abramovich's £60m bid for Chelsea's shares caused a huge stir, which has been increasingly dominated by one club and its debt-free balance sheet. The first sign of over-excitement came from Ken Bates with the ink barely dry on the deal. The Chelsea Chairman, who is cashing in his stake for nearly £18m, began to talk about a pot of cash for player acquisitions and the elimination at a stroke of the club's £90m debt. Bates later revealed, 'It's costing Mr Abramovich £200m, that's the truth [taking into account the shares, the debt and the new training facility to be built]. After 2004, our debts would have been paid off on the players, and the idea was modest and regular improvement until 2007, when the bond we took out would have been paid off or refinanced. Mr Abramovich has brought all that forward by four years. We have a lot of money but it doesn't mean we are going to fritter it away.'

But not even Bates knew precisely how much Russia's second-richest man planned to spend on players; it was estimated at an astonishing £150m–£200m over the next two years.

Instantly, there was talk of a £50m bid for Thierry Henry, the Russian's favourite player, the £30m purchase of Wayne Rooney in the summer of 2004, and a succession of high-priced big-name stars started arriving.

So why did the man who turned the soccer summer on its head decide to buy himself a football club, and a Premiership one at that? 'I want a team that wins the league and Europe. The goal is to win. It's not about making money. I have many much less risky ways of making money than this. I don't want to throw my money away, but it's really about having fun and that means success and trophies.'

He chose a UK club 'because I can afford to fly in and out and back to my job in Russia. I enjoy England and I'd like to see every Chelsea game, but that may not be possible.'

His business life took off when he first traded in oil products using the Swiss-based 'vehicle' company Runicom, now absorbed into Sibneft. 'I used my own money,' he insists, 'I didn't use State money through bank loans. My most important deals were when I was unknown. Now you have to be a known name to be a success.'

In the early '90s, Abramovich consolidated the oil business in the Omsk region so successfully that when the most powerful oligarch of that time, Boris Berezovsky, conceived the idea to create Sibneft, an amalgamation within the oil industry, he made Abramovich his first choice for the Board and then head of the Moscow office. After Berezovsky's exile to London, Abramovich was left in sole charge of his own and his former boss's shares. The pair are now no longer on speaking terms due to Abramovich's loyalty to Berezovsky's sworn enemy, President Vladimir Putin, and it is rumoured that he also wields huge influence in Moscow's corridors of power. With his close friend from university, Eugene Shvidler, Abramovich has built Sibneft into an integral element in the recent merger creating the fourth-biggest oil company in the world. Shvidler is now Chairman-designate of YukosSibneft, the joint company owned by Mikhail Khodorkovsky and Abramovich. Shvidler is also one of Abramovich's insiders at the new Chelsea.

The web of companies owned by Abramovich is largely controlled by a British-registered holding company, Millhouse Capital, based in Weybridge, Surrey, which is, in turn, controlled by a Cyprus-based organisation called Electus Investments.

In May, Sibneft's Board decided that, based on a total net profit of $1.161bn, $1.09bn would be offered in dividends to shareholders. Abramovich is thought to own in the region of 50 per cent of the company, and received several hundred million dollars in dividends. Next, he gained a huge slice of the $3bn paid by YUKOS, which is buying 20 per cent of Sibneft. (A remaining 72 per cent of Sibneft, held by Abramovich and partners, is being exchanged for 26.01 per cent of YUKOS, to be renamed YukosSibneft. Buyout or share exchange terms haven't been announced yet for the other 8 per cent of Sibneft held by minority shareholders.) So Abramovich's wealth is not merely estimated through the value of his companies, it is actually money in the bank ... well, vast amounts of money in many different banks, to be precise.

He has two yachts, a Boeing Business Jet, enjoys Chinese food and films such as *Straw Dogs* and *Pulp Fiction*, and the music of a Russian band called Spleen.

Abramovich doesn't smoke or drink, and describes himself as a 'family man' and 'a Jew first and a Russian second'. He and Irina are considering educating their five children in the UK because the British education system has 'hundreds of years of educational excellence'.

It looked as if he was on a mission to expand his empire when he moved into football, but Abramovich insists he is not driven to rule the world. He explains, 'I have no Napoleonic dream. I'm just hard-working and pragmatic.'

In 1992, after the collapse of the Soviet Union, 55 railway wagons of diesel fuel that were part of a deal in which he was involved 'disappeared' between Siberia and Moscow, ending up several hundred miles to the west in newly independent Latvia. Abramovich was investigated but no charges were ever pressed. Despite all the suspicions as to how someone so young could have amassed so much money, there was nothing else on his 'file'. Abramovich currently counts Citigroup among his advisers, formerly the famous City name Schroder Salomon Smith Barney. The firm has worked with him since 1997 and provides the credibility banks have demanded.

So how did he become so wealthy, so quickly? He says, 'I bought a company that was not the largest back then,' – referring to the rapid privatisations of the 1990s that made billionaires of a few supporters of the former President Boris Yeltsin in return for their support in the 1996 elections – 'and it is important to remember that the people who took part then were willing to take a risk and there were all kinds of risks. I was not part of a system that would take care of me, I had to survive. In 1995 [when Sibneft was privatised], $250m was a lot of money that people in Russia couldn't fathom. An apartment then cost $5000.' Most of these companies were bankrupt, extremely inefficient and poorly run, not competitive in a market economy, and it was extremely important to save them quickly because thousands of jobs were at stake. The peole who made it rich were the ones who didn't sit back and skim money off the enterprises they bought, but instead brought in good management, Western techniques, and invested in new technology, thus creating shareholder value for themselves and minority shareholders. There are plenty of enterprises out there that were privatised by non-famous (because they aren't as rich) people that are languishing.

Richard Creitzman, Abramovich's right-hand man at the Bridge after the Boardroom shake-up, says, 'He is a special guy, but he was in the right place at the right time, as were a number of others,' referring to the post-Soviet privatisation which created oligarchs such as Abramovich, Oleg Deripaska and Mikhail Khodorkovsky.

Abramovich's men on the Chelsea Board were concerned when Bates made some early remarks about the transfer policy. Bates said, 'It'd be madness to buy players and throw them in willy-nilly.' At the time, Bates was trying to defuse the first story that broke regarding Chelsea's aquisitions, a purported £35 million 'bid' by Chelsea for Alessandro Nesta, of AC Milan, which turned out not to be a bid at all! Then Bates' press briefing during the pre-season tour soured internal relationships when he criticised Eriksson. In addition, the now-over commission with Zahavi and the appointment of Peter Kenyon caused more friction. But Abramovich tried not to get involved in internal politics too much. He was having too much fun buying new players.

Abramovich's intentions are simple, according to his advisers. The Russian wants to win trophies – particularly the European Cup. To do that, he will need top-class players.

It was an unpredictable situation dictated by the personal ambition of an oligarch. But while Abramovich is a law unto himself, the Board at Old Trafford are beholden to shareholders. The Russian can overpay for a player because it is his money; the United directors must justify every pound spent or risk affecting the share price.

As if to underline the point, members of the United Board were, by coincidence, in the City of London at the time of the Chelsea takeover, explaining to analysts how they intended to turn the club's 53 million fans around the world into paying customers. What they had to say was impressive. Demand for tickets at Old Trafford continues to be so strong that the club has sold out for next season; an average of 1.1 million people use the website each month and more than 3 million United-branded items have been sold in the past ten months under a new £303m merchandising deal with Nike. All pretty impressive, but not half as much fun as having a mysterious billionaire, with a penchant for camouflage gear, ready to splash out on glory. Abramovich says that he is ready to spend whatever it takes to achieve it. If he lives up to the hype, the fans are in for the ride of their lives.

Fans of English football, too, should be glad of Abramovich. His wealth has not only prevented, potentially, the first administration of a

Premiership club – a move that would have prompted much soul-searching at the top of the game – but it has added a runner to a two-horse race. Although Arsenal came close last season with much-reduced resources, it is unlikely, with a new £400 million stadium to finance, that they will be able to mount much of a serious challenge in the years ahead. Chelsea are the new foil to United.

Passing judgement on Abramovich, the ludicrously young and outrageously rich new owner, is bound to be open to debate.

Abramovich speaks excellent Russian, but little English; he is a shy man, who clearly likes to use his shoulders more than his mouth to express himself. His wife speaks excellent English.

His first message for the fans? 'I will do everything possible to ensure that you enjoy the game as much as me.' It was a mantra he continued in the match day programme for the first game of the new season.

Abramovich says his intention is to make Chelsea a halfway house between Real Madrid and Manchester United. The Spanish team is noted for its spectacular buying of top talent, while Manchester United is seen as a great developer of young players. 'It [Chelsea] should be an international team,' he said. 'The best players need to play. What they nearly have now is a top European team. I am prepared to invest in the club and see the club be successful. And, of course, I will be looking to buy players.'

Asked which players he most likes and might like to buy, Abramovich is quick to mention Thierry Henry of Arsenal. But then, after some discussions with his advisers, he says, 'I also like Sol Campbell.'

He went on, 'I'm not going to tell you other players because their price will just go up.' Queue laughter all round, from Abramovich and Eugene Tenenbaum, his close adviser and interpreter. But even Abramovich's almost bottomless pit of money hasn't been able to prise away Henry ... not yet, at least.

When looking for an English club, Abramovich originally called on Daniel Levy, who controls and runs Spurs. The conversation went well, but at a later date Levy asked for £50m to buy a 29 per cent holding in the club. Instead of Spurs and Levy, he chose Chelsea and Bates where the 'working-capital issues' were easier to deal with. Little needs to be done to Chelsea's infrastructure, apart from the establishment of a new training ground.

Any fears at Stamford Bridge that the Russian's motives were suspect were dispelled in his homeland, where he has pumped millions of dollars into his adopted ice hockey club. Abramovich has turned a bunch of debt-ridden no-hopers at the Avangard club in Omsk into a team which is challenging for the top honours. Club spokesman Arkadi Alekseev said, 'We are so grateful that Abramovich decided out of the blue to help us. Since he bailed us out five years ago, the team has changed beyond recognition. Now we can go out to get the best players. This year, the Coach of the Russian ice hockey team, Sergei Gersonsky, started work with Avangard. It's the equivalent of Sven-Goran Eriksson taking over as manager of Chelsea. We have made great progress since Roman appeared in our life, climbing high in the league. I think this is a great chance for Chelsea. The players and fans should be very happy that Abramovich chose them. It means only the best in the future and lots of victories.'

Abramovich's takeover caused shockwaves in Russia with some ice hockey fans in Omsk expressing fears that now he has Chelsea as his new toy, he will neglect their little club. Deputy local governor Sergey Shelpakov said, 'We hope very much that Roman Abramovich will not abandon this team.'

Russian Football Federation President Vyachelsav Koloskov is furious that Abramovich shovelled his cash into Chelsea. He said, 'Russian money should be put into Russian sport for the Russian fans.' The Mayor of Moscow, Yuri Luzkhov, one of Russia's most prominent politicians, who had previously not always seemed eye-to-eye with Abramovic on other matters, remarked, 'They spat on Russia by buying Chelsea.' Luzhkov, an avid amateur soccer player, told a gathering of the city government, 'In buying Chelsea for such a huge amount of money, they abandoned our Russian teams, which needed support.'

Former Prime Minister Sergei Stepashin, now head of Russia's auditing chamber, criticised the purchase as 'unpatriotic'. But John Mann, spokesman for Sibneft, said the tycoon carefully considered Russian teams before investing abroad. 'He looked at several Russian teams over the last couple of years, but there were no deals available that met his requirements.'

It has also been noted that Russian teams lack transparency in ownership and operations, making it difficult to carry out a complete takeover confidently. Also, it would be hard to get a Crespo or Mutu to transfer to a Russian team because the level of competition in the league isn't as high as in the UK, thus hindering the team's ability to prosper.

Abramovich countered such objections with a pledge to build new stadiums in Russia, including a £65m state-of-the-art football stadium in Moscow, a new 50,000-seater complex with a glass roof that can house leading club CSKA. He said he'd like the stadium to house three teams and to be economically viable. Besides CSKA, he named Spartak and Torpedo-Metallurg as not having modern facilities. The new stadium was proudly announced by no less than the Mayor himself. No more spitting then, eh?

But as Stamford Bridge they adore their new owner, who doesn't conform by refusing to wear a tie on match days, does high fives with his Russian pals when 'his' team score, orders takeaway sushi from plush Mayfair restaurant Nobu to enjoy in their £1m executive box as he prefers that to the boardroom and directors' box.

Abramovich is different, very different. Who would have thought the club that once was unknowingly a breeding ground for National Front recruitment is now owned by a Russian Jew?

Now other clubs are wishing Abramovich had bought them instead – certainly Spurs after his meeting with Levy and definitely Aston Villa, whose chairman Doug Ellis commented: 'If Mr Abramovich had come in the summer I would have been a hell of a good listener. I would have learned Russian in a flash. When you are talking about the kind of money he has invested in Chelsea, anyone would listen.'

THE BATTLE FOR CONTROL
AND A HARD SELL

ROM AN OBSCURE 1920S German Government Bond worth £225m linked to two ex-pat 70-year-old Colombians in Norwich and Germany and a Venezuelan ex-FIFA ref, to one of the world's largest pension funds in California, to an American-backed deal to sell off Chelsea's advance TV rights, to a City financier and mad Chelsea fan recommended by David Mellor, to Celtic owner Dermot Desmond ... the offers to bail out Ken Bates were as diverse as they were bizarre.

For 18 months, Bates had been wrestling with the precarious finances of Chelsea Village. A wonderful vision of the future was stuck in a financial mire; Chelsea Village, with its gleaming hotels, an abundance of restaurants, flats, health club, nightclub and offices was Bates's master plan for diversying a football business away from the peculiarities of results on the field to a balance sheet that would reflect a multi-purpose complex.

Gone were the concept of pop concerts and playing host to team sports such as rugby; Bates sweated blood to build the Chelsea Village concept despite 20 years of fierce battles with property developers who wanted the prime land for their own profits. He wasn't going to give it up easily, so it is fascinating to examine why the point was reached when he sold out completely. The conclusion is that he had no alternative.

When Chelsea Village was completed and Chelsea floated on the Alternative Investment Market (AIM) for a market price of 55p a share, Chelsea Village had taken out a £75m Euro Bond to finance the Bates Vision.

But there were three key problems that led to a cash flow crisis that could no longer be papered over, but required major refinancing. First, the slow build-up of business for the hotels and restaurants was a drain on the resources; second, the interest repayments of the bond were at a crippling 9 per cent; and to exacerbate the situation, under the former Chief Executive Colin Hutchinson, the club ran up £50m worth of salaries with players like Winston Bogarde on £40,000 a week for basically doing nothing, and Jimmy Floyd Hasselbaink signed a contract that guaranteed him a weekly salary of £80,000 a week in the final year of his deal.

Over the quiet summer break, with wages at the same level but the income stream reduced, in the main, to the season ticket take-up, Bates knew time was running out to pay the rapidly approaching £23m debt, including £5m worth of roll-on loan from the Harding Estate, which they threatened to withhold; not for the first time, the situation had become dire.

The urgency to sort out the finances was being addressed by the 71-year-old Chairman on a daily basis from his lofty bridge office perched just over the entrance to his Chelsea Village complex. It was not an arduous journey to work, as Bates took the private lift from his penthouse he shares with Suzannah, to his well-proportioned HQ with the walls covered with cartoons chronicling the Bates era of command. In the final months before the eventual sale, the canny Bates knew he needed new investment, whether it was an individual like the late Matthew Harding, or a company, or an overseas investor. He didn't have time to be too particular, yet he didn't want to accept any injection of capital unless it was good for the club.

In fact, Roman Abramovich's takeover occurred on a Tuesday; the £23m was due the following Friday.

Prior to the point of no return, and the potential to run into administration or even worse, Bates had been plotting alternatives for many months. He was sitting on £165m worth of assets at Chelsea Village and knew that if he could turn the financial corner, the club would be worth far more than £60m, probably as much as £300m, and no doubt will be sooner rather than later under Abramovich.

There were four basic options before the Russian rode over the horizon to the club's rescue. The first was securitisation. Schechter and Co Ltd had been organising securitisation deals for a multitude of football clubs and was even consulted when the FA ran into its own cash flow difficulties.

Stephen Schechter presented a proposal to raise a £120m 'securitisation' deal for Chelsea when their debts reached a peak of £99m. The deal, basically involving advance season tickets sales for the next 25 years, would have cleared those debts and still left them with £26m in the bank. Overnight, Chelsea could have switched from the club with the biggest debts to the only club with cash reserves in the bank. Chelsea would be able to pay off the £5m outstanding loan to the Harding Estate, pay off Multiplex, the Aussie construction company currently rebuilding Wembley, who are owed £12.5m on the West Stand at the Bridge, pay off the £75m Euro Bond issued in 1997, and meet cash flow obligations with £5m to be paid to Barcelona on Petit and Zenden. With £26m in the bank, Claudio Ranieri would still have had his pick of some of the best international stars.

Spurs secured a £10m securitisation deal and have a further £65m available with the money earmarked for a new academy centre, and either to revamp White Hart Lane or move to an alternative site. Arsenal explored advance funding to meet the £100m extra required for their Ashburton Grove new stadium project. Manchester City have a 24-year, £44m securitisation with an interest rate fixed at 7.27 per cent with Bear Stearns, who also organised a £30m injection at Everton. That follows the £60m refinancing of debt-ridden Leeds United, and one of the reasons for the sale of Rio Ferdinand to Manchester United was to ensure the club could meet its repayment schedules.

In the north-east, there has been a £55m mortgaging of Newcastle United which Schechter secured n 1999 on future revenues from an expanded St James's Park. Another Premiership club to go down that route was Southampton (£25m), while leading names from the Nationwide League, Ipswich (£25m) and Leicester (£25m), have also concluded such deals.

Chelsea's securitisation deal would have been by far the biggest in football. While Bates was confident of a deal going through, he declined to sell Hasselbaink to Barcelona whose £6m offer he described as 'derisory'. Gudjonsson's agent was agitating for a pay rise, while Gallas had an escape clause and that needed to be addressed with Arsenal sniffing around.

Freddie Shepherd, the Newcastle Chairman, borrowed £50m, compared to Leeds's £60m in similar securitisation loan deals. Shepherd says, 'Yes, we have securitisation but it is chalk and cheese when compared to Leeds. They are two completely separate and different packages. They borrowed £60m to buy players and their biggest problem is that, when they fell into difficulties, they sold players at substantial losses. We borrowed £50m to rebuild the stadium, not to buy players. Our assets remain in bricks and mortar, very much like a mortgage on a house, and every time a season ticket holder renews his ticket, it is taking our debts down, it is paying for itself.'

Leeds embarked on a fire sale of players to lower their £77m debts, but are still in deep water, and events at Elland Road put off those who would have backed a similar securitisation deal at the Bridge. Yet Leeds rented their ground, and had no assets apart from their players, compared to Chelsea's assets of the ground plus all the extras. Chief Executive Trevor Birch travelled to the States in the hope of buttoning down a deal, but time ran out as it would have 'taken another month to lock up'. Faith in football clubs' securitisation deals had faltered, and Chelsea became the victims of what had happened at Leeds.

The second option was the Californian Pension. Schechter introduced the pension fund known as CalPers (Californian Public Employees' Retirement System) to Chelsea as an alternative to his securitisation proposals. The injection of funds would have been formidable but a condition of their purchase of Chelsea Village was that Bates had to 'retire' and they would put in their own people to run the complex, including the football club. The prospect of Californians describing Chelsea Village as a 'great lee-sure investment' filled David Mellor with dread when his close friend Bates confided in him the growing urgency to refinance and how the American-based pension fund wanted to buy total control and develop the hotel, restaurant and health club aspect of the complex. Mellor decided he had to act to prevent a group of investment bankers utilising their pension funds in a football club without any 'feel' or commitment to the sport.

The third possibility came about through Paul Taylor, Chief Executive of Rotch, a London-based property company; he was a serious player and earmarked as Bates successor, even though initially he would take a minority shareholding.

Taylor is a 'thoroughly decent man' according to Mellor, the former politician-turned-media golden boy, who hosted Radio 5's 606 show and supplied columns in the Evening Standard and the Sunday People. Mellor told me, 'I had every faith and belief that Paul Taylor, in the long run, would become the new Ken Bates.' Mellor had done all he could to achieve that aim, and was only thwarted at the very last.

Rotch was not involved in any shape or form. Taylor was acting purely as a Chelsea fan in his own right. The Taylor proposal was an immediate £10m injection of cash, a loan against the Sky TV income that would be due in August, as a sign of good faith, and a prelude to the purchase of a stake of up to 29.9 per cent. Sky were in the final year of a three-year contract and on the point of securing a further three years in a new bidding process at the time. The money from the third year of the present deal was higher but, because it was not due until the start of the new season, it came too late to deliver Chelsea from their cash flow crisis. In addition, Taylor would utilise his impressive array of banking and City connections to refinance the club with a further injection of between £25m to £30m in the first three months to begin the restructuring and rid the club eventually of the Euro Bond and its inhibitive repayments.

The Taylor proposal had gained Boardroom acceptance and was going ahead with his purchase of the 30 million new shares that raised the total number of shares to 200 million, plus a part of Bates' holding. The offer came in at 25p a share, some way off the 40p a share offered by a rival consortium led by London-based lawyer Mel Goldberg. The Goldberg-inspired offer, in fact, was even higher than the 35p that Abramovich eventually bid. Little wonder that Bates would have loved Goldberg to have got his client's act together. But Bates and the Chelsea Board felt the Taylor–Mellor proposals were a far more realistic proposition.

At this juncture, brokers appointed by the Taylor camp made an offer of 18p per share to the Harding Trust for their 23 per cent stake reducing the need to buy too many Bates shares at a premium price. Taylor could only afford, though, to buy a maximum of 29.9 per cent, as anything above that magic figure meant there would have to be a full-scale bid for the entire company, which was beyond Taylor's financial scope.

Mellor was convinced that Taylor and Birch, along with Bates, could all work harmoniously together in the short and medium term, and the long-term plan was for Taylor to take control from Bates. Taylor was born in Mellor's south-west London former constituency, and had a love for the club that Mellor felt was appropriate for a smooth succession.

But Birch was worried. He came to the conclusion that the financial predicament was far more serious than he had at first diagnosed, and that the Taylor deal would have meant waiting three to four months for a major refinancing programme, and the realisation set in that the club did not have anywhere near that amount of time left. The black hole of debt had deepened. The subsequent introduction of Abramovich eventually overtook the Taylor–Mellor bid.

A fourth option for Bates appeared in the shape of Dermot Desmond, the owner of Celtic. Having bought shares in Manchester United, Desmond had made it clear that he felt his club and rivals Rangers should be involved in the English Premiership. That was not going to happen, so he was clearly keen to look to invest in Premiership clubs. He was interested in a minority stake, less than the 10 per cent threshold that would have been acceptable while he retained his controlling interest in Celtic. Over convivial dinner and lunch dates with Bates, many suggestions had been put forward but little substance came of them. Desmond would probably not have been content with a 10 per cent stake and so it didn't really develop too far.

A fifth saviour, lawyer Mel Goldberg, had been in talks with Bates for three months on behalf of a Venezuelan-backed investor. Bates was never quite convinced about the Goldberg initiative, but talks appeared to be quite advanced. Time marched on, though, while meetings were cancelled, and problems arose about getting the validity of the 1920s German bond and how to release the funds. The Chelsea Chairman grew increasingly impatient, his confidence in its credibility decreasing with each hold-up.

Goldberg, an Arsenal fan, was keen to move on to the Board and oversee the investment. The Venezuelan consortium offer was to buy 29.9 per cent of the shares for £25m. A large part of the shares would have been Bates's, and he was prepared to dilute his shareholding as the offer from the South Americans was a good one on paper. But as problems arose over, apparently, obtaining government approval to release funds out of the country, Bates asked more searching questions about the origin of the money.

Billionaire Gustavo Cisneros, the 58-year-old businessman dubbed 'the Rupert Murdoch of Latin America', was named by the *Mirror* as the mystery investor who was subsequently having talks with Aston Villa Chairman Doug Ellis when the Chelsea deal fell through. Goldberg issued a statement denying that he was acting on behalf of Cisneros, whose chain of supermarkets had made him the second-wealthiest man in South America, but the paper didn't take much notice as they had already given huge prominence to a profile of the South American billionaire, whose fortune was estimated at around £4bn from his range of businesses.

However, it emerged that a Venezuelan ex-referee from Caracas was the real investor. There were three names on the 1920 German bond: that of the Venezuelan ref and two female pensioners. The pensioners had no plans to be part of the consortium to buy Chelsea and were investing their money in property development and the construction of schools and hospitals. One of the 70-year-old ladies lived in Norwich, the other in Germany. Goldberg never dealt with the two old girls directly, only by email, and has been deliberately left in the dark about their origins. However, there is one clue – they do correspond in Spanish, and the theory is that they are Colombians. Although German bonds from the '20s were regarded as 'junk bonds', this one had the authenticity of the Federal Reserve Bank of the United States and the highly respected Citibank were acting on their behalf. With part-ownership of the German bond, the offer from the Venezuelan ref and his consortium came in at 40p a share, when the shares were trading at under 20p, so it was a tempting offer for a minority stake. They did not want to run the business, merely to invest in it, and naturally Bates was anxious to accept it, but had little faith it would ever come off, despite Goldberg's enthusiasm.

Mellor and Taylor knew they had competition from Goldberg's consortium, and vice versa. Neither knew anything about the Russian connection until it was too late.

Goldberg tells me, 'We were two days away from completing a deal and I knew there was another party involved, but Ken Bates wouldn't tell me who it was. I suspected that it was someone connected to the Rotch group, and I had an inkling that they were close to a deal to buy 15 per cent of the shares for £10m. But we were going ahead with the purchase of 29.9 per cent of the shares for £25m. Yes, we were two days away from completing the deal, due diligence was holding the contracts up, we knew we were in competition with someone from Rotch, but what we didn't know was that the Russian would come along and blow us all out of the water.'

Lino Duran is the Venezuelan ex-ref, and together with two others had a meeting with Bates. Goldberg said, 'He likes English football ... I took him to Chelsea and he loved the Chelsea Village complex and he wanted to replicate the concept in three or four different South American countries and, in return, offer first option to the best South American players.

'The deal didn't come to its conclusion quite quickly enough, but we met Ken about ten days before Abramovich completed his deal, and we shook hands on our deal. We had dinner at Fishnets restaurant in the Chelsea Village ... I was present with Lino and a number of his colleagues who would have been involved in the consortium. We had our first meeting with Ken back in March.'

Goldberg has not been put out by the wrong guy being linked to Chelsea. He says, 'Gustavo Cisneros got in touch with me as a result and he has now become a client! As for Lino, he is still interested in acquiring a holding in an English club, and we did speak to Villa and have been interested in half a dozen clubs, although four clubs from the Continent have also been in touch.'

But Mellor was highly sceptical of Goldberg's ability to pull off a deal, as he said, 'We are led to believe that a group of mysterious Venezuelans, represented by lawyer-cum-agent Mel Goldberg, have £40 million to invest in a Premiership club. This is particularly bizarre because they are apparently willing to put this money in for a minority stake. Who in their right mind would do that? It gets worse. They were negotiating with Chelsea for some weeks and, had they met agreed deadlines, they would have owned 29.9 per cent of the club while the Russians were still dozing on the Steppes. At no stage in the process was it ever proved they actually had the money. And, if you ask me, they don't.' Mellor was convinced that the Goldberg option was the 'joker' in the pack, and Bates was exasperated with the problems surrounding the release of funds connected to the exotic German bond.

Birch, meanwhile, had meaningful discussions with Zahavi, an Israeli agent who represents Rio Ferdinand and who had been instrumental in taking the centre-half from West Ham to Leeds and then on to Manchester United. Zahavi had been particularly active in the summer, representing Joan Laporte and Sandro Rossel in Barcelona's abortive deal to secure the services of David Beckham, the England captain. The ubiquitous Zahavi brokered Barca's official bid for Beckham, and in the process at least ensured the presidency for Laporte. But Zahavi had an even bigger deal up his sleeve with Abramovich, first recommending him to purchase Spurs and then settling on the move for Chelsea. Bates could have retained control with Taylor, but Birch knew the best option was the Russian ... and so did his Chairman.

After Bates met Abramovich for the first time early on Thursday evening at the Dorchester for a glass of Evian, they shook hands on the deal after about 45 minutes. Bates returned to the penthouse at Chelsea Village to confide in Suzannah that it was time to hand over the reigns after 21 years. Bates made his confession with a tear to Suzannah as he flopped back in the huge, comfortable sofa opposite his giant plasma TV screen set in the wall. Bates and Abramovich had planned a Tuesday morning announcement to the City after talks dragged on through Monday afternoon and early evening but, with the media having got wind of a deal, it was brought forward to 9.45pm. Bates couldn't believe his luck that someone wanted to invest so heavily in a football club. He told me, 'Because of what has happened at Leeds, football has become a dead duck as far as clubs getting bank loans and investors interested.'

*   *   *

Mellor's mobile phone emitted its usual trill as he was enjoying the company of a dozen family and friends in a Thai restaurant on Wimbledon Common after a pleasant day out out at the tennis. His dear old friend Bates was the caller. Not unusual, they were in constant touch and they have shared many an intimate dinner date together over Ken's favourite Pouilly Fuisse. On this historic occasion, Bates was calling from his Chelsea Village penthouse. Bates chirpily informed Mellor that it was time to break open the Dom Perignon; he had just struck a deal with a Russian multi-billionaire and Chelsea was saved, rescued from the financial noose just as the trap door was about to open. Not that Mellor could have found a bottle of upmarket bubbly at the local Thai. Bates explained to Mellor that he opted to sell out to a man with incredible resources, rather than to take the route that Mellor had been advocating and negotiating for months. Bates was convinced that selling to Abramovich would take the club on to the next level and enable them to compete seriously for the Champions League as well as becoming realistic title contenders. All very well and good, but it wasn't exactly what Mellor wanted to hear. Of course, he wanted the best for Chelsea, but he had other irons in the fire that he was convinced would soon provide the security they had all been working so hard to achieve.

Bates wanted Mellor to rejoice along with him. But the Red Thai Curry, Phad Noodles and Stir Fry Vegetables had lost their edge. Mellor could hardly celebrate along with Bates at news of such immense importance, as the realisation set in that his own rescue plan fronted by a wealthy fan with City and banking connections had been thwarted at the last minute. Mellor cast his mind back over months of behind-the-scenes toil to bring to Bates a potential saviour. Mellor had done all he could to achieve that aim and was sure he had helped to pull off the takeover coup ... until that call on his mobile informing him that Taylor had been gazumped by the Russians.

When more details emerged with non-stop media coverage from the front to the back pages, incorporating the City desks in between, Mellor was less and less convinced that it was the right direction for his beloved Chelsea. He was deeply concerned that Chelsea had been captured by a dubious foreign investor. After a few more weeks, and one meeting with Abramovich, his views began to change, and after six weeks and more than £100m invested in 11 new players, he was a convert.

But now Mellor had to deal with the repercussions of his aborted attempt to install Taylor.

In the two weeks prior to the takeover, Chelsea Village shares shot up 40 per cent on their AIM listing, and jumped a further 7p 24 hours before the announcement to close at 35p, after Abramovich agreed to buy 84.9m shares from Bates. Dealers noted that 270,000 shares changed hands in the day leading up to the late-night announcement when its usual daily turnover would be in the low tens of thousands. A total of 1.27m was traded that day before the news broke. The London Stock Exchange, which regulates the AIM, asked the FSA to investigate.

Rumours soon spread that Mellor had made a huge killing with insider knowledge. In fact, nothing could be further from the truth, and Mellor has provided the full facts and, together with Taylor, acted honourably and without any devious offers to the Harding estate to make a fast buck.

Taylor, in fact, is the 'mystery' man who made the offer to the Harding Estate to purchase their 23 per cent block shares, the second largest to Bates.

Conspiracy theorists always have a field day when the subject turns to Bates. Add Mellor's name to the mix, and it becomes an intoxicating cocktail for the media. The Chelsea takeover, even by Bates's standards – he is no stranger to the unexpected and mischievous – put the rumour factory into overdrive. While the back pages were preoccupied day after day with the identities of the Abramovich transfer targets, the sub-plot was the FSA investigation on two levels. Did anyone profit by insider share dealing? And who really owned the Chelsea shares and were they acting in tandem when they shouldn't have been?

The second question was one for Bates and is dealt with later, but the investigation into insider dealing became an issue for Mellor with innuendo flying around that somehow he was involved. A hit list was circulated by the FSA of those under suspicion of insider share dealing prior to the takeover, and the names of five individuals and two companies were on that list. Mellor's name did not appear on the list of suspects, but he did find himself being 'doorstepped' by a reporter from the *Daily Mail*. After a heated call to the *Daily Mail* City desk to convince the newspaper that their tip was inaccurate, the story was 'spiked' – not used.

The solicitor of Ruth Gist, widow of the late Chelsea tycoon Matthew Harding, fielded questions from the media as to whether Mellor was involved in a bid to buy the Harding Estate shares weeks before the takeover. Laurence Graham represented the Harding Estate, and was asked by Mrs Gist's solicitor – Richard Parry at Farrer's and Co – about the identity of the bidder. It was not Mellor. It had, in fact, been a broker representing someone else. Bates had spoken with Mellor about the attempts to implicate him in potential share dealings. Bates's theory was that it was inspired by hostile forces to blacken his name by association.

For some time there had been little to no interest in purchasing the Harding shares as no one really wanted the second-largest block of shares because they would then have to work, somehow, alongside Bates, who would have blocked a position on the Board. The sudden interest raised suspicions. Mother-of-four Ruth, 49, confirmed that she had considered selling her stake when the surprise offer materialised. But Ruth, whose millionaire husband Matthew – killed in a helicopter crash in 1996 – had helped keep Chelsea afloat, decided at the eleventh hour not to sell. Ruth, or rather the Trust on her behalf, eventually took up Abramovich's offer for the value of £12.6m. Had Ruth's shares been sold prior to the takeover, the buyer could have made an astonishing profit.

As the *Observer* reported, 'The attempted purchase is to be investigated by the Financial Services Authority, which has launched an insider-dealing probe into the way Chelsea's share price surged just before the Abramovich deal was announced on 2 July. A few days before that announcement, Ruth Gist, widow of the late Chelsea tycoon Matthew Harding, received an offer for her 21 per cent shareholding in Chelsea Village, the football club's parent company ... Richard Parry, Gist's solicitor, confirmed that the approach had been made but declined to comment further. However, Gist is "relieved" that she did not sell, because the value of her stake has since risen by some £4 million. Parry refused to identify the would-be buyer, citing commercial confidentiality. He is thought to have no known previous connection to Chelsea. A spokesman for the FSA declined to comment. According to insiders, however, the City regulator is keen to make sure that the mystery speculator had no prior knowledge of Abramovich's intentions. Before the Russian stepped in, Chelsea was saddled with £90m of debts and facing a cash crunch.'

The offer came from Mellor's associate Taylor and the pair were involved in their own talks with Bates. Mellor was naturally alarmed by the innuendo that he had attempted to trade illicitly in Chelsea shares. 'I am very protective of my commercial reputation,' said a forthright Mellor.

The reality is that the Harding Estate had been desperate to sell for some time. The pressure was mounting because Matthew's mistress, Vicky Jaramillo, needed the money for her children by the former Chelsea Vice-Chairman, and was urging a sale. Ruth, too, was a beneficiary, but so was another of Matthew's girlfriends who had another child.

A broker made approaches and it was clearly advantageous for Taylor to buy the stake, and it was a reasonable and seemingly fair price at the time, considering neither the Harding Estate, nor Taylor or Mellor, apparently knew of the impending offer from Abramovich. The offer for the Harding share was perfectly legitimate and Mellor has every right to feel aggrieved that he has been the victim of a whispering campaign. He told me, 'My involvement was merely to bring Paul Taylor and Ken Bates together.

I introduced Taylor to Bates because he has a formidable influence with the banks, and he was ready to loan the club £10m to keep it going, but he didn't have deep enough pockets to bail Chelsea out of their debts; the Russian did. Taylor was nowhere near as liquid with his funds. I cannot blame the Chelsea Board, or Ken, for taking that deal because you only have to look at the finances involved to see why they did, rather than go in our direction which would have, in all honestly, been applying the sticking plaster to the problem.'

At the time of the Abramovich takeover, Mellor felt naturally bitter after 18 months of hard work for no reward, in attempting to help resolve the club's financial predicament. At first he felt it was the wrong image for the club. He said at the time, 'I don't think it is good in the long run for a football club of Chelsea's standing to be owned by a foreign billionaire, even if he turns out to be an eminent one. There are consequences for football in the broader sense, and ramifications for the Premiership as an international brand. Naturally, I was furious when the Russian tied up a deal and it all happened so quickly, because I had been trying to help sort something out for the past 18 months – (a) because I am a friend of Ken's; (b) because I am a Chelsea fan; and (c) because when Ken decided to go, I would have preferred somebody to replace him that I got along with and believed in. Paul Taylor was that man. He had the potential to become Ken's favourite son, so by the time that Ken felt it was right to retire he would would have had somebody there to offer the whole of the club. I am just so very upset that it didn't happen. But as it turned out, Ken met the Russian on the Thursday and the whole damn thing was done by the following Tuesday, and nobody knew outside of those involved.

'It was an unpleasant experience when I was informed that the deal had been done, and there have been some potentially damaging assertions made that are not true. Someone has been loose-mouthed to suggest that I have been involved somehow in trying to buy the Harding Estate shares, and it appears that my name is being dragged into it. I knew that Paul Taylor was making an offer to buy them because it was the best strategy to getting the first foothold into Chelsea and the cheapest way in, because they were available, the share price at the time was 18p and, on the face of it, it was not a bad price, particularly considering that there had been some interest in the shares at one time, but absolutely no interest in them for a long time.'

Even though the Harding Estate rejected the proposal, Taylor, with Mellor in the background, continued his talks with Bates, right up until Abramovich stepped in.

Yet Mellor was sure that the Taylor talks progressed smoothly enough. Mellor continued, 'Taylor was told that everything was confidential, and that is the way it has remained, and the deal would have been done had it not been for the Russians arriving late on to the scene.'

Mellor added, 'Taylor was ready to go for it, and the Chelsea Board approved the deal, but Trevor Birch, when the Russian deal was put on the table, just threw his hands up in the air and knew it was the best one for a company under so much financial pressure. The scale of the debts were so high that Taylor had no chance of meeting them. In fact, his plan was to restructure the debt and that would have taken him at least three months. He needed that time to sort it all out and there wasn't even a guarantee that he could have pulled it off, while the Russian had the resources to do it.

'It was a problem for Taylor because of what we called "the Leeds disease". However well connected he was with the banks, brokers and financiers in the City, they had all lost confidence in football and the value of their shares after the disaster that befell Leeds United.'

At the outset, Mellor had reservations, warning against the perils of toying with the fortunes of the Premiership club. Mellor was concerned about what could happen if it did not go as planned. Mellor said at the time, 'What I think that we have to hope, as Chelsea fans, is that the kind of investment that is being talked of will give Chelsea a good run-out in the Champions League. The club faced the prospect of not being able to do much in the transfer market this year ... given the pressure of some of the debt repayments ... and that's why I think Ken Bates was looking towards a person for whom a couple of hundred million is mere bagatelle and, in Mr Abramovich, he appears to have found such a guy. This is a power-play by an extremely wealthy man ... and as far as he is concerned, Chelsea Football Club, with their entrance into the Champions League, is a fitting vehicle for his ambitions ... and what he will want to do will be to put his resources into the club and, if money can buy success, there is a fair chance that Chelsea might achieve.

'I think the worrying thing is that when people buy football clubs that they regard as a plaything, which the rest of us have invested quite a lot of our life interest in, they can become bored. Mr [Mohamed Al] Fayed came in, he chucked a lot of money around, over £100m, Fulham achieved some success, but now we have moved beyond the point of investment, to disillusionment, disenchantment and I would not be at all surprised if Mr Fayed doesn't disengage from Fulham some time during this season leaving them to return from whence they came.'

Tony Banks, Labour MP for West Ham, is an outspoken and loyal Chelsea fan who raised objections. 'I want to know if this individual is a fit and proper person to be taking over a club like Chelsea. I would have preferred that the takeover of Chelsea had taken place after these questions had been answered. We know that Chelsea is in financial difficulties and that a deal has been arranged with an individual we know nothing about, with a background we know nothing about.'

The former Sports Minister remained sceptical despite all the signings and a promising start to the new season. 'It is still quite difficult to come to terms with. It is like winning the Lottery three weeks running ... you can't quite believe it. The man clearly has the money, he is worth what he says he is, but you can't help wondering why this has happened to us in such a short space of time. Being one of life's great pessimists, I wonder what price we're going to have to pay. I suppose that comes from having been a Chelsea supporter for so long. I always work on the assumption that if something sounds too good to be true, it probably is.'

Banks called for the takeover to be investigated by Sports Minister Richard Caborn. But Mellor insisted, 'At the end of the day, rightly or wrongly, private companies are there to be bought and sold by other private people and whatever reservations all of us may have about this turn of events, it isn't really a matter for Ministers.'

Mellor also felt that Bates had little option but to look for an investor if Chelsea was going to maintain its place among the top sides in Europe. He reflected, 'The difficulty of servicing that debt as well as meeting the aspiration of fans – the players' wages were costing him millions each year – was becoming a bit of a nightmare. For better or for worse, this is petty cash to Abramovich, but quite what he is going to make of it remains to be seen.'

American John Mann, who speaks for Abramovich and who is an executive at Sibneft, responded, 'In Russian business, especially in the murky mid-1990s period, a lot of people went out looking for stuff. Sometimes it was politically motivated, sometimes commercially.' With reports of two investigations into Abramovich's activities coming to light, Mann added, 'All I can tell you is that law enforcement officials of any country have never filed charges against him.'

A leading City source laughed at Banks's suggestion that there should be an inquiry into whether Abramovich has the right credentials to own a Premiership club. The respected City figure told me, 'If we wanted a test to decide who is fit and proper to run a football club, we would have a very big orphanage!'

Mann added, 'Roman Abramovich, like Mr Banks, shares a passion for football. He is committed to Chelsea and, like Tony, wants the very best for the club. We have written to Mr Banks in order to introduce Mr Abramovich to him, and have offered further dialogue to assuage his concerns.'

The 60-year-old Banks has been following Chelsea since he was a 10-year-old on the terraces, and has held a season ticket for 30 years. 'I was one of those lucky people who managed to see all of Chelsea's home matches in 1954/55 – I've still got all the programmes – and that was the last time, in fact the only time, we won the championship. Hopefully, I shall see them do it again before I die.' Thanks, perhaps, to their new Russian godfather about whom Banks has so far been so sceptical!

Banks retains the belief that the deal still needs further investigation. 'What I said at the time it all happened wasn't just a knee-jerk reaction. When I was Minister, I said that no football club should be taken over until the football authorities had satisfied themselves about the bona fides of the proposed new owner, whether the intentions are honourable. If the FA are not satisfied, they should be able to say to him, 'You will not have a licence to operate a football club.' One of the other things they could do is insist that a surety bond is deposited with them, surrenderable should the new owner decide to play dirty. This should apply not only in the case of Chelsea but to every professional club, because they are not simply economic entities, they are also institutions which go far beyond capitalisation on the stock market or how much they are worth in shares. They are part of people's lives, whether they are Chelsea or Cheltenham.

'My real worry is that here is someone who has taken over a club with which he had no previous association. I've heard Chelsea described as his rather expensive executive toy, and that is a matter for some concern. I've invested 50 years of my life in Chelsea FC and I'm concerned about what happens if he loses interest in his toy. And on what basis is the money being provided? This is what the FA should be finding out. I think the Sports Minister, Richard Caborn, should be asking some serious questions. Who will know what is going on at Chelsea now there is just a single owner?'

Banks did not talk with his pal Bates about it in the first few weeks after the deal was struck, 'principally because I don't want to be told to eff off.

But I might risk it when I next bump into him. Of course, when Ken himself appeared from nowhere and took over the club we wondered what the hell he was going to do with Chelsea. We had no idea whether he was in love with the club, but he stayed around and grew to love it, and we have to make sure that's what happens with Mr Abramovich. Whatever his intentions are, we must hope that if it is a toy, he will learn to love it and, like a kid's teddy bear, will hold on to it for ever. That's the hope, but there's always the fear.

'I just hope he's true to his word, that we win the Premiership and become the greatest team in the world. If so, I'll kiss his boots.'

Mellor, meanwhile, has mellowed in his objections to Abramovich. He explained, 'Having met him and his entourage, they are very pleasant people. If there was anything untoward arising from the smears, we would have read about it by now. The way he conducts himself around the club is impressive; he is modest and unassuming, and very pleasant. It is a smart move putting a Londoner, Richard Creitzman, on the Board, and he is working well with Trevor Birch and Ken Bates.

'Let's face it, it is incredibly exciting these days ... they have bought sensibly with a clear strategy of recruiting half home-based players and half from abroad.

'One Saturday over dinner, Trevor told me it was wonderful to be part of it and that within five years there was a genuine chance of winning not just the Premiership but the Champions League. He also said that you cannot be taken seriously unless you buy one of the world's top five strikers and they've done that.' However, Mellor was shocked that Birch was replaced by Peter Kenyon and Bates had not been informed of the negotiations to recruit the Manchester United chief executive. Mellor might now approve of Abramovich but he ahs been at loggerheads with agent Pini Zahavi and the pair exchanged words at half time in the directors' box at the Spurs match. Mellor had criticised Zahavi once too often in his *Evening Standard* column, and the agent found himself sitting one row behind Bates' friend. But Mellor was all smiles at the 4-2 win that kept Chelsea's title hopes going.

In fact, in honour of Abramovich, Mellor is attempting to find someone technically minded to work out how to play the Russian national anthem when his mobile phone rings!

DRIVING A HARD BARGAIN ...
AND A BENTLEY

KEN BATES'S ONE LUXURY item to celebrate his financial windfall – a new lilac–silver Bentley. No yacht? 'I can hire a yacht for a month if I want to. Why bother with all the hassle of being ripped off by the captain and paying through the nose for harbour charges?' No private jet? 'Not worth it if it's only going to be used now and again.' Why a Bentley, Ken, when you already have one? 'Well, my one hasn't got some of the extras I want, such as a hands-free cellphone, and I know I can have one installed, but with all the time and fuss that will take, I've decided to treat myself to a new Bentley.'

Ken discovered a dealer in Weybridge that offered him a 10 per cent discount. 'Everyone wants your business these days, and its not difficult to drive a good bargain.' For the man who bought Chelsea for £1 and avoided financial meltdown at the Bridge plus a £17.5m cheque from Roman Abramovich, it makes sense to strike a bargain for the next Bentley.

The 71-year-old former Emperor of the Bridge concluded the deal with Abramovich over a glass of Evian over dinner at the Dorchester Hotel on Thursday, 26 June, and it's been champagne ever since.

During the course of one of the biggest football announcements of all time, I had around a dozen conversations with the outgoing owner, who afforded me the first of many interviews over the next weeks, and daily contact between us became commonplace.

In one of his relaxed moods, I asked Ken to encapsulate what the past 21 years as Overlord of the Bridge meant to him. He told me, 'Fantastic experience, wouldn't have missed it for the world, I have loved every minute of it.'

It's been quite an experience for everyone else as well! Football life won't quite be the same with Bates making plans for his eventual retirement.

It is part of football folklore that Bates bought the club for just £1 in 1982, but that is misleading because he also took on debts that were crippling at the time, to the value of £1m. Bates told me, 'I took over when the club was bankrupt and bottom of the Second Division with a crumbling stadium, and it is great recognition of my achievements that when this guy wanted a football club he looked at Manchester United, Arsenal and Spurs, and he chose Chelsea because we had the most potential; we have a great ground, not necessarily the biggest but the best, and we have a good team.'

Bates concedes that it has been mostly a struggle to keep Chelsea going. 'I spent the first ten years fighting to keep Chelsea at Stamford Bridge and the second ten years battling to build the best stadium complex in the country, and in all that time I have striven for the ultimate goal and that is to develop the team into one of the élite in England.'

Now, after two decades of colourful years at the helm, he is winding down. 'I won't go on for ever and, at some stage, I'll want to sit back and retire. I'll enjoy the fruits of my past labours and Roman's future labours.'

Bates has often wondered who would succeed him. 'I'd been looking for 18 months and thinking, "Who do I leave it to? Who will I hand the club over to when I retire?" Now, in due course, the new owner will nominate the successor to replace me. At other clubs, people hand their stake in the club to their children, who might have no interest in football. None of my kids are really interested in football and certainly not interested enough to do it full time.'

Bates is keen to emphasise that his power was not total. 'Contrary to the popular conception, I've never been the total decision-maker,' he added. 'It's always been the Board reaching a consensus.'

It is going to be tough to get to grips with the reality that he is no longer master of Chelsea Village, his baby, his vision which comprises lavish hotels and a banqueting complex in one of London's trendiest areas.

Abramovich may decide to offload the extras, as he says, 'If I decide they are burdens, I'll look at other options.'

Bates is fortunate that the Russian decided to buy an English club rather than a Continental one. 'We like England because it has the most competitive league in Europe,' Abramovich said. 'It's easier to buy here because many of the clubs are publicly quoted. We examined several and chose Chelsea.'

Bates met Abramovich only once before the Russian launched his £59.3m bid to purchase every Chelsea Village share, in addition to taking over the £90m debt and injecting another £100m immediately for new players, with a pledge of a total of £150m–£200m over the next two years to make the team one of the best in Europe. Such an injection of cash immediately opens up the possibility of developing a championship-winning side, something that has eluded Bates throughout his time as owner.

Bates says, 'Roman is putting £200m into the club in total. Do you think he'd spend that just to pour it into the Thames? That demonstrates this guy means business and we have got a great future now. We'd been looking for a partner investor for almost a year. That's why, at our EGM, we got our shareholders to agree to issue 30,000 more shares. We were talking to four suitors and, of them, three actually approached us out of the blue. Roman wanted to get involved in Premiership football and looked at four clubs – but thought we were head and shoulders above the others. We're a good team and in the Champions League, which must have influenced him.

'When Trevor Birch first met them, he was amazed they knew as much about Chelsea as he did. We arranged to meet last Thursday and did the deal in 45 minutes. He is a young man and his wealth is quite phenomenal. He is the right man to take this club on to its next stage of its development. He feels that Chelsea is the only club in this country with real potential and, once we got talking, it didn't take us long to thrash out a deal. We have been working on it non-stop for the past few days and I am exhausted.'

Bates is not perturbed about the jibes that selling out to a Russian will start a trend of overseas 'sugar daddies'. Bates pointed out, 'There are several clubs already owned by Scandinavians while an Egyptian owns Fulham. If there is a trend, and I don't think there is one, it won't have started with this transaction.'

Neither does Bates believe that Abramovich would be railroaded into paying inflationary transfer fees. 'This man is a billionaire and hasn't become that by making silly, emotional decisions. It will be evolution, not revolution. We're only four or five weeks from the season and it'd be madness to buy players and throw them in willy-nilly. But we are looking to strengthen, as we're one or two short after letting a few go at the end of the season. We're looking for quality players and were looking for them before last Thursday. You'll be pleasantly surprised when the first-team selection is announced.' Bates was either bluffing, or even he didn't realise just how much Abramovich was prepared to spend.

Bates believes the takeover is 'a marriage made in heaven. Let's be honest about it, I have always had to run Chelsea on a shoestring. We could have continued to pootle along or we could go into the big league. I feel I have taken Chelsea into that big league, that élite in this country, but if we want to compete with the likes of Real Madrid and Barcelona, then we need more money, much more money. Because of what happened at Leeds, football is now a dead duck when it comes to loans and investment, rightly or wrongly, that's how it is. Now here comes along this man with plenty of money who wants to invest in Chelsea. With his financial muscle behind us we can compete on the world stage and you know that has always been my main ambition – it has been the reason for all my hard work at this club.

'This is a great deal for the Chelsea fans. They are not too bothered who owns the club, they are mostly interested in how much money we can spend on new players. We are now entering a new era. Despite all our handicaps over the years, I have made Chelsea into one of the top four or five clubs in this country. With this guy's help and financial muscle, we can be one of the top four or five clubs in Europe. You have got to look at the wider spectrum, and he will sit back and have the pleasure of being associated with a club that can hit the heights – and know that he has made it possible.'

Abramovich won't even be on the Chelsea Board, as Bates explained, 'He can't come on the Board because he is a Governor of one of the Soviet provinces and that precludes him becoming a director.'

Bates knew when to get in, and he knew when to get out. His timing was perfect when he arrived as Chelsea's saviour in the early '80s and fought off the property developers. There are those who love to hate him and have savaged his reputation, and Bates has kept Peter Carter Ruck, the nation's best libel lawyers, in lucrative overtime.

But for those who label him a loser, he walks away with plenty of profit for a £1 investment and Chelsea have collected plenty of silverware in recent years, having recruited players of global distinction from Ruud Gullit to Franco Zola, and World Cup winners in Marcel Desailly, Frank Leboeuf, Didier Deschamps and Manu Petit.

Regrets? 'No, not really. Nothing goes completely to plan in this game.'

Bates gave short shrift to claims that he sold Chelsea as the club was running out of money. 'I never comment on those reports because most of them are rubbish anyway,' he said. 'But our problems were behind us, apart from short-term cash flow which had actually been arranged to be covered anyway.'

Two loans in particular were proving difficult to service – a £5m facility with the Royal Bank of Canada and an £18m syndicated loan led by Barclays, although Bates later told me that it was the refusal of the Harding Estate to continue with their £5m facility that proved to be the difficult issue.

The offer document confirmed that the company was facing 'working capital constraints' and that its takeover would result in 'a substantial injection of new funds'. Chelsea Village reported a loss of £16.6m for 2001/02. Bates pulled off a master stroke in selling up to Abramovich, whose personal fortune makes Chelsea's debts 'an irrelevance'. As Bates confided, 'When I told him he should clear the debts, he asked how much we were paying. I told him 7 per cent. He told me not to worry – in Russia they pay a lot more!'

Bates originally asked for 40p per share, but settled at 35p. An Abramovich insider told me, 'He could have bought Chelsea for half the price, but he didn't want to harm the club, waiting for it to go into administration before buying it. He could have got it much cheaper but he is a man of honour.'

Abramovich observed, 'It is the right price. I don't feel like I saved the club.'

The purchase of Chelsea was relatively simple. From day one, Abramovich assumed control by buying Bates stock for £17.5m and, in addition to Bates's 50 million shares, the Chairman knew of a further 35 million shares. From 1 July 2003, Abramovich was in control, irrespective of whether other shareholders accepted the offer.

The FSA were concerned as to the owners of five offshore trusts that sold the other shares to the Russian. The issue, for Huey Evans, the Director of Markets and Exchanges at the FSA and one of the City's most feared investigators, is whether certain shareholders, hiding behind nominee accounts, were acting in concert or were connected in some other relevant way. If they were, then their identities should have been revealed under company law.

The FSA inquiries into the ownership of the shares did not affect Abramovich's takeover. The FSA's publicly stated concerns that investors 'may have been misled' brought an angry response from Bates. The investigation into the ownership structure of the club was separate from the ongoing investigation into possible insider dealing in the club's shares before the takeover was announced, and the rise in the price of Chelsea's shares immediately before the deal with Abramovich was made public.

The Stock Exchange's takeover panel issued a statement revealing that the FSA are looking into 'the nature and status of certain shareholdings in Chelsea Village Plc in the period preceding the announcement of the bid' by Abramovich. The statement added that the takeover panel understood the inquiries were 'unconnected to Chelsea Ltd', the company set up by Abramovich to buy out Bates.

The Harding Estate have accepted the share offer; so, too, have Sky, so now the Chelsea company purchasing the shares has over 90 per cent and may compulsorily request the rest. Now this FSA statement is both unsatisfactory and unacceptable, all innuendo, nudge-nudge, wink-wink. They use phrases like "may have been inaccuracies" and "may have been misled", suggesting that they have been misled. So let them say who has been doing the misleading and what the facts are. It should not be on the lines of the usual Government spin-doctoring exercise. We don't want politics involved here. It's simple as I see it – the FSA should put up or shut up.'

Bates said, 'The question of Chelsea's shareholders was first looked into when we went public in 1996 and it was accepted by the Stock Exchange. The FSA then held an inquiry about a year ago and found nothing wrong. I am now fed up with this innuendo. I want to know what evidence they are supposed to have received and who the source is.'

FSA inquiries of this nature are not uncommon in takeover cases and should 'matters come to light', the takeover panel will conduct their own inquiries 'at the relevant time'.

An FSA spokesman warned that any breach of the disclosure rules presents serious problems. He said, 'The market should have all the information on companies available to us because then you get into the area of possibly creating false or misleading impressions, you don't know what may be going on.' But he cautioned that, as yet, the FSA has not launched an official investigation. He added, 'We know enough to begin conducting enquiries. We haven't actually moved to a formal investigation. We are still at the making enquiries stage.'

The FSA faced a daunting task in trying to unearth the ownership of certain shares in Chelsea Village. Some use a Guernsey-based company run by Patrick Murrin, a non-Executive Director of Chelsea Village since July 1996.

According to Chelsea Village's last annual report, Murrin owned 100 shares as of June last year. He is also a director of Seymour Pierce Group Plc, a City-based firm that acts as Chelsea's nominated stockbrokers and financial adviser. Seymour Pierce acted for Chelsea Village Plc in the Abramovich deal. Keith Harris, a member of the Board of Wembley National Stadium Ltd when Bates was Chairman, and former independent Chairman of the Football League, as well as being a Manchester United fan, is Seymour Pierce's Executive Chairman.

The other major known shareholders are the estate of Matthew Harding which holds a 23.5 per cent stake, and BSkyB with a 9.9 per cent stake.

Once Bates had pocketed the £17.5m, the next question was how long he would remain as Chairman. Bates said he would stay until 2005. He first addressed the question on arriving in Kuala Lumpur where Chelsea competed for the Asia Cup, saying, 'It seems to me that my enemies are stirring it up for me ... I am enjoying my life at Chelsea very much at the moment. I have all of the pleasure and none of the pain. I'm going nowhere. I've got a job to do and I've started it and I'll see it through to the end. I'm not on my way out. No way.'

Bates, who was also in Rome for Chelsea's 2-0 defeat by Lazio, is clearly excited by the stream of new arrivals at the Bridge. He was particularly taken with £6m teenager Glen Johnson's performance in Italy. 'He is an extremely talented young player with a tremendous attitude,' said Bates. 'He made a big impact.' As Damien Duff and Wayne Bridge joined their new team-mates for the inaugural FA Premier League Asia Cup, Bates advised Chelsea fans against getting carried away after the arrival of four stars for £36.5m. Bates argued, 'The expectations of fans are always impossible. I'm a fan myself. My expectations are wild but as a Chairman they are more realistic. Money alone does not buy you success. There are a few clubs who have bankrupted themselves trying to do that.' Bates added, 'Every Chairman wants to win everything – if they didn't, they'd be in the wrong job. But Chelsea has never expected to win silverware, so it is a bonus when we do. We hope to do better than we did last year. We got to two quarter-finals and went from sixth to fourth. We'd like to improve on that.'

Bates backed Claudio Ranieri to handle the new-look team. 'To be a manager you have to be a fool or a strong man and we have 20 of them in the Premiership. Ranieri has a proven track record, both at Chelsea and previously in Europe, of being a shrewd judge of players.'

Bates also defended the spending. 'So far, we have spent £34m on four players, only £4m more than Manchester United spent on Rio Ferdinand last summer. Last year, Claudio Ranieri didn't spend a penny and took us from sixth to fourth place. In the process, he blooded five youngsters.'

And as far as the club heading towards financial meltdown was concerned, Bates was keen to dismiss the idea. 'Our fans have been reading we were 24 hours from bankruptcy. What a complete load of crap. We had already rescheduled our debts, it wasn't a problem. By 2004 all our debts on players would have been paid off and then the plan was that, until 2007, we would carry on with gradual progression and modest improvement. After that, Chelsea would have been a cash cow. It was always going to be that way. What Mr Abramovich has done is allow us to accelerate that by three years.'

Bates insisted Abramovich is in it for the long haul and no one is going to rip him off. 'How has Mr Abramovich made his £5.4bn? He's a shrewd businessman. People seem to forget all of that. It would cost him £200 m to walk away. If he's worth £5.4bn then we are still talking about a significant amount of money. It would cost him five per cent of his wealth. Why would he have started something if he didn't want to see it through? He has his advisers. They know what a good buy Chelsea Football Club is and they know the potential here. The balance of power could be shifting; there is certainly a more level playing field now.

'I was very interested in what Graeme Souness said about us the other week. He said that teams would not roll over and give us points. We know we are going to have a fight on our hands and people will raise their game against us. We know that every game is going to be like a cup final. Even if we are playing a workmanlike, journeyman team they are going to be fighting us for everything.

'It has helped us to disturb the established order. Instead of viewing it as Manchester United, Arsenal and 18 others, it is now Manchester United, Arsenal, Chelsea and 17 others. In fairness, that's harsh on Freddy Shepherd and what he has done at Newcastle. They have hoovered up the best players out of places like Ipswich and Nottingham Forest. And they have got Bobby Robson, too. God will probably retire before him and they've got the backbone of the side for the next five years. And there's Liverpool. They have improved their squad – so there's probably five of us now and there is always room for a surprise package. Arsenal might not have any money, if you believe what you read, but they have a very strong team. They might not have a new ground and they might not have the corporate facilities that they would like, but they still get 38,000 for every game. And, though I'm talking through gritted teeth now, they won the FA Cup last season and the Double the year before. Not exactly on the breadline, are they?'

And finally, the thoughts of Chairman Ken as he reflects on the most momentous takeover in football and all the ramifications for himself, Abramovich and the club...

'I'm very happy, very happy indeed about what has happened to Chelsea. Chelsea is a success story, it was a success story before Mr Abramovich arrived, a great success story, and now he has fast-tracked it far further and it's just great.' Look back to season 1984–85 when Chelsea went head to head with one of the teams of the day, Sheffield Wednesday. What has happened to Sheffield Wednesday? They're in the Second Division, while Chelsea qualified again for the Champions League. Remember the Big Five of two decades ago – Manchester Untied, Arsenal, Spurs, Everton and Liverpool? What has happened to two of them? Spurs and Everton are now Premiership strugglers.

'When I look back over the 21 years I feel we have done a pretty good job, and that is why it was the most exciting club for Mr Abramovich to buy: there was a platform on which he could build.

'The day Ranieri arrived here he told me that, as he came from the Continent and wanted a Continental approach, he wanted two players for every position. We tried to accommodate him but I am sure he is now pleasantly surprised by the quality of players he has for every position.

'I am delighted too. I know that, with no financial restraints, there is no limit to what Chelsea can achieve.'

Bates is too often shown in a bad light. 'Just he other week someone wrote that I cut a lonely figure on the end row. Well, I am in my usual seat, the one I have had for 20-odd years. I continue to host the directors' suite, the board room and the directors' box. Mr Abramovich comes along with all of his mates. He is not interested in the politics of football; he has put his money up to enjoy his day out and, believe me, he enjoys himself. But he sits up there in the box with his friends and he has a ball. He doesn't come down to the directors' box – he is not interested. He is like a very rich punter, there for the fun of it, and I am enjoying it too.'

Bates not only sold his shares but reached agreement with Abramovich on the timing of his final farewell. 'I am chairman until 2005 which is also our Centenary, then I become life-president, stepping back another stage. We won the title in 1955 and it would be great to win it 50 years later so it coincided with our Centenary. But believe me, I won't have any problems if we win the Premiership this season as well. Two in a row? Yes, that would do me just fine.'

A DONE DEAL

ROMAN ABRAMOVICH WAS INTRODUCED to Pini Zahavi by the Israeli agent's close friend German Vladimirovich Tkachenko, owner of Russian club Sovietov Krylya, in Samara since 1999. Tkachenko is an influential member of the council of the Russian Federation, the equivalent of an MP. Zahavi told me, 'I was introduced to Roman a year ago by German. German is a good friend, we have known each other for a few years and I have been involved in meeting people in Russian football for 15 years. German is my main contact with Roman, he is a close friend of Roman's ...'

Zahavi had become acquainted with Abramovich in a series of meetings throughout 2002. Zahavi knows him well enough and told me, 'Roman is a serious guy, he talks to people, listens to their opinions and can then make his own mind up separating the serious from the non-serious.'

Abramovich was told by Tkachenko, the 33-year-old who runs two major aluminium companies and who is even now influential in his football dealings, 'Pini is a guy you can trust, more than anybody in the world ... he is discreet and gives you honest opinions.' Through German, Pini has gained the trust of Abramovich. Born in Donetsk, German was educated at the Gorlovsky Institute of Foreign Languages.

Zahavi has become, mostly due to his activities in the summer, one of the most powerful wheeler-dealers in the game. So what are his connections, background and contacts?

Zahavi grew up in Nes Ziona, a small country town a few miles outside Tel Aviv. The son of a shopkeeper who sold building materials, Zahavi became a sports journalist and started a sideline in agency work. Now 59, Zahavi belies his age with a youthful approach to life. He is very close to influential figures in Israeli's large immigrant community and one of his best friends is Eli Azur, who runs a string of Russian-language newspapers in Israel. Together, they run a company called Charlton, which buys up worldwide football rights, including the Premiership, to be sold on to Israeli broadcasters.

Zahavi's amazing global connections in the most unlikiest of locations gave him a head start in the Russian transfer market following the collapse of the Soviet Union. He has made regular trips to Moscow and Kiev for the past ten years. After being introduced to Abramovich, a friendship grew, cemented by the pair's Jewish roots. Abramovich has a Knightsbridge penthouse, Zahavi an apartment near Marble Arch.

After spending his Christmas holiday in 1979 following his favourite club, Liverpool, he found himself fog-bound at Heathrow Airport while waiting for a flight home. There he spotted Peter Robinson, the Liverpool Chief Executive. He walked over and introduced himself and suggested a player in Israel he should sign, Avi Cohen. In the deal that subsequently took the full-back from Maccabi Tel Aviv to Anfield for £200,000, Zahavi convinced Robinson to let him act as the middle-man.

After the Cohen deal, Zahavi built a relationship with Graeme Souness and all the backroom staff at Anfield. When Souness became Manager of Rangers, two of his early signings were Cohen and Bonni Ginsberg, another Zahavi player.

Towards the end of the 1980s, he was making friends with Alex Ferguson, who had recently arrived at Manchester United and was looking for new players. Another was Eriksson, then only recently installed as manager of Benfica.

'The one thing he does have is a very good knowledge of football worldwide and an extensive network of influential contacts,' says Maurice Watkins, a director of Manchester United, and a friend of Zahavi for ten years. 'The fact that soccer is a global game now means it is essential that clubs have good contacts. Pini has those contacts. He has correspondents in every major footballing country feeding him information on players and helping fix things.'

Euro '96 brought Ferguson further proof of Zahavi's footballing judgement. As they sat together at Villa Park before the Czech Republic–Portugal quarter-final, Zahavi told Fergie to watch out for Karel Poborsky. Poborsky lobbed Vitor Baia to score the goal of the tournament. Within a month, the Czech winger was checking into Old Trafford with Zahavi as deal-broker.

Parallel to Zahavi's rise has been that of Jacob Shahar, President of Maccabi Haifa during a decade in which they had become Israel's richest, most successful and most powerful club. Shahar and Zahavi are friends who grew up together. Maccabi led a successful drive to renegotiate the television rights for the Israeli league. The main beneficiaries were Maccabi and Zahavi's company, Charlton. In October 1996, Maccabi's biggest asset was their brilliant young playmaker, Eyal Berkovic. Zahavi convinced Souness, then Manager of Southampton, to sign the player despite reservations that Berkovic was too lightweight for English football. Berkovic was a success, and his subsequent move to West Ham brought Zahavi into contact with Rio Ferdinand, who was being chased by half the agents in Britain. The pair became such close friends that they went on holiday at the same time to the Red Sea resort of Eilat.

A dream came true for Zahavi in September 2002 when Maccabi played Manchester United in the Champions League. At Old Trafford, Zahavi and Jason Ferguson (Sir Alex's son and also an agent) were walking in and out of both dressing rooms together.

His biggest player client is Rio Ferdinand, thanks to a chance meeting with the then 15-year-old centre-half at West Ham's Chadwell Heath training ground. Zahavi secured Rio's £18m move from West Ham to Leeds United and then on to Manchester Untied, both deals smashing the British record. Even before Ferdinand moved to Old Trafford in a deal brokered by Zahavi, the agent was involved in many major United deals, including Juan Veron for £28.1m. He is so trusted by Ferguson and Abramovich that each is comfortable with the fact that he is working for both.

Zahavi works alone. Fellow agent Barry Silkman, who was one of the Israeli's first deals in 1980, said, 'When you're a one-man band there can be no leaks. When the big conglomerate agencies do a deal, 20 people know about it. That's why clubs trust him to handle their big business.'

He was also involved in David Beckham's £25m transfer to Real Madrid.

He bolstered the successful election bid of Barcelona's new President, Joan Laporta, by facilitating his conditional £30m offer for Beckham, a move United welcomed as a way of driving up the price for the England captain.

Zahavi got another of his clients, Turkey goalkeeper Recber Rustu, a new job in the process. Laporta agreed to take on Rustu, who was out of contract with Fenerbahce, even before he got the presidency.

Johnson's departure from West Ham means that Anton Ferdinand, Rio's younger brother, can establish himself as right-back at Upton Park. Chelsea, through their Mr Fixit, are watching closely. The Ferdinands have the same agent.

Old Trafford, April 2002

Abramovich's passion for football was activated when he went to the World Cup Finals in Japan and Korea. But he was interested in the sport before that, as he explains, 'I'd also watched a few games in Russia and enjoyed the environment.'

Nine months later, Abramovich set his heart on owning a club when he sampled the atmosphere of Old Trafford and thought seriously about buying Manchester United.

Zahavi, through his multitude of contacts at Old Trafford, arranged tickets for the Russian. Zahavi's close contacts are Sir Alex and (at the time) Chief Executive Peter Kenyon with whom he has done a great deal of business in the past, including the transfer of Rio Ferdinand for the current British record fee of £30m.

Zahavi arranged tickets in the directors' box, but no one that night at the quarter-finals of the Champions League at Old Trafford knew the unfamiliar face watching the Manchester United v Real Madrid game.

Graeme Souness, another of Zahavi's many friends, contacts and business associates, picked up Abramovich from the airport as a favour to the Israeli agent and took both the Russian and Zahavi to Old Trafford. When Souness spotted Abramovich's features plastered all over the national papers the day he bought Chelsea, he was straight on the phone to Zahavi. Taking Abramovich back to the airport was none other than Rio Ferdinand. In Rio's car was also his four-year-old brother from his mother's second marriage. The boy loves to sing and, throughout the journey from Old Trafford to the airport, he had Abramovich joining in the songs. Zahavi went with two other friends of Abramovich to a Manchester restaurant awaiting Rio's mission to take Abramovich back to the airport.

Abramovich says, 'That's when I decided I really wanted to be involved in football. The whole atmosphere got to me and that is when I knew I had to be involved. On the way back to Moscow, I couldn't stop thinking about it. So I said to my people, "Find me a football club. "'

England captain David Beckham had been controversially left on the bench but he came on and scored twice in United's 4-3 European Cup quarter-final, second-leg victory, but the Spanish club progressed 6-5 on aggregate.

Abramovich added, 'It was a very beautiful game and I realised I couldn't pass it by. I decided less than a year ago to get involved, and looked at ten clubs in England, of which four were "possibles".'

May, 2002

A short-list of five clubs was drawn up which comprised Lazio, United, Arsenal, Tottenham ... and Chelsea.

Abramovich first met with Spurs chairman Daniel Levy to discuss 'general issues', and the question of whether Levy would be interested in selling his shares did crop up. Levy confesses: 'Yes, we did have a meeting at his request because he wanted ENIC's perspective on the European football market. It is important to note, however, that at no time did we discuss, either then or subsequently, his desire to acquire a Premiership club.'

Abramovich closely examined the possibility of buying Spurs but any deal was difficult because it would have been a problem to buy out both Levy's shares and the 13 per cent still in the possession of Sir Alan Sugar.

However, Levy received a telephone call from Zahavi, who made a more formal declaration of intent, asking whether he would be keen to sell and at what price. Levy made the mistake of asking far too high a price for the shares – £50m for 29.9% of the club, which he valued at £150m. At the time, the share price was 18p, valuing the club at just £20m.

Ironically, a further appointment had been made for the day after the announcement of the Chelsea takeover. Naturally, was there was no need for that second meeting, in fact no need to even cancel it!

The Russian's advisers felt that too much investment would be needed either to build a new stadium or to renovate White Hart Lane, while Stamford Bridge was redeveloped. Spurs is also going through a particularly unproductive period, with the team requiring radical surgery.

As the Russian's private helicopter took him across London after his meeting with Levy, he spotted a football pitch, stadium and complex. 'That looks a damn sight better than the ground I've just visited,' said

Abramovich. At that stage, he was still not totally convinced about buying an English club, according to insiders. When he eventually made up his mind to buy a club, Abramovich recalled his helicopter journey and knew it was a wise move to go for the Bridge rather than White Hart Lane. Spurs fans will be green with envy now that they have discovered how much the new owner has been willing to invest in players.

In making his decision about finding a club in England, Abramovich considered that Arsenal was a non-starter because leading shareholders such as Danny Fiszman, the Carr brothers and David Dein would not contemplate selling.

Manchester United would have been too costly and also tricky. Outside the élite, long-standing club owners such as Doug Ellis of Aston Villa and David Murray of Glasgow Rangers wanted to sell out, struggling to keep up.

Abramovich said, 'I looked at a lot of clubs in England and one in Europe, but after studying everything and talking to my advisers, Chelsea was the one I wanted to buy. It was the obvious choice for us once we'd studied all the facts surrounding it ... now we have to build something special here.'

Jonathan Clare, Deputy Chairman of Citigate Dewe Rogerson, public relations advisers for Abramovich, said he had looked at several clubs before opting for Chelsea. Bates told me, 'This guy looked at four clubs, two of them in London, and felt there were too many problems.' Bates took great pleasure in the fact that one of the clubs was clearly Arsenal, where he has put one over his great adversary David Dein.

Abramovich adds, 'Being in the Champions League was also important. It helped, but it was not decisive. There were four or five other factors that helped me make up my mind. I love London and Chelsea is in the centre of London ... that was important to me. The English word "fun" sums it up for me. It is not about business. I want to be at every match,' but unable to ignore the value-for-money element of his investment, he adds, 'the price and quality of Chelsea made it the optimum choice.' And he is willing to commit to years of ownership. 'I see it as a very long-term commitment,' he says, although he refused to disclose the limit on funds he was willing to pour into the club, explaining that by doing so would push up the price of future contracts.

There is also no doubt that Abramovich came exceptionally close to buying Manchester United. One of Abramovich's advisers on the finance side tells me, 'Yes, he was very, very close to buying Manchester United until his advisers told him it would be too difficult.' Abramovich was told that the Irish connection would prove an obstacle as they held a significant slice of the shares, and that he would encounter problems with Sir Alex Ferguson who could be more difficult to deal with. Chelsea was a much cleaner, less complicated transaction. Certainly he could have afforded the £650m it would have cost to buy Manchester United and he had no compunction in paying the price as he explains that rich Russians enjoy spending their money lavishly. 'There are lots of rich, young people in Russia. We don't live that long, so we earn it and spend it.'

Richard Creitzman knew that the purchase of Chelsea was made easy because they had to deal with only one man – Ken Bates. He said, 'The fact that Roman loved central London helped, but we also took into account the fact that we would only have to deal directly with one person rather than go through the process of talking to numerous shareholders. The others were seriously considered but, once we did our homework, the appeal of purchasing Chelsea became even greater.

'Roman went to the Champions League quarter-final between Manchester United and Real Madrid and his takeover of Chelsea snowballed quite quickly from there. He then said, "Come on and have a look at football," and that was it. From then, we started focusing in on what he wanted to do. We set up some meetings, had chats with the banks and they put out some feelers to see what was out there. The banks came back with a definitive report and said this is the story on the three or four clubs that had come through from the discussion process.

'It wasn't just the shares. He likes London, so that was a plus for Chelsea. Financially, it depends how you look at it, but if you are coming in to buy, and someone is in a weaker position, then it is better for you as a buyer.

'They [Chelsea] are in the Champions League, as are Manchester. They have a good squad, Manchester have a very good squad, as have Arsenal and Newcastle from the teams that were above Chelsea last year. But here is a very strong team. [Carlo] Cudicini, I think, is one of the best goalkeepers in the League. Ranieri is one of the top managers. I am not going to go through the whole team, but there is a very strong side and the people we have bought are very strong and the key thing now is to get them all to gel together.

'We prepared information for him about various clubs; he took out the ones he wasn't interested in and there were a few left, most of them English. We got a bank on board to show the turnover, debt, players, league positions, stadium information, non-football business and so on of the clubs. Then, one Wednesday night in Moscow, we sat down and he said, "Right, we are flying over to England tomorrow." We weren't coming to buy a football club but we had focused in on two, one of which was Chelsea, and we had the meeting with Chelsea first. We met Ken Bates on Thursday evening; on Friday, lawyers got involved and, by Tuesday, bang, that was it.'

Abramovich got his first taste of the football bug while at Old Trafford. He sat in a corporate box, behind glass. According to his right-hand man, the decision to place a barrier between the privileged few and the raw atmosphere of the stadium is something that Abramovich felt was a mistake. The glass boxes on Stamford Bridge's East Stand are being looked at; the Russian is considering opening them up to the elements.

Wednesday, 23 April 2003

Jonathan Barnett represents some of the country's leading players such as Kieron Dyer and Ashley Cole, and he is highly influential in some of the big transfers and player contracts. When Dyer opted to re-sign for Newcastle United, it was Barnett who thrashed out a lucrative deal that enabled England's promising star to rush out and buy the latest £100,000 car. A contract worth £75,000 a week put Dyer among the country's highest-paid players.

'Jonathan is a nice guy and a friend of mine and he afforded an introduction for me to Chelsea's Managing Director Trevor Birch; he has good connections in the game,' says Zahavi.

Lunch was arranged at Les Ambassadeurs Club in Hamilton Place, Park Lane, where Barnett, Birch and Zahavi enjoyed a convivial lunch paid for by Zahavi. It proved to be one of the most significant lunches in the history of the English game.

Barnett explains, 'I arranged the lunch at Les Ambassadeurs on behalf of Pini to meet Trevor Birch, who wanted to discuss some players he wanted to move out of the club. The conversation got round to Chelsea's precarious finances, and Trevor mentioned that Chelsea were in need of money and quickly. Pini said that he knew somebody. It all moved on from there. There were several meetings or conversations between Pini and Trevor. Pini and Trevor had their own agreement over commission and I had an agreement with Pini. It would not be uncommon, would it, for agents such as Pini and myself to be on a commission for this sort of introduction?' Clearly the Zahavi-Birch-Barnett meeting was the catalyst for the Abramovich takeover, but the issue of commission has become a contentious one.

Zahavi tells me, 'We discussed players, and Trevor wanted to know if we could help move some of his players out of the club.'

The background is that Chelsea had, over the past few years, acquired some world-renowned superstar names who had been approaching their sell-by date by the time they pitched up at the Bridge, but had now become highly paid accessories the club could do without.

Zahavi refused to name names, but it doesn't take a genius to work out that Winston Bogarde was hardly earning his £40,000-a-week salary, for ever on the treatment table or in the reserves; that Manu Petit might have a World Cup winner's medal but was no longer the player who dominated midfield like he did at Arsenal; and that Jimmy Floyd Hasselbaink's contract was based on expensive annual pay rises, making him the top earner at £80,000 a week with the Manager never quite sure whether he was a genuine world-class goalscorer or not. Try as they might, Chelsea could not rid themselves of the crippling financial burden of one of the most expensive wage bills in the Premiership while also carrying debts of £90m. As the financial crisis deepened, it was imperative to unload some of this surplus playing staff as discreetly as possible.

As the lunch progressed, it was clear that the financial problems at the Bridge were worsening and that, while the aperitif was about the players, the main course was whether Zahavi had sufficient worldwide contacts to find a suitable buyer for Chelsea.

Zahavi did have a few potential buyers. The ultra-well-connected Israeli knew the likes of Spurs fan Phillip Green, who might be persuaded to invest in a club, although he was more inclined to look to the one he followed rather than a London rival. But through Zahavi's supreme connections in Russia as well, he knew that Roman Abramovich particularly would be keen on such a sporting investment.

Zahavi was willing to explain to me the finer details of his conversation with Birch on the topic of finding a suitable buyer, saying, 'I made a point of asking Birch whether he had the authorisation and whether he was talking on behalf of Bates and the Board. He told me that he did. After the lunch, I said to Birch to give me a couple of days.'

In fact, it was more than two weeks later when Zahavi called Birch to inform him that he had somebody interested. The delay was because Abramovich had looked at Spurs first, and examined the feasibility of buying either Manchester United or Arsenal. 'Listen ... I have an interested party,' Zahavi told Birch.

Friday, 30 May 2003

Rio Ferdinand and his close friend and agent Zahavi travelled to Moscow for a working holiday. There, Zahavi had the opportunity to discuss with German Tkachenko the possibility of involving Abramovich in a takeover of a Premiership club.

Other topics of conversation included whether Zahavi could help Tkachenko to bring Manchester United to Samara.

Monday, 23 June 2003

An 8.00am meeting was arranged for Birch to come to the Marble Arch flat of Zahavi. The value of the Chelsea Village shares at the time were languishing below 20p and Zahavi wanted to know the price required to buy the club. Birch demanded 40p a share, but conceded that if Zahavi's man was serious, the price would be negotiable. Zahavi passed on the information to Abramovich in Moscow via a call to his friend German. The call came back to arrange a meeting to conclude a deal.

Thursday, 26 June

Stamford Bridge was the venue for Birch to meet the Russian delegation of Abramovich, German Tkachnko and Eugene Tenebaum. Birch was on the line virtually every minute to Zahavi to keep him fully updated about the talks. No one had any doubts about Zahavi's pivotal role in the deal.

The deal was done in about 20 minutes.

They broke up at 11.30am and decided to go out to lunch to celebrate. Birch was teased over lunch that they didn't really want to go ahead with the deal to buy Chelsea, they were just interested in a free lunch!

Later that day, Zahavi received a call from Birch. Could Roman meet his Chairman Ken Bates?

Through German, Zahavi persuaded Abramovich to delay his flight back to Moscow to meet Bates. The meeting was arranged at the Dorchester Hotel. Zahavi didn't need to attend that meeting between Abramovich and Bates as the deal had already been done.

At 7.10pm, Bates marched along the narrow corridor, past the check-in for the coats, and on to the plush Dorchester bar, frequented by the rich and famous, a favourite pre-dinner cocktail haunt of Sir Alan Sugar and Lady Anne, to greet Abramovich and his entourage. Bates and Abramovich drank Evian water, and nibbled the delicacies on the table. Forty-five minutes later, they had shaken hands on the deal. Bates had a dinner date later that evening when he celebrated with champagne. If the strain of the past few days and weeks was taking its toll, Bates was hiding it well.

Friday, 27 June

Richard Creitzman, Eugene Tenenbaum and Roman Abramovich met with Chelsea's fnancial advisers and stockbrokers Seymour Pierce at a hastily arranged meeting at Chelsea Village.

Seymour Pierce Chairman Keith Harris has seldom seen a deal go through so speedily. He tells me, 'It was break-neck speed, I have never experienced anything as quick as this. I thought the deal to buy the *Express* by Richard Desmond was quick, but we had to raise the money.

'We arrived on Friday afternoon, around 4.00pm, and were told of the meetings the previous day. It was all relatively straightforward, the finances were in place and verified by Citibank who knew Abramovich from deals in Russia, so I had no problem with them.' Estimates as to his fee for his advice on the Chelsea deal totalled a cool £1m for his firm, of which he owns a 20 per cent stake.

Harris looks back and now says, 'This deal has lifted the shadow over the entire football industry. Everyone was down, forecasting gloom and doom and suddenly it all looks a bit brighter. Whether or not more Russians will end up owning football clubs over here is an interesting point, but Abramovich has shown he is deadly serious with the welter of player purchases and that can only encourage others to follow suit. All the accusations that it is a toy, well, anyone who commits to something like half a billion dollars is hardly playing at it. That shows commitment in my book.'

Harris suggested that Abramovich snubbed Manchester United because it would have cost £700m to take over. Harris said, 'There was a great deal of research done by him and his advisers before going for Chelsea. He looked at a number of Premiership clubs. They were Manchester United, Arsenal, Spurs and Chelsea. I can understand why he chose Chelsea for a host of reasons. Why not Manchester United? If you think of the sums of money involved, United are the most successful financially. They would have cost £650m–£700m. That's a huge chunk of change. He paid £60m for the shares outstanding at Chelsea. But buying the company meant assuming responsibility for the debts and that was another £80m. So he got Chelsea for £140m.' Although the debts were £90m, there were reserves of £10m so Harris is right to put the real debt figure at £80m.

'As for United, what can you do with them, how can you improve them? At Arsenal, you would have to spend to buy and build a stadium. You have all that problem ... and it would be expensive. Spurs have spent on the ground but is it big enough and in the right place? And how much would you have to spend on the team?'

Harris, who was still working on takeover possibilities at Old Trafford, said, 'You look at Chelsea ... the assets are in place and they have spent a lot developing the ground into one of the best in the Premiership. The infrastructure of the team is good. Sure, there is money to be spent but the backbone is strong. Only time will tell whether it was money well spent. One suspects this is an investment.'

Bates said, 'He went to United to watch a game but he didn't like the atmosphere. He decided he wanted a club in London and opted for Chelsea as they had more going for them than other teams. We have no problems with stadium redevelopment.'

Wednesday, 2 July

Zahavi accompanies Sven-Goran Eriksson to Abramovich's London flat, but it wasn't until a photographer realised the significance of the pictures that the front- and back-page story broke a few days later when Roman's wife Irina went on a much publicised two-hour shopping trip to Harrods – but, apparently, there was no bid for Fulham! Zahavi was less than pleased to be so high profile when, normally, he only wants his clients to hit the headlines – he likes to remain well and truly in the background. It was an uncomfortable time for Zahavi, but even so the real focus was on what precisely went on over tea inside Abramovich's London base.

Already, the headline CHELSKI had been used on the front page of the *Sun*, and in as diverse journals as the *Guardian* and *Evening Standard*.

Thursday, 3 July

The famous Abramovich Wish List of transfer targets contained more than 30 names, a *Who's Who* of world football stars. It was a question of discovering whether players could become available at the right price and it soon became clear that all the money in the world couldn't prise away players such as Henry and van Nistelrooy, while clubs were demanding far too much for players at the age of 30 such as Vieri.

Nesta was not on the list even though he became the first name linked with the new wave of potential targets.

The identity of the person who had compiled the list has been a subject of feverish media debate. Was it Eriksson ... Ranieri ... Zahavi? No doubt Ranieri confirmed every single candidate, but the only decision maker, at the final point, was Abramovich.

Zahavi then embarked on a whirlwind, feverish tour of some of Europe's most glamorous footballing cities. In week one alone, the seemingly ageless Zahavi did a tour of the Continent – on Tuesday it was Paris; Wednesday, Turin; Thursday, Milan; and Friday, Monaco, pursuing Europe's finest footballers on behalf of Chelsea's new billionaire owner.

And all the while, Zahavi was networking. It is not simply a matter of one agent pulling off a deal. The player has an agent, and sometimes another agent has the authorisation for the transfer. Transfers can be complex, and might involve numerous agents, who all work on a commission basis. For example, in the Geremi transaction, Barry Silkman, a friend of Zahavi's, knew the agent who represents the Cameroon international in Spain. By introducing the agent to Zahavi, the Spanish agent would have paid Silkman a commission. So the deal proved to be a highly lucrative one for the man known as 'Silky', even though he played a small part in the overall transaction. One by one, Zahavi contacted the web of connected agents.

The emergence of Abramovich has sent football agents into a frenzy. Just as they might have been looking for alternative employment with the transfer market in its most depressed state for a decade, along comes a 36-year-old with the express purpose of having 'fun' and more than sufficient cash to finance all the fun he wanted. The floodgates opened.

The £6.9 million signing of Geremi, Real Madrid's Cameroon midfielder, was handled from Zahavi's Monaco hotel room by fax. Zahavi was behind the surprise deal with West Ham for their 18-year-old defender Glen Johnson, and on the same day he and Abramovich made Chelsea's initial offer for Vieri. After he helped to tie up the deal for Geremi, that evening in Monaco he met Juventus Vice-President Roberto Bettega and Executive Director Luciano Moggi to attempt to thrash out a deal for Edgar Davids.

Zahavi knows how much Abramovich wants to turn Chelsea into the finest club side in the world. 'He wants Chelsea to be the best, the kings of Europe – run like Manchester United and more successful than Real Madrid.'

'Chelsea have livened things up a bit,' says Silkman, the former Crystal Palace and Manchester City player. His relationship with Zahavi goes back to the time when the Israeli brokered a deal to take Silkman to Maccabi Tel Aviv in the 1980s when he was still a player. They have remained friends ever since, but have never been partners.

Silkman says, 'Chelsea have been good for the transfer market. They wanted Damien Duff, and with some of the money Chelsea spent, Blackburn bought Steven Reid, and that has left Millwall with cash. So the money is filtering through. At the same time, Chelsea have sparked clubs into action. Maybe they had been leaving money aside for a rainy day, now they are not reining in so much. They were also waiting to see what happened with the TV deal. As long as clubs are sensible, they will be OK. Look at Southampton, they now have £5m–£6m to spend.'

Following the sale of Wayne Bridge, bids went in for Neil McCann from Rangers at £1.5m and Sunderland's Kevin Phillips for £3m.

Chelsea did, he says, pay over the odds for Duff – but he says Duff's agent was the reason for that. 'They ended up paying £17m. There is no way they wanted to pay more than £10m,' Silkman says. 'No one has benefited apart from Blackburn. If the player was worth that much, then why was he not already being paid £50,000 a week? That is a question for his agent.'

Wednesday, 6 August

Bates and Zahavi meet for the first time. Zahavi was at Stamford Bridge helping to finalise the arrival of Veron. The meeting took place in Birch's office in the presence of Abramovich's chief aide Richard Creitzman. The Chairman walked into Birch's office and over to Zahavi, shaking his hand. Zahavi remained seated. Bates told me, 'We were introduced for the first time and I simply said, "Nice to meet you at long last."'

It was anything but an amicable encounter. Ever since the deal had been struck, Zahavi met with a stone-wall approach from Birch and a failure to gain any sort of recognition from Bates. Put quite simply, Bates told me that he had not met Zahavi, that he had not commissioned him in any way and that, if Birch had given him the impression that he could speak for all the shareholders, including himself, then the Chief Executive was mistaken.

In other words, Bates had no intention of listening to Zahavi's case for commission on the deal. Equally, Zahavi had enlisted the aid of Barnett and Phillip Green to contact Bates in a bid to make Chelsea comply with his demands for commission. Little wonder the first meeting was a touch frosty. Bates offered the opportunity for a 'chat' but Zahavi was not included to talk, he just wanted to be paid. Bates, in turn, disclosed that he was recommending that Zahavi be paid commissions from certain Chelsea transfer transactions. Zahavi countered that he was offering something he already had!

Zahavi was 'pissed off'. He was involved directly or indirectly with all the Chelsea transfers and was consulted about them.

Barnett is similarly upset over the non-payment of any commission. 'How did Roman Abramovich come to buy Chelsea? Did he just turn up in a taxi one day? Of course not. Pini and I worked on the deal from the start and I am far from happy about the fact that no commission has been paid.

'Pini and Trevor no doubt had some arrangement while I had one with Pini. I am not prepared to discuss how much commission I had agreed with Pini but you could put it in seven figures.

'I have spoken to Ken Bates about this. I was shocked at the behaviour when he claimed he knew nothing about it. Ken insisted he knew nothing about it, but he must have found out somehow. Somebody surely afforded the introduction? It's all a mystery to me why no commission is being paid.'

Barnett ended up moving two of his clients to the Bridge – Johnson and Bridge, – but as he said, 'Yes, I will get my commission on two transfers, but from my clients, not from anyone else, so that has nothing to do with the way Bates has behaved toward me and Pini.'

Bates tells me, 'I got a call from Phillip Green who said he wanted to act as the honest broker, but I told him there was nothing to broker, and that was it.' Indeed, it was true that Bates had not met Zahavi, who had dealt with Birch, but the issue was a running sore.

Monday, September 7

Zahavi planned a long break, a return home to Israel, followed by a well-earned holiday in the States, and then to Brazil for business before thinking about the re-opening of the transfer window in January 2004.

But Zahavi had a very important and contentious side-issue to deal with. He had been consulting with his legal advisers for some time and, although he had attempted the route of genteel persuasion through a variety of intermediaries, myself included, he decided not to act. Zahavi did not want to take the route of legal action, in order not to embarrass Abramovich and Chelsea Football Club.

Some top people in English football suggested to Zahavi that he should sue Bates. I can reveal that one of them was Bates' fierce adversary David Dein of Arsenal and FA vice-chairman. Barnett says: 'Pini has behaved unbelievably well. In all of our discussions I wanted to sue Bates straight away but Pnin was more restrained. David Dein said, "he's a big bully – sue." But Pini doesn't want to cause any embarrassment to Abramovich.'

Zahavi turned up in the Chairman's room before the match with

Blackburn with a host of his entourage, which took Bates by surprise. It was Zahavi's way of saying he was still around, had some clout at the club, and was awaiting some recognition for the vital role he played in pulling off the Abramovich takeover.

Bates has powerful allies in the media, none more so than David Mellor, who wrote in his *Evening Standard* column on 18 July, 'One thing is certain amid the swirling eddies at Chelsea, and that is the sooner Pini Zahavi gets on his bike, the better. And that may happen now that his cunning plan to help out his best mate Sir Alex Ferguson by palming Juan Sebastian Veron off on Chelsea has come to nothing. Veron going for £14m only looks a bargain because Ferguson was rash enough to spend £28m on him. Looked at in the cold light of recent experience – two years of being a bit-part player at Old Trafford – that kind of money looks exorbitant for a player soon to be 30. Then there's the small matter of his personal terms, believed to be in the region of £5m a season. Chelsea are saying thanks, but no thanks. And the sooner Zahavi takes the hint, the better.'

Could that have been partly inspired by Bates? On 25 July, Mellor was still not convinced about Veron when he wrote, 'Last week, it looked like the Pini Zahavi-inspired campaign to get Juan Sebastian Veron to Chelsea had foundered, but a week is as long a time in football as it is in politics. The torch has been re-lit on the back of some encouraging words from Claudio Ranieri, though I suspect the Veron he likes is the one he knew at Lazio.

'I doubt Ranieri has seen much of him at Old Trafford and, if he had, that his enthusiasm would have survived. Only one question need be asked: given the vacuum at Old Trafford after Beckham's departure, if Veron is any good, why isn't Ferguson building his new midfield around him? Veron didn't start against Celtic and looks likely to be as much of a bit-part player next season as he was last. That's unless Alex's friend Pini can pull off a trick. And he's trying, believe me, he's trying. But wiser heads will know that if Ferguson has lost confidence in Veron, there's no reason for anyone at Stamford Bridge to have any. And at £14m and £100,000 a week, Veron doesn't come cheap.'

At least Mellor had the good grace to admit he was wrong about Veron, after the Argentinian played a blinder in the opening Premiership game. Mellor's column on Friday, 22 August ran, 'As for Veron, I am a sinner come to repentance. I worried that he was spoiled but an early encounter with another sceptic changed his mind, and should have changed mine. Well, before Sunday's Premiership encounter my friend reported how fit and determined Veron was. Which was exactly how he looked, with end-to-end running and accurate passing, not to mention that goal. Already, Chelsea are building themselves around Veron and this could be a season to rival the one with Lazio three years ago where some of the most unforgiving fans in the world hailed him as a hero amongst heroes.'

But Chelsea's new directors are not happy with the conflict. One director confronted Mellor at the Spurs game. The feeling among the directors is that it is unfair. Mellor's a guest at matches, eating and drinking free of charge and at the same time criticising Zahavi, one of Abramovich's chief aides, on behalf of Bates. Mellor had once again, the day before the Spurs match, attacked Zahavi in print.

5

ROMAN'S ARMY

R OMAN ABRAMOVICH'S RIGHT-HAND man at the Bridge is Londoner
Richard Creitzman, but all key decisions require one man's approval
– the new owner.

The Board of Chelsea Ltd consisted of five members: non-Executive
Chairman Ken Bates, now a figurehead; Chief Executive Trevor Birch;
Richard Creitzman, Abramovich's personal adviser; Eugene Tenenbaum,
who runs the Russian's worldwide investments; and Bruce Buck, a senior
partner with the City law firm Skadden, Arps, Slate, Meagher & Flom, who
acted for Abramovich during his takeover. The Russian Revolution took
place in the boardroom as well as in the dressing room. The first major
change was the recruitment of Peter Kenyon to replace Birch.

Birch, an insolvency specialist and former Liverpool trainee, joined
Chelsea from Ernst & Young, where he built a career in accountancy
after his dreams of becoming a footballer faded. Birch was involved in
all the £110m recruitment of the 11 new stars, and he says that all the
transfers done in the summer of 2003 started with the Manager.
Working with Zahavi, Ranieri identified target players he wanted to
bring to the club. It was then down to Birch and Zahavi to make contact

with the relevant clubs and players. Zahavi is understood to have carried out all negotiations with West Ham for the transfer of Glen Johnson and Joe Cole. In the case of Veron, Zahavi made the initial running with Manchester United Manager Sir Alex Ferguson, a close friend, before Birch kept talks going with the then Old Trafford Chief Executive Peter Kenyon. Little did Birch know at the time that he was negotiating the Veron transfer with his own successor! With one playing the official role and the other working more discretely, the pair would haggle over fees and personal terms until they were agreed in principle for each of the 11 new faces. It is at that point that Birch would call Creitzman, one of Abramovich's most trusted allies. Creitzman, described as a charming, typically English City trader, has been working from an office at Chelsea since the summer. He returned to Moscow once the transfer window was shut.

When Abramovich was happy with each of the deals, Creitzman talked to Tenenbaum, the Canadian Managing Director of Millhouse Capital, the Weybridge-based investment vehicle that controls the Russian's interests. Tenenbaum is the real power on the Chelsea Board. Thirty-eight years old and married with three children, it is he who controls the access to Abramovich's funds, and who acts as Abramovich's interpreter, as well as a key adviser. The Canadian has been living and working in London and Moscow for the last ten years and is described as being very cautious and serious. At the point when each of the deals has been concluded, Tenenbaum releases the funds from one of Abramovich's numerous bank accounts straight into Chelsea's current account. 'Roman isn't actually signing any cheques. It's all sorted by Tenenbaum.'

Birch said at the time he was the chief executive, 'The business works at the speed of light now. We tell Roman what it costs, and he sorts it out. Simple as that. There's such a buzz around the place.' Construction was under way immediately on the fifth floor of Chelsea's office block inside Chelsea Village for Abramovich's new headquarters, and those of his chief aides on the newly constructed Board.

Ranieri has been regularly consulted over the player acquisitions. However, it is apparent that the new owner makes up his mind about how much is spent and on whom. He enjoys it. As he said, he bought Chelsea to have fun.

'There are a lot of discussions with Claudio,' Creitzman insists. 'Roman knows the players who have come in. He does not know them inside out or tell you how many goals they scored last year. But he watches videos and goes through cassettes on a lot of players. Agents all over have been sending him cassettes, and if Claudio says 'yes' then they go ahead. Videos get sent to Roman and he talks to Claudio and he talks to other people.'

One of those people is Creitzman, a Director of Chelsea Ltd, now owners of Chelsea, and one of three Abramovich appointees on to the Board. 'I speak to Trevor [Birch] a lot and Roman fairly regularly, and there are a couple of other people involved on the Russian side and they have access to Claudio. And Roman can call up Claudio if he wants to. He's got his mobile number.'

Is it money well spent? 'The players we have bought will play for the club for three, four, five years, and I think they will be very successful, and their value therefore will not necessarily fall away,' says Creitzman, before adding, 'What we have bought is the entity of Chelsea Village. There are bars, restaurants, a hotel. It is a fantastic venue outside of the football. So if you say are we looking to sell it, we are not, but I think it was a good investment. It is difficult to make money in football. I don't think he [Abramovich] is going to go out of this making billions of dollars because that is not realistic, but I think he wants success.'

So what kind of return does Abramovich expect? 'I am not going to put a time on it, because he wants to enjoy himself and he would love to be successful,' Creitzman says. 'But if they are not successful, then he understands, he has run businesses, he runs a hockey club in Russia. He knows what sport is all about. It is an emotional thing.'

Abramovich is clearly a fan. 'He was at the World Cup last year in Japan,' says Creitzman. 'He went to some of the European Championship games in 2000. Last year, Lokomotiv [Moscow] got into the Champions League so we went to some of those games. He likes his sport.'

Creitzman also acknowledges suspicions over Abramovich's motives. 'He is used to it ... I get it when I come home too. It was always, "Here is the dodgy boy from Barnet," but it's just down to a lack of knowledge about Russia and what has gone on.' Not that Creitzman is worried. 'I answer to Roman,' he says, 'not anyone else.'

Creitzman is a Barnet supporter who was born and raised in London, educated at Surrey University, and then left England to work in Moscow and become part of the new Chelsea owner's business empire. Creitzman has worked for the billionaire since 2001 as Head of Corporate Finance at Sibneft. It was Creitzman who prepared the initial report on how the Russian might buy into a football club. Creitzman says that Abramovich 'takes a strategic look at management and is not so hands-on'. Creitzman is now Abramovich's eyes and ears at the Bridge and therefore a major power broker in English football's Russian revolution.

Creitzman, one of three new Chelsea directors, became part of Abramovich's inner circle, a trusted aide who overseas the day-to-day running of Chelsea. Creitzman knows the way Abramovich thinks and acts. Is Abramovich intent on making Chelsea the world's biggest club? 'He doesn't have an ego like that ...' Creitzman says. Abramovich has apparently said 'no' to acquisitions 'several times when the price wasn't right ... People ask how soon Roman expects to win something, but you can't put a figure on it. Roman wants to enjoy himself. He wants to win but it doesn't mean he will chuck his toys out of the pram if Chelsea don't. For him, Chelsea's another challenge and that's what he's all about – pushing himself.

'If they [Chelsea] are successful, then even more reason to stay in it, because he will want to maintain that success. He has not said to me, "I'm doing this for two years or for ten years," it was just, "I want to buy a football club." And he has done it. A man who does what he says.'

Creitzman, who insisted that Abramovich's infamous meeting with Sven-Goran Eriksson was 'only social' said, 'Roman will be at games and has discussed the players we've brought in with Claudio, because his knowledge of football isn't small. He will run Chelsea like he runs all his other businesses – setting his managers targets and letting them manage. Claudio knows what he has to do and he wants success as much as Roman does. In oil and aluminium, his managers have certain targets to meet and get rewarded for those targets. There is a regular contact between Claudio and Roman, and Claudio wants success as much as Roman does. They've discussed players and we have to get the green light from Roman for players we have signed. We'd say, "Duff is going to cost £17m. Yes or no?" He said "yes" on that deal but he's said "no" on a number of occasions because he felt the price was too high.

Just how much precisely is Abramovich investing in Chelsea? The reality seems to be however much it takes. There have been suggestions he has invested £200m, £220m, maybe as much as a quarter of a billlion. The real figure is far more complex.

Look a little deeper and the Abramovich pockets really are the deepest in football, not just in this country, but anywhere in the world. But that doesn't mean he has actually thrown anywhere near as much as has been reported at the club. Abramovich is a shrewd and successful businessman and not as 'crazy' as Adrian Mutu, one of his more expensive purchases, described him.

The main investment has been the purchase of the entire company but, relatively speaking, he has bought a prime Premiership club on the cheap, for just under £60m, first buying Bates's shares and those of the five offshore trusts to give him control from day one with 57% of the shares and then bidding for the entire company to de-list it from the AIM on the Stock Exchange to take it private.

Abramovich's company has taken on the £90m debts, but the majority of that is a £75m Euro Bond, which is not due to be paid in full until 2007 and, should it be paid off early, would invoke expensive early redemption payments.

As for the purchase of the players – virtually an entire new team for just over £110m – only a part of that is paid up front, with the vast majority of the outlay paid over a period of four years. It was always preferable to buy abroad because clubs could then negotiate the repayments terms, usually over the four or five years of the player's contract, sometimes even longer, but it was always negotiable. In the Premiership, since its inception 11 years ago, the rules have stated that clubs must pay 50 per cent up front and 50 per cent within 12 months. That rule changed only this season. Now, like transfers abroad, the fees are payable over the period the clubs negotiate. That means that buying between Premiership clubs could become more affordable, certainly in the short term. So when Chelsea bought from West Ham, for example, their first purchase of Glen Johnson was for £3m plus £3m after certain clauses kick in, and even that £3m will be staggered over a period. In the case of Bridge, the Zahavi-Birch negotiating team reduced the price but paid 90% of the entire £2m 'within two days' and LeSaux was given a lump sum settlement to move on to Southampton as part of the deal.

In addition, Abramovich's company has technically 'loaned' the money to Chelsea and, although he won't be charging any interest, it is still a loan that could be repaid. No bank would now loan a club any serious money for player transactions, so without Abramovich there would be no transfer kitty. It means that Abramovich has only had to put up a proportion of the £100m transfer budget immediately.

Trevor Birch explained at the time, 'The important factor is that his arrival has had an impact on the game because it has sparked such massive transfer aquisition, but it also true to say that all the transfer fees are staggered payments. In reality, Abramovich has bought Chelsea for a bargain. No, he doesn't have to pay the debts straight away, he has simply acquired the debt. As for the transfers, again, only a proportion has to be paid.'

Abramovich has also acquired one of the 15 super executive boxes in the new Millennium West Stand. Birch says, 'He is not a director, he is the owner, so he will be entertaining his guests in the executive box.'

Bates originally put the best boxes up for sale for £1m a season for a minimum ten-year lease. Needless to say, there were precious few takers. Bates had difficulties in shifting them, even though Chelsea cater for a super-rich type of fan who might have been able to afford the £1m-a-season facility. As it turned out, Sky TV, who owned 9.9 per cent of Chelsea before the takeover, took a couple and so, too, did Emirates Airlines who are the shirt sponsors.

But when the Russian Revolution began, Abramovich acquired one box, and four companies associated with him also took boxes. Port Vale fan Robbie Williams was impressed when he saw them but he bought one of the smaller boxes that cost £60,000 a season.

Birch could hardly believe the speed of the Russian Revolution as he observed, 'This is the job that I came into football to do. I never imagined it at the level it's escalated to here, but being able to run a football club with big sums available is wonderful. It's completely different from what I was doing two months ago. Last pre-season we brought in only de Lucas on a free transfer and, all of a sudden, we have a menu of the world's best players. It's a dream job. To have all these funds available is great. Any club in the world would want to be in that position. Before Roman Abramovich took over, we had made preparations for restructuring and rescheduling our finances. That's what we had been working towards for 16 months.' Little wonder Birch was stunned when he lost his 'dream' job.

Chelsea are also committing a further £20m for a new state-of-the-art training facility for the future benefit of the club, and as Birch pointed out prior to his shock exit, 'That will be a club expenditure that will raise the level of debt, presumably.'

Besides buying in expensive footballers, the club also want to build for the future to leave a lasting legacy. A new training ground and youth-development facility was crucial to ensure that they can have a home-grown team by 2010. Chelsea currently use Imperial College's sports ground at Harlington, near Heathrow Airport, and many new signings have been shocked to see the facilities there, compared to state-of-the-art bases such as Manchester United's at Carrington. Chelsea have been trying for some time to clear planning hurdles preventing a new base but now, with Abramovich behind them, they are looking to ensure their youth structure matches their ambitions in the transfer market.

Bates said, 'We've got a great youth policy at Chelsea but we haven't had the facilities. We have just got a place which we've exchanged contracts on and we are planning for December. The first thing I told Roman is that we need a new training ground. We've got a £17m–£20m project and you can rest assured that this guy didn't become a millionaire by doing silly things. I'd like to think that, by 2010, we will have a home-grown team and won't be buying expensive players. We've got a good record with youngsters coming through. Money itself doesn't buy success, as we know. I can think of a few clubs who tried to buy success and failed and were in financial difficulties, which take 10 to 15 years to come out of. Our plan before Mr Abramovich was that we were going to have a difficult year this year and then clear our debts off, so we have saved four or five years, really.'

Chelsea have a handful of home-grown players in their first-team squad, such as John Terry and Carlton Cole, but they have lately also turned to West Ham's emerging young stars instead, buying Frank Lampard, Joe Cole and Glen Johnson. Bates added, 'I think that West Ham are going through a sabbatical and they'll be back next year. They are a good club and they've got a great football academy.'

West Ham Chairman Terry Brown has admitted he covered up the club's financial position earlier this summer to ensure the best prices for players. 'He was quite right,' observed Bates. 'If you admit you've got financial problems, which obviously Chelsea had in the past 12 months, and you try and sell a player, then it's bargain basement fire-sale time. It's not a matter of deceiving the fans. The players needed to be sold and they got good prices for them.'

One of Abramovich's key aides must hold the record for the shortest term of office as a Chelsea Director. Eugene Shvidler, the President of Sibneft, has been credited with turning the Siberian oil company into Russia's fifth-largest crude oil producer, making it the primary source of Abramovich's vast wealth and expanding industrial empire. The 39-year-old is a graduate of the Moscow Institute of Oil and Gas, where he first met Abramovich, and has an MBA in Financial Accountancy. Shvidler is also the Chairman of the Investment Board of Millhouse Capital. But Shvidler resigned after only three-and-a-half weeks in the job because of his heavy workload. An insider close to Citigroup, the bank which advised Abramovich on the Chelsea deal, explained that Shvidler had underestimated the time he would need to spend in the role. He was be replaced on the Board by Buck, a partner at the law firm advising Chelsea.

Of the old regime, Birch remained initially as a key player in the transition. Birch signed up with Ken Bates in 2002 with a mandate from the Board to bring financial stability to Chelsea Village. In March, Bates was talking about selling a minority stake in Chelsea to cut debt. Birch's mission was to 'squeeze the assets', increasing membership of the health club and boosting occupancy at the hotels.

Birch signed a service agreement with Chelsea worth £500,000 a year and which runs until 2007. In fact, it was signed in January and is one of the longest service contacts for a listed companies Chief Executive at four years and eleven months. As Abramovich decided to terminate Birch's contract, he was in line for a golden parachute worth up to £2.25m. If Birch were to be dismissed for 'failing to perform his duties to a reasonably satisfactory standard to the Board', he would still receive 18 months' pay, triggering a £750,000 pay-off. He also gets a £1,000-a-month car allowance and petrol costs, plus private health insurance for him and his family. Birch must have been grateful to Bates for such handsome pay off terms!

Birch's remuneration and perks were disclosed in the offer document, which had to have full financial disclosure of the bid by Abramovich when he made his formal offer of 35p, the price he paid Bates, to all existing shareholders. It was also disclosed that Chelsea Pitch Owners, the body that owns the freehold to the ground and the stadium, owes £9m to the club's holding company Chelsea Village. The loan is supposed to be reduced by selling shares in the CPO to fans for £100 each, but the supply of new investors has virtually dried up, raising concern that the loan will never be repaid. The debt actually reduced by a mere £13,500 in the year ending 30 June 2002, the last full period for which accounts are available. The CPO was set up by Bates to protect the status of football at the club's Stamford Bridge ground. By owning the freehold, CPO's 12,000 shareholders have a veto over whether the site could be redeveloped for an activity other than football. The freeholder originally intended to borrow £7m although it was actually lent £11.1m, as part of a wider £75m ten-year Euro Bond issue on the part of Chelsea Village in 1997.

The borrowing by the CPO is interest free and the repayment date is 'unspecified'. Advisers to Abramovich know of the CPO conditions and ownership of the ground, and are 'comfortable' with it.

The offer documentation values the club at £59.3m and detailed the resignations of six directors, including Finance Director Christopher Alexander, Operations Director Simon Arthur, and Commercial Director

Lorraine O'Brien. Michael Woodhead, Deputy Chairman and a non-executive director, appointed on a three-year contract, also left, receiving £36,000 in lieu of one year's salary. The other two Board departures involve non-Executive Directors Mark Taylor and Patrick Murrin. Taylor, through his legal firm Mark Taylor & Co, was paid £107,478 in legal fees by Chelsea Village last year. Taylor and Murrin were also Directors of Fulham Holdings, when it was acquired for £523,000 by a Chelsea Village subsidiary in the financial year to the end of June 2001.

The offer document reveals that Chelsea has 30 dormant subsidiaries, including Chelsea Pacific, Chelsea Pensioner and Chelsea Football Club Dot Com. There are 13 trading subsidiaries, including the football club, the management company for the Chelsea Village hotel and nightclub operator.

Under the new owner, Chelsea Village is to be owned by a British Virgin Islands-registered company.

Chelsea Ltd, a special-purpose vehicle, registered in England, was formed to buy Chelsea Village, but it is just an intermediate entity. Chelsea Ltd is wholly owned by Isherwood Investments Ltd, a company incorporated in Cyprus, which in turn is wholly owned by Taverham Holdings Limited, a company incorporated in the British Virgin Islands. Abramovich is the sole beneficial owner of Taverham.

To add to the complex corporate structure, it is thought Taverham will be ultimately owned by Millhouse Capital, a holding vehicle for all of Abramovich's assets which is registered in this country and has its office in Weybridge, Surrey. Millhouse shares are all owned by an entity in Cyprus.

Russia and Cyprus have a tax treaty which makes the Mediterranean island an attractive place for wealthy Russians to keep their money. But Abramovich's advisers stressed that this company structure was the best way to organise his interests rather than to hide anything. Everything is owned by Abramovich and there are no other hidden investors, the advisers claimed.

Security is another key area for Abramovich, who surrounds himself with bodyguards, including former KGB men, and travels in bullet-proof vehicles, the price he has to pay for amassing a highly lucrative business empire. In the aftermath of the changeover from the old Soviet systems, the nature of Abramovich's deals in the former Soviet Union and other Eastern European states has naturally brought him into contact with some of the most dangerous underworld figures in the region. Less than five years ago, his Aston Martin was found riddled with bullet holes in France. At his Moscow base, he travels in an armour-plated Mercedes flanked by other protected vehicles. Abramovich feels he and his family will receive greater protection in England. Perhaps that is one of the reasons he has bought a football club, and he is clearly enjoying the experience.

Despite the claims of those in positions of power around him, global domination also seems to be part of the game plan. As part of this worldwide expansion plan, prior to the appointment of Kenyon, the club joined forces with Auckland club Football Kingz in a deal aimed at giving the big-spending Premiership giants direct access to some of the best rising talent in Oceania. Kenyon, no doubt, had far more grandiose plans for Chelsea's global expansion. The Kingz, who play in Australia's National Soccer League, will also be used as a breeding ground for Chelsea's youngsters in a partnership that will open up further commercial opportunities for the London club. 'It gives the opportunity for our players to gain experience in a different environment playing in the Australian National League, gives Chelsea access to the best talent in New Zealand and Australia and opens up playing and coaching exchanges,' said Chelsea Chief Executive Trevor Birch. 'It will give a pathway for players in New Zealand, Australia and Oceania to a world-class football team. We have seen players such as Harry Kewell, Mark Viduka, Brett Emerton and others come through the region and New Zealand players such as Danny Hay at Leeds and Wynton Rufer at Werder Bremen.'

Newcastle have links with Chinese club Dalian and are starting up a new team, Hong Kong United, as a joint venture, while Manchester United have a long-standing tie-up with Belgian club Antwerp.

The inaugural Premier League Asia Cup was partly intended to give the three Premiership clubs – Chelsea, Birmingham and Newcastle – a foothold in an Asian market so dominated by Manchester United and Arsenal. The commercial value of links with the rising football nations are crucial and Birch is confident that the new partnership with Football Kingz will prove fruitful for the Chelsea brand name and their sponsors. 'The partnership will drive the Chelsea brand in the Australian region, opens up merchandising opportunities and, because the Football Kingz are 10 per cent owned by Sky TV – as are Chelsea FC – we can exchange TV content, run competitions for both sets of our supporters and add value to our sponsors such as Emirates,' he said. 'The partnership will also continue to lift the profile of football in the region, especially with the driving force of Sky TV behind it.'

Creitzman pointed out, 'If we win, there might be more Romans out there who want to win as well ... Roman knows football is emotional. But he is very honest, very direct, very successful, very focused ... and I have never seen Roman emotional. I don't know him that well, I'm not one of his best friends, but in the meetings I have had with him he is very focused, calm and collected, and that is how he is. And that is one of the reasons he has been so successful.'

SIGN HERE ...

ROMAN ABRAMOVICH WANTS CHELSEA to produce, as well as procure, its talent and a new £20m training complex complete with enhanced youth facilities is now affordable. 'I don't believe the model of Real Madrid would fit in the English structure. I see Chelsea being in between Manchester United and Real Madrid,' the Russian said. 'At Manchester United, there is an academy that is preparing future players. But when you have to make a purchase, you do.'

Abramovich might say his purpose with Chelsea is simply 'to have fun', but for men as successful as he has been, fun tends to involve winning. 'Buying Chelsea is a way to realise my ambitions,' he said. 'Chelsea is near the top of its league. It's one of the best teams, and England is a very competitive league. For me, that was a very important criterion. My message to the fans is I will do everything possible to ensure they enjoy the game as much as me.'

Supporters concerned that his real interest is Chelsea's property portfolio should be reassured by Abramovich's record with Avangard Omsk, his ice-hockey team. Abramovich has been serious about investing in Omsk and, under his sponsorship, they have gone from provincial also-rans to a leading power in Russia's superleague, with an annual wage bill of $15m, which approaches pay levels in North America's NHL. Omsk is a city deep in Asian Russia, out on the West Siberian plain, but Abramovich's money has attracted top players.

John Mann, spokesman for the new owner, is also keen to reassure Blues fans. 'Chelsea fans should not worry. He is a very serious guy and has good intentions.'

Bates and his Chief Executive Birch had originally set up secret option transfer deals for Scott Parker at Charlton and Joe Cole at West Ham, both at £6m. Bates told me, 'We couldn't afford to take up the options, mind!' Roman Abramovich told Claudio Ranieri he wanted more seasoned internationals and that was a bitter blow to Cole who wanted to leave West Ham for the sake of his England career. He knew he had to play in the top flight to keep his England ambitions alive, and he approached Sven-Goran Eriksson for advice. Cole was on the top of Ranieri's wish list and Bates negotiated a £6m option before Abramovich's arrival. Bates hinted at Cole's possible arrival when, replying to a fan's question, he said, 'You will be very surprised to see who will be playing in the centre of midfield next season.'

But it looked as though Cole had been passed over for higher-profile players on the Continent. Eventually, Cole was signed, becoming part of a feverish acquisition of new talent. Suddenly, not even Manchester United are in Chelsea's spending league. In London, with Fulham once more impoverished, West Ham relegated, Tottenham up for sale, and Arsenal in a financial straitjacket, Chelsea leaped ahead as the main challengers to Old Trafford's supremacy. They have the highest turnover and stadium capacity of the London clubs and, long before Mohamed Al-Fayed promised to make Fulham 'the Manchester United of the South' from a base in west London, Bates talked of doing the same.

Chelsea's new owner has a good knowledge of football and, on his arrival, drew up a wish list of transfer targets that eventually brought him Joe Cole, but only after exploring a number of world-class alternatives.

Many of the players on the wish list have not arrived, but that is not to say they won't be at the Bridge eventually. First, the new Chelsea had to convince a number of those players that they really would become the force within European football that the new owner promised.

Abramovich's philosophy was startling, so much so that no one believed it at first when he said, 'This is not a business venture. I am focused on the game, the beauty of the game. This is simply for my love of football. Buying Chelsea is a way to realise my ambitions myself. Through a great team you can realise your ambitions through a great game. Chelsea should be an international team. The best players need to play. What they nearly have now is a top European team. I am prepared to invest in the club and see the club be successful and, of course, I will be looking to buy players.'

Abramovich is an aggressive mega-spender, one who reaches for the superstars like Real Madrid's Florentine Perez, so the new Chelsea owner needed someone to pull back the reins at times. Abramovich made it plain that money was no object in securing the players of his choice, although Zahavi told me, 'I won't allow him to be ripped off.'

But like the Bernabeu President, he directly influenced the decision over which players will wear his club's colours. Asked whether he would get involved in team matters, Abramovich said, 'This is what the pleasure is all about, to participate in the game and the selection process.' He was referring not to team selection, but to the selection process of the acquisition of new players. He explained, 'The Coach will determine which areas are in need of new players. I will participate in that process, discussion and analysis.' Note 'the Coach' as opposed to 'Claudio Ranieri'. Abramovich promised to meet the Italian 'in the very near future', but it was four days before he finally did met Ranieri. Abramovich took over with a neutral opinion of Ranieri, and so it was hardly surprising that Fabio Capello, Sir Alex Ferguson and Sven-Goran Eriksson are being linked to Stamford Bridge. A Chelsea insider reaffirmed, however, that none of these men were offered the job.

But before a final decision on the Manager, the players started to arrive, almost on a daily basis. A spoof email circulated the inner sanctum of the Stamford Bridge hierarchy 48 hours after the Abramovich takeover: 'Now we are owned by a man with £5.4bn, we are in the market to buy just about any top player in the world ... and the first one he's bought is Heskey.'

With a world-record budget of £150m–£200m, Abramovich set about the task of buying in talent by taking soundings on his transfer targets from a wide range of opinion, not just from Ranieri and his Mr Fix-It, Zahavi, or maybe even Eriksson, but also from Russian sports journalists and supporters of the west London club. 'Their opinion is very important to me,' he said. 'They understand more than the press.' Two days after buying Chelsea, Abramovich received a letter from a ten-year-old fan. 'He described the situation in the team perfectly and three of his five suggestions for new players we were already thinking about,' he said. Abramovich was impressed. 'I couldn't even write at that age.'

The famous Abramovich Wish List comprised the élite of football's most exciting talent in the UK and abroad:

- *Full-backs*: Wayne Bridge, Glen Johnson
- *Midfield*: Patrick Vieira, Steven Gerrard, Pavel Nedved, Kieron Dyer, Edgar Davids, Damien Duff, Emerson, Geremi, Juan Sebastian Veron, Mekelele, Rivaldo, Ronaldinho, Harry Kewell, Joe Cole
- *Forwards*: Thierry Henry, Ruud van Nistelrooy, Raul, Michael Owen, Wayne Rooney, Ronaldo (senior) at Real Madrid, Ronaldo (junior) at Sporting Lisbon, Christian Vieri, Herman Crespo, Cissé, Zlatan Ibrahimovic, Andrei Shevchenko, Patrick Kluivert, Adrian Mutu

From youngsters such as Portuguese wonderkids Christiano Ronaldo and Wayne Rooney, to players valued at £50m or more like Thierry Henry, Michael Owen, Stephen Gerrard and Raul, the team headed by Zahavi and Trevor Birch set out to discover their availability and price. Even if they didn't make it this time, there will be a next time for some of them. Chelsea would have taken Ronaldo from Real Madrid if he had been available – he wasn't. They will take Raul if the price comes down as his contract nears its expiry. Ronaldo was signed by Manchester United from Sporting Lisbon with Barcelona in the race, and Chelsea backed away, even though they would have offered Jimmy Floyd Hasselbaink in part exhange. The price doubled once Manchester United got involved, and they had the edge as they have a link with Sporting Lisbon. Zahavi told me, 'He will be the best player in England inside two years.' Chelsea opted not to go for him although he was one of Zahavi's choices. Zahavi added, 'He is world class, can play on the right or left, and although he was one in my head he is only 18 and he was thought to be too young for the position.' United had been tracking the Portuguese Under-20 star for some time but pushed the deal through when they became fearful of a bid from Barca.

Top of the hit list were Thierry Henry, Spanish football's icon Raul, Wayne Rooney and Michael Owen, all of whom would have signalled Abramovich's intent to build a team of superstars to rival Real Madrid and Manchester United. In midfield, Abramovich wanted to pair Patrick Vieira with Steven Gerrard. Of course, the brilliant Czech Pavel Nedved at Juve was also a target. In addition, Leeds United's Harry Kewell, Juventus midfielder Edgar Davids, Roma's Brazil captain Emerson, Paris Saint Germain's Ronaldinho, Christian Vieri and Harry Kewell were on the list, but all proved to be unattainable – at least for the time being.

Others were there to be signed, including a host of English players: Glen Johnson, the teenage full-back sensation at West Ham; left-back Wayne Bridge at Southampton; and Real Madrid's Cameroon international Geremi who had a year's experience in the Premiership with Middlesbrough.

Discreet enquiries were made about all of these players, including Henry and Vieira. The response was that Arsenal's star striker simply didn't have a price; Vieira was untouchable and would sign a new £100,000-a-week contract. Instead, Arsenal offered Freddy Ljundberg and Francis Jeffers, a far cry from the two Gunners that the new Chelsea wanted.

Liverpool issued a 'hands off' warning for Gerrard as Manager Gérard Houllier prepared his squad for the new season at their Swiss training camp. The England midfielder, 23, made headline news as a £50m target, even though only weeks earlier he made it clear he wanted to stay at Anfield for life and, along with Michael Owen, was due to sign a new deal. But the usual behind-the-scenes mumbling suggested that he might at least listen and, of course, such a stance would only enhance his contract negotiations.

A Liverpool statement directed at Chelsea said, 'The player is not for sale at any price. He is a central part of Gérard Houllier's plans so they would be wasting their time.'

In any case, the transfer policy was that Chelsea would not be seduced into offering outrageously inflated prices, but would play a more patient waiting game.

Owen was another star negotiating a new contract and Chelsea were monitoring developments. Houllier said, 'I wouldn't sell any of my major players, no matter how much was offered. Maybe I am one of the few Managers who has the confidence to say that. It's because of the quality of the Board of Directors. I am confident about Gerrard and Owen signing new contracts.'

Abramovich is the one man in world football who can afford Henry or Raul, for example, but the players would have to want to sign, first and foremost, and players of this calibre would rather wait and see how it all developed at Chelsea before committing themselves.

Chelsea were approached by Raul's agent and quoted an astronomical 100m euros, £71.4m, in addition to the wages for the Real Madrid ace goalscorer which were 12m euros a year, around £8m. The £100m package for Raul was presented to Chelsea because the Real star striker had fallen out with President Fernando Perez. Raul was angered at the purchase of David Beckham, telling Perez that Beckham is overrated and will create a media circus that could destabilise the team. He was also smarting over the sacking of Vincente del Bosque, and the way captain Fernando Hierro heard the news that he'd been dumped on the radio.

There is a 180m euro buy-out clause in the player's Real contract, and Chelsea could trigger a move if they were willing to pay that much. At least Chelsea have stopped to consider a bid for Raul while Manchester United dismissed it out of hand as far too steep even for their considerable resources.

Raul's internal dispute with Perez is such that the Real legend is refusing to sign a new contract. His present deal expires in 2005 and the prospect of Raul walking away on a Bosman free transfer is too much for Perez to contemplate. Raul's agent, Gines Carvajal, says, 'Raul is in no hurry to talk about a new contract. It is not in his interests.'

Again, it made headline news that Chelsea were involved in Raul, but it was way off the mark to suggest there had actually been a 100m euro bid as some of the tabloids suggested, but Arsenal manager Arsene Wenger and Manchester United boss Sir Alex Ferguson feared the power of Abramovich's cheque book. The rumour was fuelled that the world-busting bid had been made when the player's agent, Gines Carvajal, said, 'Roman Abramovich has made an offer of 100m euros (£71.2m) for Raul and they want to pay him 12m euros (£8.4m) a season, double what he is earning at Real Madrid. FIFA agent Marc Roger, on behalf of Chelsea, asked me if Raul would be interested in entering negotiations for a transfer to Chelsea. I spoke to Raul and he said "no". He is not interested in leaving Real Madrid. Raul's buy-out clause is 180m euros (£128m).'

Raul previously insisted the only club he would leave the Bernabeu for would be Manchester United, and even that would not be for years to come. The striker dismissed any suggestion that he was seeking a move away from Madrid, where he is a cult figure. 'There are two years left on my contract and when we have to talk about [extending] that, we will,' said Raul. 'The club knows my intention is to stay and, in my opinion, all we have to do is sign and seal it.'

Marc Roger, the FIFA agent, denied he was involved in an attempt to bring Raul to Chelsea, but that he was involved in the deal for Claude Makelele. 'I do not deny that I have been in touch with Carvajal but that was about other matters than Raul,' said Roger. 'I am not working for Chelsea.'

Ranieri made light of some of the more glamorous and outrageous names linked with his club. 'Raul tonight, tomorrow it is Rivaldo,' said Ranieri. 'Maybe Raul must renew his contract.'

The astute Italian was aware of the behind-the-scenes moves to patch up Raul's differences with a bumper new pay deal.

Sir Alex Ferguson has always valued the Spaniard. He said, 'You can buy Figo, you can buy Zidane, you can buy Ronaldo – but the best player in the world just now is Raul.'

Chelsea, perhaps, will bid for Raul next summer when they might also have Rooney in their sights, and these players might look at events at the Bridge and believe the Russian Revolution can challenge Manchester United domestically and Real Madrid in Europe.

An adamant Arsenal Chairman Peter Hill-Wood and Vice-Chairman David Dein made it clear, when Chelsea put the feelers out without actually making a formal bid, that neither Henry nor Vieira were for sale at any price. Hill-Wood told me, 'I'd be very reluctant to sell at any price, whether it is £50m or £70m. It's only money, after all, and we are trying to build a team here at Arsenal – not destroy one. We cannot replace Henry because he is simply irreplaceable, and so it doesn't make sense to take the money for him, however much it is, however much it may seem tempting. I know people are looking at our move to Ashburton Grove and our current liabilities and assume we need the money. All I can tell you is that the finances are containable ... put it this way, I am not losing any sleep over them. If we can raise the money for our move, it is self-evident that people are not going to lend us the money unless they are pretty well convinced that our business plan makes sense and that we are not driving ourselves into the ground.

'I understand that everyone is also assuming that the economics of the game are on a downward spiral and that any club would be foolish not to take such a large sum of money. But I don't believe this fellow at Chelsea is that much of a fool that he will throw so much at just one player. So far we have not received a bid, so it is all very much hypothetical, but as far as I am concerned, Henry is not for sale because he is so fundamental to our plans. We shall have to wait and see if Chelsea do make such an offer and what the overall view is about it, but you now know mine.'

Clubs feared their top stars not be safe from Abramovich. But Manchester United Chief Executive Peter Kenyon says there is one player even Abramovich's millions could not tempt them to sell ... van Nistelrooy. Perhaps now he may think differently.

The Dutchman's strike record since joining United in a £19m move from PSV Eindhoven two years ago is sensational. In 101 appearances for the club, he has netted an incredible 80 times. Kenyon, when still at Old Trafford, said, 'Chelsea's bid is mind-boggling. £71m is something you can't even contemplate getting a return on. Manchester United is recognised as one of the most profitable football clubs and businesses in the industry and that figure would not even register. We could not do that. Clearly, Ruud is not for sale at any value from our point of view. He's an essential part of our squad. We have to look at where our squad is, and what ultimately drives all our business and all our activities is the football team and the success. You could not replace a van Nistelrooy – there isn't another one around – therefore he's not for sale. The way that you could measure Ruud is that he is an exception to the rule, and we hope he will play for United for many years to come.'

The 36-year-old former England keeper Nigel Martyn was targeted as cover for first choice Carlo Cudicini. The modest offer of £500,000 was described as 'derisory' but cash-strapped Leeds would have ended up taking it; the player declined a move south. Manager Peter Reid declared, 'I have had a chat with Nigel and, take it from me, he is staying put.' Martyn, who has only a year left on his £25,000-a-week contract, now intends to win a new deal to take him through to retirement. His agent Phil Graham said, 'As things stand, he wants to be Leeds' number-one keeper. Last season has gone – it's a new period now and Nigel knows he has a chance to be first choice at Leeds again. He still thinks he is the best keeper at Elland Road and he has the chance to prove that.' Yet, remarkably, at one stage, one newspaper actually reported he had 'signed' for Chelsea! Originally Reid dealt him a double blow by telling him Paul Robinson would be his number one and the club could not afford to keep him. Reid is under strict orders to raise money, and with Robinson likely to stay at the Yorkshire club, he reluctantly decided to cash in on Martyn.

Chelsea signed two keepers over the summer. But former Sunderland player Jürgen Macho damaged his ankle ligaments in training and will miss most of the season, while Ranieri is believed to have doubts over the quality of Italian Marco Ambrosio. Chelsea also recently released the former England Under-21 international keeper Rhys Evans.

A number of players were desperate to jump aboard the Abramovich bandwagon, realising the salaries on offer. Parma's Japanese icon Hidetoshi Nakata was one of them. Following an approach from Leeds, he told reporters that the English club he wants to join is Chelsea.

Assembling a world-class midfield is an essential stepping stone to securing the services of the game's top strikers. Nakata was not on the list, but Veron was, although he did not warm to Chelsea's overtures at first and told boss Alex Ferguson he does not want to leave Manchester United. He said, 'It has never been my intention to leave Manchester United. I want to stay and I have made my intentions clear. But I do not know what the club want to do.'

Veron came on as a second-half sub as the Reds beat Celtic 4-0 in a pre-season friendly in Seattle. He was clearly not part of the first-team picture any more, yet he was willing to fight for his place.

Ranieri, at first, suggested he knew nothing about a bid for the Argentinian international, telling Italian reporters, 'We've not spoken to him [Veron]. I don't know what people are on about.' It was a mere smokescreen.

Central to Ranieri's plans was the signing of a combative central midfielder and, while Patrick Vieira and Steven Gerrard would be anyone's primary targets, they were unavailable. Davids is a suitable holding midfielder in Juventus' back-to-back Serie A title campaigns, although with only 12 months remaining on his contract, Juve were still holding out for a large fee. Chelsea's interest in the Dutch star did not tempt him into leaving Juventus, according to the player's agent Robert Geerlings, who told Italian sports daily *Gazzetta dello Sport* that the Premiership side had attempted to sign Davids even before Abramovich had taken control of the west London club. When asked about Chelsea's desire to bring Davids to London, Geerlings said, 'We don't know anything about this. We have not had any other offers from Chelsea since Edgar said no to them in June, but things can change. Juve could reach an agreement with Chelsea. We will see. What is certain is that Edgar wants to stay in Turin and hopes to discuss his renewal soon.'

Manchester United sounded out Newcastle over Kieron Dyer, who was also on the Chelsea wanted list. Newcastle slapped a £25m tag on Dyer's head, and that put any move for Dyer from Chelsea on hold. Newcastle Chairman Freddie Shepherd moved to end speculation. 'Kieron Dyer is not for sale. Every player has his price but we don't want to sell him and I don't think even Ken has enough roubles to buy Dyer.'

But there were plenty of alternatives. Ranieri, speaking in Kuala Lumpur, said, 'We need players with good motivation so that we can continue to blend the team into one that can challenge Manchester United and Arsenal seriously at the top of the Premiership. But with the squad I have now, we will be very, very close to the bigger teams.'

With Chelsea preparing for the Asian Cup tournament, he insisted there is no end in sight to the spending. 'It is important that the team continues to grow, and it is important we continue to pick up the best players. While the team we had was good, we needed something more and the four new boys will surely add to the team.'

The latest additions at Chelsea – Duff and Bridge – arrived in Kuala Lumpur to join the team. Ranieri added, 'We have to win, we want to win and we will try very hard to win against Malaysia, who I know will also be trying very hard to stop us.'

After Roma's win over Fulham, the club issued a statement that Emerson was not for sale and that they were angry at what they described as an illegal approach. Roma Sporting Director Franco Baldini said, 'It's true that we have received important offers for him, not only from Chelsea. But we will give everyone the same answer –this season Emerson won't move. But the thing that bothers us is when the player is contacted personally and not through his club. We are not going to ask for FIFA help, but this thing has to be stopped. Roma want to extend the contract with him; we will speak about it soon.' Baldini claimed that Chelsea offered the 27-year-old Brazil captain personal terms of £21.34m over six years. An incensed Baldini insisted, 'The situation is simple. Chelsea offered Roma 27m euros for Emerson and we answered that he is untouchable. At that point, Chelsea went straight to Emerson with an offer outside the market – a contract for six years and 30m euros. You can understand the turbulent frame of mind the player is now in. But Emerson has been correct in his behaviour because he told us everything. I have spoken with the player. We have told him we consider him irreplaceable and we want to renew his contract and offer him more money. He answered that Chelsea, too, clearly have great belief in his ability given their offer. I realise he has seen a train laden with gold going past his door, but he will just have to do the right thing.'

Emerson was sorely tempted by Chelsea's massive offer. Baldini added, 'The fact that they contacted him before us is annoying. I'm not saying that we are going to get in touch with FIFA but this story has to finish, they have been very incorrect.'

Emerson's agent, Gilmar Veloz, flew into London to discuss the personal terms even though Roma insisted they still had not given Chelsea permission to talk to their star. Baldini remarked, 'It seems that Chelsea are continuing to go to the player directly despite our warnings. I understand Emerson's agent is in London right now, but nothing can happen without Roma's say-so. Even if Emerson says he wants to move, that does not mean we are going to let him.'

The problems surrounding the abortive luring of Emerson to Chelsea only intensified the prospect of a move for Makelele. The Real Madrid player was about to fall out with his club over his wages, more so with the arrival of Beckham, and Chelsea knew he would be more readily purchasable than Emerson.

As for the strikers, there were no negotiations to buy Real Mallorca's Samuel Eto'o, even though he was on the list, and he was offered to the club.

The stumbling block with hard-up Mallorca was that half of any transfer fee must go to the player's former club Real Madrid under a sell-on clause. In any case, there were players ahead of Eto'o in the list of strikers and despite much media coverage he was not pursued as much of a priority.

7

ZOLA'S EXIT ...
AND A SWIFT RETURN?

R OMAN ABRAMOVICH MADE AN amazing attempt to bring Gianfranco
  Zola back to Stamford Bridge just 24 hours after the greatest player
in the club's history signed for Cagliari.

The Russian offered the 37-year-old striker a contract worth a
staggering £3m a year immediately after he had signed for his home-island
club Cagliari. Although Zola hadn't kicked a ball for the Serie B club,
Cagliari were offered £1.25m to tear up their contract with the player.

Incredibly, Zola refused to 'do the dirty' on Cagliari, even though he
will earn just £350,000 a year there, and would have played in the
Champions League at Chelsea instead of Serie B. Even more remarkable
is that just 24 hours before the takeover at the Bridge, Chief Executive
Trevor Birch refused to budge on the offer to Zola of a 50 per cent wage
cut in last-ditch talks with Zola's lawyer. Zola was seeking just a little bit
more. 'The differential was so minimal as to be almost irrelevant'
according to Italian sources.

Then, as soon as the takeover occurred, an offer in excess of his
previous year's salary was on the table – too late, as Zola honourably stuck
to his agreement with Cagliari. Zola revealed, 'I think I have made the right

decision. My reputation with the Sardinian people was at stake, and I knew that they were expecting a great deal from me.'

Abramovich's representatives twice contacted the Sardinian President Massimo Cellino with offers to buy out Zola's contract. Cellino staked his reputation on making Zola the spearhead of his club's promotion campaign. Cellino revealed, 'Abramovich sent Zola a fax offering him 4m euros (£3m) a season. I have seen it with my own eyes – it is all true. He also contacted me by phone via an Italian middle-man, offering me $2m (£1.25m) to tear up Zola's contract. I was really taken aback. I thought Zola knew nothing of what the Russian was doing. But, in fact, he told me in full about what had happened to him. I got another call from Abramovich, this time offering me £1m to call off the deal. I told him "no" straight away, and even joked about him offering me less money this time.

'Bringing Zola back to Sardinia is a beautiful fairytale, which could not be allowed to end before it had begun. It is too important for Cagliari and the whole island. Zola told me the offer he'd received was genuine, but said I should not worry – the salary I was offering him was worth ten times as much. I told him that if I had that kind of money to spend, I would offer it to him, too.'

Bates was taking the brunt of the criticism for losing Zola but made it clear he has not dealt personally with players' salaries for some time, first handing over to Colin Hutchinson and then recruiting Birch for that role.

Zola also turned down a £4m deal from the Middle East in favour of going home to Italy. There can be no more deserving recipiant of FIFA's Fair Play Award than England's former Footballer of the Year.

Bates says, 'When Gianfranco signed a two-year extension in 2001, we increased his salary by £1m a year. We felt our new offer was all we could afford, given the financial constraints we had until the takeover. Now he's gone to Cagliari for less than he'd earn here. He could also have gone to Qatar and earned £4m tax free in a year. But Sardinia is his home and he wanted to go and play there. We'd love him to come back with Cagliari for a charity match, at the end of the season. I'd like him to wear a Chelsea shirt for 45 minutes and a Cagliari shirt for 45 minutes.'

Chelsea were so desperate to keep hold of Zola they considered buying Cagliari and enquired how much it would cost to turn it into a nursery club, but the approach failed.

Zola's agent, Fulvio Marrucco, refused to comment on the exact nature of the proposed package, but said, 'Chelsea were desperate to keep him and would have done almost anything to get a deal.'

Claudio Ranieri was deeply upset that Zola had left. 'I really wanted Franco to stay but he and the club could not agree over wages. I'm not surprised about what has happened because I talked to him two or three days ago and things were going in that direction.Chelsea should have made a bit more effort to keep him but maybe they were involved in other matters. From a technical point of view, we have lost a great player and a great ambassador. Everywhere we went we made friends because of him and I think he has been the most loved Italian in England.

'When the Queen decided she should arrange a dinner for Italians in the UK, Zola was on the list. It's going to be impossible to replace him in the hearts of the supporters. His loyalty, generosity and technical skills were all put at the disposal of our club and he was a vital leader in the dressing room.

'I remember when I first met him in Naples. I was in charge of Napoli and Maradona had just left. We needed somebody to replace him and I told our Chairman that whoever came from abroad it would be impossible to replace Maradona, so we should just go directly for Zola. He was a brilliant success and has been ever since.'

Zola preferred to end his career with Chelsea, but grew tired of waiting for an improved offer to stay for another year. By the time Chelsea came up with the cash, Zola had already given his word to Cagliari. Zola said, 'This was the hardest decision of my life. What decided it for me was wanting my son Andrea to understand what life is like in Italy. Cagliari is the club I supported as a kid but even that did not make my heart-breaking decision any easier. Only people who have lived for so long in such a great city as London can understand how it feels to turn my back on seven great years there. I have had the time of my life and walking away is very painful.'

But a close friend revealed, 'Franco really wanted to spend the final year of his career in England. His family were happy in London and he wanted his children to complete their education at their present school. He expected Chelsea to make him an offer at the end of the season and was surprised when there were no talks arranged before he went on holiday. He was left with the impression that the club weren't really making an effort to keep him and, when they finally came up with an offer, it was less than half his present salary. It was never about the money because he could have gone to Qatar and picked up £4m for playing 20 games. But the longer it went on without Chelsea opening serious negotiations, the more he started to think they didn't really want him to stay. So he told his agent to start investigating other opportunities and the Cagliari offer developed very quickly after that. By Tuesday, he had already shaken hands on a deal to go back to Cagliari, where he started his career. It was just after that that he received a phone call from Trevor Birch at Chelsea with a massively improved offer. But because Franco is a gentleman he felt he could not go back on his word to Cagliari.'

Zola scored 80 goals in 302 games in his seven years at Chelsea and Birch added, 'We tried to find a solution and when the new investors came in it was the first issue on the agenda. As a result of additional resources available, we offered terms which satisfied him but we felt that having given his word to his home-island club he would have to join them.'

At his farewell press conference at the Bridge, Zola was asked if he would have stayed had he received an improved offer before 1 July. 'Yes. I wasn't thinking of leaving and had put all my offers on standby. But the renewal of my contract went on and on until 1 July, when my contract expired. Then I had to do something. I couldn't keep the other people waiting as that would have been disrespectful to them. So I decided to go. Chelsea made me a better offer on 2 July, when the transaction between the old owners and the new owners happened. They came to me with a better offer and that gave me a really bad couple of hours. But, unfortunately, it was too late. It wouldn't have been correct to take it, because Cagliari had followed me for such a long time. The renewal of my contract happened at a bad, bad moment. Chelsea were in a bad situation and we couldn't make an agreement. But I'm not putting any blame on Chelsea as they had so many more important things going on than renewing my contract.

'To play in the Champions League again would have been very attractive. But I made a choice. I know what I'm losing but I made my choice for other reasons. This is not just about playing football – it's about doing something I believe is right. Money is important but some things are even more important. This is the longest I've been at a club. I'll miss my friends here and the everyday life – and my children will miss it as well. But I care about the people in Sardinia. Football is very important in their lives and I want to share it with them.'

Zola carved a special place in the hearts of Chelsea fans and he wanted to return to say farewell to his Blues team-mates, Ranieri, club staff and friends. Zola also explained how he almost joined Napoli in the summer of 2000 after his row with Luca Vialli. 'One of the most important people for me at Chelsea was [former Chief Executive] Colin Hutchinson,' he said. 'Three years ago, I was about to leave – and he said I had to stay. Without

Colin, I'd have gone. I was very close to going to Napoli. We'd just won our second FA Cup but my situation was uncertain and not clear. It was a family matter as well, but we decided to carry on with the adventure here.'

The new challenge made him 'feel alive', agreeing to captain the side. 'I want to go back where I started. I'm going to a place where everyone's going to be very demanding of me. It makes me feel alive because of my reputation going in after many years. I like the challenge, really. I feel I can do something for the people who supported me in the first place.'

On leaving Stamford Bridge, Zola said, 'I feel bad. I feel sad. It's the place where probably I received the most satisfaction of all; it's the place that made Zola so important football-wise, it's the place where I received everything I was first dreaming of when I first started playing football. I'm not going to get anything like that anywhere. Even the best things have to end. I'm delighted, because in the last year I've given satisfaction to my supporters and I've received satisfaction from them.'

Bates fiercely denied pushing the fans' hero out of the door. He claimed, 'Franco leaving was nothing to do with money. He has taken a pay cut to go back to Sardinia. And he could have gone to Qatar for a lot more money if he wanted. It was a family decision by Franco. His kids have been brought up in England and educated here. He was worried that if he didn't go back home now, his kids would feel like foreigners by the time he did return to Italy. We're very sad to see Franco go – he has been such a magnificent servant.'

Thierry Henry would be a good signing according to Zola. He joked that Henry would be the perfect replacement for him – if only the Frenchman could match him for speed!

So who could replace Zola? 'I can't give advice, I'm just a miserable football player! I think there are players around, more than one, who could replace me. It's finding them and getting the team that owns them to release them. But with the financial potential that the club has got now, they can force many things.'

As we have seen, Chelsea were linked with a world-record £50m bid for Henry which would have eclipsed Zinedine Zidane's £46.5m move from Juventus to Real Madrid two years ago. But an Arsenal spokesman said, 'We're not in the business of selling our best players. There's no logic selling players to help other clubs prosper.'

Zola said of Henry, who is contracted to Highbury until summer 2007, 'He'd be a good man for Chelsea but I'm not sure he'd be very willing to do it. I've been surprised by the big names linked with the club. Chelsea need to find a player who the young players will look up to, as it's important to have motivation and create enthusiasm. It's important to find a player with those qualities. And I think that's a priority for the club. If Chelsea do that, they can create the right atmosphere and environment to be successful.'

Zola urged Abramovich not to make a rash decision on Ranieri, who steered Chelsea to fourth place in the league in the 2002/03 season guaranteeing Champions League action. 'I can understand that these people, as they've put money in, will be very demanding with the Manager and everyone. But, hopefully, they will also understand that things don't come straight away in football. I've seen teams in Italy spend huge amounts of money, not have success and then sack the Manager. In football, you need time, patience and the club to support the team. The new man has a big responsibility on his shoulders. Hopefully, Chelsea are in good hands ... I hope he does the right things for the fans. I have not met him but what has happened at Chelsea in the last few days is an incredible story and I pray he loves this club and gives the supporters the satisfaction they deserve.'

Zola discovered a club in turmoil when he returned to the training ground to say his goodbyes. He explained, 'There is a lot of uncertainty and I can understand that some players will be feeling anxious. Everything has happened so quickly and the players need someone to reassure them. I don't think the team needs too many changes, maybe a couple of new players, but I'm sure the Manager is aware of what is needed.'

Zola urged caution in the transfer market. 'Money can give you many things – a new car, a new team – but it can't buy everything. To win things in football is not just about buying big players, but creating the right environment for the team to work. The financial potential the club has now means it can do many things, but I don't think this team needs too many players to improve, just ones in certain positions. Chelsea came fourth last season and were in contention for the title until Christmas. A couple of players in the right place will make them very competitive.

'For Chelsea to win the league depends on who they are going to buy and how they settle into the team. Obviously, the players in the camp now are anxious and that is understandable. There might be a bit of uncertainty because things have happened so quickly. They have read many things in the papers, but hopefully the club will give them stability and reassure them because Chelsea need to carry on along the same lines.

'The new owner wants to make Chelsea a big team, but it's very important to create the right atmosphere at the club and he needs to make things clear to people who are already there now.'

Fan Dave Johnstone, of the Chelsea Independent Supporters' Association, queued up for hours to kiss Zola's feet as he arrived at the ground for the press conference. Zola joked, 'That cost me a lot – I had to pay him! My greatest achievement has been the way the people of England regarded me off the pitch. There are many foreign footballers who have come here and achieved great things in the game. But the people here also respect me for my behaviour and as a person. That is something of which I am very proud. Money can give you many things in life like a new car or even a new football club. But it can't buy you the sort of relationship I have enjoyed with the Chelsea fans for the last seven years. My greatest satisfaction has been off the pitch, for the respect people have given me. Many footballers excel in games but when you have something like that, it's very special and I'm very proud of that.'

He departed with vivid memories of great goals, such as the one that won the Cup Winners' Cup in 1998. Zola felt particularly appreciated by the fans at the 2002 Cup Final when he was a substitute; his name was the first one chanted by the fans. 'It meant a lot because these supporters have been incredible. I've said many times it's not only about cheering you on when you are winning and everything is going well, it's also about supporting you in difficult moments and I've had all of it, which has been incredible for me. As a sportsman, I really care about those things.

'Many years ago, we played in a game against Bolton. We needed a draw for the UEFA Cup and they needed a draw to avoid relegation. We beat them 2-1 but after the game their supporters were clapping us. That says a lot. That will be something I tell everybody in Italy and Sardinia. If only we can acquire that, it will be a great thing.'

Zola insisted that if it hadn't been for the fans, he wouldn't have been playing at such a competitive level at his age. 'For me, football is not just about playing for money. I've made sacrifices from morning to evening, I've dedicated my life to football and just ask the people to consider that, and then the result sometimes can be good, sometimes can be bad, but I always do it with the maximum of professionalism and, you know, when someone recognises that, you have achieved something important.

'The way I have been welcomed from day one is incredible. What I liked above all was this kind of attention towards the team. I wasn't used to it. That is the best thing you can have as a sportsman because as I said many times, there are many competing and you can't always win, you might come second, third or last, but when they support you all the time, it's crazy, it puts extra life into you and that was really something that I appreciate more than anything else.'

Oddly enough, Gianfranco Zola was not as popular in his homeland. 'No. I think I was popular, I think I was very much appreciated, but the dimension I reached over here with this club is certainly unbelievable. And I must say thank you very much for that. The people they stop me and say, "Thank you for everything you've done for this club," but it should be me saying, "Thank you for what you made me become," and I do believe that.'

Recalling his first day at Harlington, Zola says, 'Well, I was a little bit lost, if I can say that, because I was in the middle of a new country, surrounded by people who couldn't talk my language, and I couldn't understand them. So I felt confused a little bit in the beginning, but then I went to the pitch and started playing and started training ... I saw my game come alive. And I saw the faces of my team-mates, you know, quite surprised by my qualities. And it made it even more ... it reinforced my choice, really.'

It was hard, at first, to learn English when there was so much Italian spoken. 'It wasn't easy, especially because if you consider that there were so many players from abroad, plus the English players, you had to change from Cockney to the Scottish, to the Irish, there was everything. Jesus Christ, it took me seven months to understand Dennis Wise and Steve Clarke. It wasn't easy but it was worth it, because I've had a wonderful relationship with them, they've been great friends for me, but it took a lot, really.'

He has made many personal friends. 'Absolutely, I've got my best friend Kevin Hitchcock, who has been the closest, along with Dennis, Steve Clarke ... I've had a lot of really good friends. I'm going to leave a lot of friends over here, which is nice ... you can move from one country to another and still have a lot of good friends in both, which is fantastic, very good friends, I must say.'

His greatest achievement at Chelsea? 'On the pitch, I think winning the first FA Cup was the most important thing because, by doing that, we had set another standard. Chelsea wasn't the same team as the years before, it was a team aiming to win the Championship, competing for all the competitions, so it was a new reality for them, it set the standard. I think that victory was the most important.'

So the 45 minutes against Liverpool in the fourth round was particularly memorable. 'Oh, that was unbelievable, I still think I never played a game where the air was full of electricity like that, and it was unbelievable. In the second half when Sparky came on, oh, what a game that was ... That moment, I started to realise how important the FA Cup was to the supporters over here. Before that, I wasn't sure.'

There were many other great moments. 'The year we played the Champions League we had such memorable moments. Obviously, when we played Barcelona over here we beat them 3-1, that was one of them. There were a few others as well. I remember when we beat United in the League 5-0, it was another great moment. I'll go for the Barcelona one because that moment we felt like we were one of the most important teams in Europe.'

At the end of his emotional press conference, the media afforded Zola a spontaneous round of applause. Zola said, 'It was good, that. But I've had good relationships with the press over the years. I really appreciate that because they respected me a lot and I appreciate that, so it's OK, I was pleased.'

How does someone these days manage to forge a good relationship with the British media? 'Well, I think trying to do your job as well as possible, with dignity and honesty and respecting their job. And doing things properly, I think I have done that.'

Chelsea now hope to organise a charity match against Cagliari at the end of next season at Stamford Bridge for the supporters to be able to say a final farewell. The Italian is almost certain to retire at the end of the next campaign. 'Fingers crossed, yes, that would be a dream for me. I couldn't say goodbye to the supporters properly ... the best goodbye I can imagine is on the pitch here, you know, I can say goodbye better with my feet than with my words.'

He promised to return to London on a regular basis. 'I am keeping my house over here and I will be over often. I would like this relationship to carry on ... although I'm not playing for the club, I still belong to the club in some ways.'

Maybe one day as Chelsea Manager? 'I still don't know if Gianfranco Zola will be a manager yet, I don't really know if I have the qualities to be a man like that. It's something I would consider in the future after I stop playing, because right now I think I can be more helpful on the pitch to the game. That belongs to the future... you know, you have to wait ... it's very important that everything you do, you do it with passion and determination and it will come only when I have to decide about that.'

In his final address to the fans, in a special interview with Chelsea TV, Zola looked into the lens and said, 'As I said before, it's been a true pleasure for me to play for this club, for this shirt. I have played good games, I've played bad games, but I've always played with passion, with care, and what I've received here is something that goes beyond what I was expecting, so it's great. Let's carry on keeping an eye on each other ... I'm going to be looking for Chelsea's results, maybe you will be looking for Cagliari's results. But thank you very much ... it's been truly a pleasure.'

8

MANAGING THE FUTURE – CLAUDIO, SIR ALEX OR SVEN?

WITH A GIANT PORTRAIT of a leopard on the dining room wall and art deco adorning the expansive reception room in the £5m Knightsbridge flat, Sven-Goran Eriksson, flanked by Mr Fix-It, Pini Zahavi, came for 'tea and a chat' with new owner Roman Abramovich.

The fact that the social gathering took place in the predominantly grey and cream two-level flat just 48 hours after the Russian's takeover of Chelsea, and a full four days before he was introduced to Claudio Ranieri, naturally set the chattering classes into overdrive.

The palatial apartment at 39, Lowndes Square was the venue for the summit with the England Coach that reverberated from Soho Square to the Bridge and right around the globe after a few opportunistic snaps from the paparazzi were published. Playing down the significance of the meeting, the 'spin' from Soho Square and from the Abramovich camp at the time was that the meeting at the luxurious private venue suggested that Eriksson merely called round for a casual cup of tea and a chat.

With the intrigue of the Abramovich takeover perfectly sufficient to whet the appetite, the possibility of a further sensation had Fleet Street drooling – was the England Coach once again thinking of defecting? After all, he had done so before when conducting talks with Manchester Untied.

Eriksson categorically denied that he has any interest in taking over as Manager at Chelsea. He said, 'I can confirm that last week I met with Pini Zahavi and the new owner of Chelsea Football Club, Roman Abramovich. The meeting took place at Mr Abramovich's property in London. Due to the intense media profile given to Mr Abramovich's involvement with Chelsea, I accept that this meeting may create unfortunate speculation. Therefore, I would like once again to categorically reaffirm my total commitment to my role as England Head Coach. I am thoroughly enjoying the current European Championship qualifying campaign and I am looking forward to leading England to success in the future.'

However, there was one major flaw in Eriksson's assertion – hadn't he made very similar assurances before that he was not involved in talks with Manchester United, prompting the then Chief Executive Adam Crozier also to issue a denial? On that occasion I had caught them out because my exclusive in the *Express* and *Daily Star* proved much later that a deal had been done with Manchester United.

Eriksson felt the need to speak out as both the FA and Chelsea were embarrassed by the wave of bad publicity. He therefore continued with his denials by explaining that he has been friends with both Abramovich and Zahavi for some time. He added, 'Pini Zahavi and I have been good friends for 20 years, since I was coaching Benfica. As Pini spends a lot of time in London, we regularly meet socially. Additionally, I have known Roman Abramovich for several months and during that time have also enjoyed socialising with him when he is in London.'

In the current feeding frenzy surrounding any speculation over Eriksson's future as England Coach, no one seemed fooled by this down-playing of events.

However, one of the precious few round the table sipping tea with Abramovich and Eriksson knows the full inside story – Pini Zahavi himself. Zahavi told me several weeks later, 'Sven was never offered the job, and I should know. I introduced Sven to Abramovich a year earlier and they had met five times before this meeting.'

If Eriksson couldn't become Manager straight away, there can be no doubt that he indicated when he might be available, certainly after the European Championships, if not before, and the chit-chat also included the England Coach's liking for a certain kind of English player, such as Glen Johnson, and a foreigner he would always select, Juan Sebastian Veron. Maybe the future would also herald the perfect partnership of Eriksson and David Beckham. The fact that those specific players became part of the Chelsea transfer Wish List is a mere coincidence. Of course it is. And Ranieri wanted both players all along. Of course he did.

Abramovich himself added to the uncertainty surrounding Ranieri by admitting that he is 'not sure' about the Italian Coach. When first asked his thoughts on Ranieri's position, Abramovich shrugged his shoulders and said, 'I am not sure, I just don't know. I am going to sit down with him in the very near future.'

Ranieri naturally expressed fears for his job, saying, 'I don't know anything about these rumours about another manager. But I know the rules of the game and that when control of a club passes from one man to another, anything can happen. It's the right of the new man to decide who he wants in charge of the team. I don't know Mr Abramovich and I would like to speak to him.'

Ranieri, who has been in the Stamford Bridge hotseat since 2000, added, 'At the moment I'm relaxed and continuing to coach my side.' Having steered the south-west London club to the coveted fourth place in the Premier League at the end of the 2002/03 season, and the promise of a place in the lucrative Champions League, Ranieiri naturally felt that achievement deserved a chance under the new owner, and he had the backing of Ken Bates.

There was more speculation that Ranieri's fellow countryman, Roma's Fabio Capello, was a target if Ranieri is sacked. Capello was unsettled at Roma to the extent that I can disclose that the Italian Coach made contact with intermediaries expressing his interest in replacing Ranieri when the time comes, should it come. Sir Alex Feguson was also linked as his successor, but a Chelsea insider later told me that this was not the case. No one knows where these rumours came from, but they cannot have harmed Ferguson's position at Manchester United. A surprise name in the frame down the line could be Graeme Souness, who knows Abramovich through mutual football contacts, and he is the type of big-time character who could appeal.

Abramovich was clearly sanctioning the transfer activities behind the scenes, a common occurrence abroad, but in Britain, managers are still largely allowed to decide who to sign and who to play.

Under-threat Ranieri even admitted that he had no idea Chelsea were in negotiations with Barcelona striker Patrick Kluivert, and it may have been an unsubstantiated rumour. 'I don't know anything about Patrick Kluivert, only what's been in the papers,' admitted Ranieri. 'But he is one of those strikers who every manager would like in their team.' Ranieri admitted that he knew nothing about Abramovich but insists his millions can help Chelsea reach a new level.

Ranieri walked out on Atletico Madrid three years ago after President Jesus Gil tried to get involved in matters on the pitch, and he also left Valencia after bust-ups with directors. The Italian Coach, who at that time had not yet met Abramovich, said, 'I don't permit interference on the technical side and, if something like that was to happen, my departure is a sure thing. The arrival of Roman Abramovich won't influence my work. Directors have not done so before at Chelsea, and nor do I think they will now. Shareholders have never advised me what to do. I've never been told what to do with the team each weekend by a director at any stage of my career. I wouldn't have let it happen.'

Abramovich has left Ken Bates as Chairman but it is clear that he wants a 'hands on' approach at the club. Abramovich said, 'This is what the pleasure is all about – to participate in the game and the selection process. The Coach will determine which areas are in need of new players. I will participate in that discussion and analysis. I like Thierry Henry and I also like Sol Campbell. But I'm not going to name any other players because their price will just go up.'

On Chelsea's original list of summer targets were Joe Cole and Scott Parker, but they were sidelined initially as Abramovich went for more spectacular aquisitions. When it became clear that clubs like Roma were not going to let Emerson leave, or Juventus were asking too much for Edgar Davids with only one year left on his contract, rather than being ripped off, the club went back to West Ham for Cole.

Ranieri has a policy of bringing in good, young English talent with West Ham's Cole and Charlton midfielder Scott Parker both fancied by the Blues Manager prior to the takeover.

At their first meeting, Ranieri was very impressed with Abramovich's love of the game, his commitment to be successful at all costs. As they discussed his plans for the acquisition of new players, it crossed Ranieri's mind that here is a guy who will not accept anything short of absolute success. The Italian said Abramovich urged him to keep faith. 'The meeting lasted one hour in which I told him straight I saw no reason for him to get rid of me,' Ranieri said. 'I simply told him the truth, that last season people called us no-hopers but we made it to the Champions League ... But I also told the new owner it was already in my plans we should do much better this season. He told me and the players he wants to be the top club in Europe.'

Abramovich has a poor grasp of English and said that this was not going to change for the sake of talking to the players. 'My simple English is good enough to talk on the phone with Claudio Ranieri,' he said. 'I met the players once during training and we agreed on the necessity of building a new training ground.' There were, he said, no plans for a change of management. Yet that will do little to quell speculation that, in time, Ranieri will make way for Eriksson, and that, in turn, would only increase the likelihood of David Beckham joining him should he eventually jet back from Madrid.

Ranieri said the pressure was now on the London club to start winning big. 'Throughout my career, I've had to fight on my feet at clubs where the situations have been tough, really tough. But at Chelsea with Mr Abramovich, the expectations are now very different and we have to start winning big trophies very soon before getting to the top of European football.'

Bates is fighting his corner. The former owner who remains in the chair for the time being told me, 'They got on very well and most of the talking was about players. Efforts are now being focused on the preliminary rounds of the Champions League, then the Champions League itself and the League. If I didn't think highly of Claudio, I wouldn't have given him a four-year contract. He didn't have a penny to spend last season because we didn't have a penny to spend, and yet he took us up from sixth to fourth and we reached the quarter-finals of both cups.'

Now Ranieri has plenty of money to spend and judgement day is not far away, but for the moment it's *Carry On, Claudio*.

Chelsea were eventually forced to distance themselves officially from speculation linking them with Eriksson from early on. Birch leapt to the defence of Ranieri, claiming that the club had no intention of tempting Eriksson to Stamford Bridge. Birch declared, 'There is no truth in the rumour we are trying to bring Sven-Goran Eriksson to Chelsea. Claudio Ranieri is the Coach, has four years remaining on his contract, has just got us into the Champions League and has already had a very positive meeting with Roman Abramovich. Together, we have charted the Chelsea path forward.' Something Birch did not mention was that it would also cost Chelsea £8m to end his four-year Stamford Bridge contract.

Birch's statement came after the FA earlier reiterated Eriksson's commitment to the England job after some reports suggested it was a matter of when, and not if, he joined Chelsea. The FA, in something of a panic, restated the Eriksson denial of Chelsea intent that had been issued a week earlier, after it first emerged he had met Abramovich along with Israeli agent Zahavi.

Ranieri criticised Eriksson's 'naïveté' at being caught by a photographer when meeting Abramovich at his London apartment. The wary Italian interpreted Eriksson's assurances that the meeting was purely social as a denial of any move to kick him out and install the Swede at Stamford Bridge. But Ranieri could not help criticising the England Coach's actions. From the club's pre-season training camp in Italy, he said, 'In my opinion, if it is true Sven doesn't have his mind set on this job at Chelsea as he has claimed, then I am willing to believe him. However, that means he was very naïve to let himself be photographed so obviously going into Mr Abramovich's house in London.'

Ranieri officially unveiled the Premiership club's first five summer signings and vowed to build a championship-winning side. The Italian said the signings of Damien Duff, Geremi, Glen Johnson, Wayne Bridge and goalkeeper Marco Ambrosio were a major step towards joining the big league.

Ranieri knows money alone will not guarantee success. 'The owner said you can buy the players but not the wins. It is important to work hard. I think we all want to win – the owner, me, the players – we all want to win. I said Manchester United, Arsenal, Liverpool? They are better than us because they have a bigger squad. But now we are building. The first step is to build a squad. This is very important. I have confidence in myself, in my players and, of course, in my new owner. We are building a good team, a team like Real Madrid, Milan, Manchester United.'

The excitable Blues boss is fed up with suggestions that the new owner dictated the biggest spending spree in the club's history. And he is insulted by insinuations that it was Sven-Goran Eriksson who identified Chelsea's transfer targets during his 'secret' meeting with Abramovich.

Asked if all the players sitting alongside him were his choice, the Italian snapped momentarily, but tellingly, 'Maybe Eriksson.'

Later, he attempted to dismiss the remark as a joke for the media. Ranieri snapped, 'Who do you think bought these players? Eriksson? That is ridiculous, a joke. That sort of speculation is not good for him and disrespectful to me and to the players. I was the man who recommended all these signings to the new owner. It is *my* team, *my* responsibility and, if it does not work out, it will be *my* downfall. Fortunately, all these players know they were my choice. The new owner gave me the opportunity to look for good signings and I have wanted to buy Geremi, Duff and the others for a long time.'

He confronted Abramovich about his future the minute he was introduced to the man. Ranieri insisted, 'I was very calm when the new owner came in. My first question to him was, "OK, do you want me or not?" I wanted to know straight away. Not because of his meeting with Eriksson and all the other rumours, but because I have a lot of experience in this game and know how things can work. When a new owner comes in he can change everything. When any new boss comes in, he can say, "I don't want you." There is nothing you can do about that. So I said to Mr Abramovich, "If you believe in me, that's OK. If you don't, why wait? Get rid of me now." Fortunately, he said I am working very well and told me to continue in this way.

'I never asked him about the meeting with Eriksson. It was not important for me. He can do anything he likes. I understand that. For me, the only problem will be if my team does not win matches.'

Mark Palios was only one week into his new post as FA Chief Executive when the Eriksson–Abramovich summit hit the headlines. A few weeks later at his first press conference inside Soho Square, Palios suggested that he had contingency plans should Eriksson walk out, although I must say it sounded pretty insubstantial as to what precisely those plans might be, other than to go for the obvious man at hand, Steve McClaren. Palios said, 'Sven and I spoke at the time the photographs were published. He has agreed the timing was unfortunate. Of course, we will have a contingency in place with regard to Sven's eventual departure, but equally I would do that for all major business risks, from what happens if Soho Square burns down to the key employee walking out.

'We'll be talking to people to find out who is valued in the game, who the players and managers like, and who is respected. As for talking to a specific target, that would be down to the specific circumstances of that person and the club he is with and the sensitivities we have to respect.'

Palios said he would open negotiations with Eriksson if the Swede were approached by a club – 'You always negotiate with key employees if they get headhunted' – but stressed that, in his opinion, Eriksson was the best England Coach of modern times and had a unique opportunity.

'Sven is one of the best coaches we have had in recent years and his only defeat in a competitive match was in the World Cup quarter-final,' said Palios at the time. 'If you remember, like me, trudging out of Wembley in the rain when Germany beat us in the last game there [in October 2001, Kevin Keegan's final match in charge], I think most England fans would settle for that. He has a great chance of reaching Euro 2004 and is in charge of an England team full of young icons, all of an age where they are coming to their peak in time for 2004 and a World Cup in 2006 in Europe. From a professional perspective, he has an awful lot in front of him. Many people in the game would like to be in his position.'

Ranieri, entering his fourth year as Chelsea Manager, knows the stakes have been raised. 'Pressure is good. If I didn't have it, I would change my job. I am used to it in Italy, in Spain and now in England. Results have been my life at every club and I am used to working hard. At the start of every season, my aim is to improve on the previous year. Manchester United, Arsenal and Liverpool are all better than us because they have had bigger squads for a long time. It's very important to close the gap on those three big teams but you must ask the new owner whether that will be enough to satisfy him.

'My eventual aim is to create a team as good as Real Madrid, Manchester United, Juventus, Milan and Inter. But we will need a lot of good champions [his synonym for world-class players] to achieve that. I have been building for the last three years and now I have the chance to put in some new champions. I am very happy with the five signings I have made so far but we are not finished yet. This is just the beginning. I'm not going to say how many more I want to sign or tell you their names because I am tired of all the bullshit.

'This is going to be a long and busy season for us. The aim is to fight it out in every competition, from the Champions League to the Carling Cup. I cannot guarantee we will win any of them but I think it is realistic to expect Chelsea to win the Premiership within the next two years. All I can do is show my best. If that is good enough, that's fine. If not, well, I'm pleased to meet you!'

While in Malaysia during the pre-season build-up, Ken Bates entered the Eriksson debate. First, Bates criticised the England Coach's substitutions policy, something he had done before, but not Abramovich's meeting with him as such. Eriksson has persisted with changing his team in friendly matches and recently had four captains in one game, including Jamie Carragher and Phil Neville. 'Eriksson? I don't think any of us are over-enamoured with him, are we? At the last FA Council meeting, I stood up and suggested England caps are awarded only to players who appear in competitive internationals. They all applauded that and Geoff Thompson agreed the international committee should consider it. It cheapens the cap. And how can you have four bloody captains in one match? The armband has been tossed to the side of the pitch and it seems whoever is nearest gets to wear it. It's a shameful way to treat something that's part of our football heritage. Being captain of England should be the ultimate honour.'

Then Bates denied that Chelsea were trying to coax Eriksson to the Bridge, adding, 'It's not a fair assumption to make. People have put two and two together and come up with 85. If a guy goes to the San Lorenzo restaurant to meet someone, so what? Does it mean he's going to buy the place? Roman Abramovich is a friend of his and that's all there is to it. All this rubbish that has been printed about him coming to Chelsea is just that – there is no record to put straight. So they were pictured together, so what? All Claudio has to do is ignore it and go about his business as usual. And that's what I've told him. All these rumours that the players we have signed are Sven's players are just crap, they're utter rubbish. Claudio wanted Geremi last summer and he wanted Wayne Bridge – and Damien Duff too, for that matter. Agents will confirm that enquiries were made.'

Bates told me that his prime objective was to defend Ranieri, but his decision to give an interview to the Sunday journalists backfired. Bates called me after he read the papers to express his annoyance, bordering on disgust.

But it proved highly embarrassing for Bates as clearly Abramovich is a friend of Eriksson's. Abramovich was far from pleased with the publicity and when Bates was asked for an explanation, he told Abramovich's aides that he, too, was livid. Bates accused the papers of distortion and was deeply regretful about how his comments had been portrayed.

Bates further tried to defuse the situation with a call to Soho Square, to Eriksson himself. Bates is, of course, an FA Councillor and had been, at one time, on the FA Executive Board. Bates wanted to extend a cordial invitation to Eriksson to dinner to explain how the headlines came about. So far, the England Coach has proved unavailable for such a social occasion but will see Bates, perhaps, at the FA instead.

But the bottom line is that Ranieri has the chance to prove he is the man for the job, not Eriksson. 'Sven is the England Manager and we're hoping he's going to win the European Championships for us. He has known Mr Abramovich for a number of years so I suppose he's entitled to have tea with him,' Bates said.

Far from looking like a manager under pressure, he contemplated being coach to the world's richest football club. Striding off to lunch with skipper John Terry at his side during the club's pre-season tour, Ranieri was beaming with relish at the possibilities that had opened up to him in his search for new players. 'I am the luckiest manager in the world ... Fucking hell, I have waited 20 years for this moment to arrive.'

Fresh from introducing £17m Duff and £7m Bridge to their first training session, he admitted he's still hasn't landed the 'big champion players the club needs', players like Inter's Christian Vieri, Herman Crespo or Juan Sebastian Veron, with Brazil captain Emerson another target.

When even more big name stars started to arrive, he said, 'I cannot believe how things have changed at Chelsea. It is beyond my dreams and I feel very privileged. I think back to last summer when I had nothing to spend and it shows that life is very strange. Before Mr Abramovich came, I could say, "I like this player and this player," but I knew it was very difficult to buy them. Now with Mr Abramovich, I can put more players on my list and we are buying some of them.

'There is pressure but I do not worry about losing my job. Everyone knows they will die sooner or later, but do you think every day, "I might die?" No, you live your life. A real problem is what I had 15 years ago, when I started my second season as Manager at Campania Puteolana. I had only 10 or 11 players and no one for the bench. The bookmakers have closed the book on me being the first manager to get the sack. They should open it again because, if they do, they will make money.'

Whatever the truth behind all the rumours and Bates's good intentions, the bookies were convinced of their validity. Ranieri was slashed from 20/1 to 7/2 to be the first Premiership managerial casualty. Ranieri has so far retained his job, albeit on 'trial', irrespective of William Hill suspending bets at one point with such intense media speculation. Glenn Hoddle was second favourite at 4/1, and new Fulham boss Chris Coleman was 5/1. It was generally accepted that the Italian had until Christmas to keep his job. Ranieri will have to deliver and mould the new signings that Abramovich wants into shape ... or else. Ranieri survived the initial takeover period but it was clear that he has to make an immediate impact or a replacement with a far higher profile and reputation will be appointed. Eriksson knows he can improve on his £3m-a-year FA deal if he moves from Soho Square to west London.

Eriksson, on his first public media engagement ahead of the international friendly at Portman Road, was quizzed about the infamous tea with the Russian. A clearly embarrassed England Coach asked the public to believe that he is just good friends with Abramovich. Fans of the national team will turn a blind eye to just about any indiscretion, whether it be liaising with glamorous television presenters or Russian billionaires, just as long as he keeps winning.

Pressed on his furtive meetings, he replied, 'I'm sorry that, during my two years here, every time there's something happening with a club, my name is linked. It's Italian, Spanish and English clubs ... but I'm also honoured by it, to be fair. And I'm still here. If we don't qualify, I don't think you want me anyway!'

Later he added, 'I said that half-joke, half-true, but I think it is more true than joke.'

He spoke in terms which hardly discouraged a belief that the Russian may have benefited from his advice on players. 'It was not the first time I've seen him ... I've seen him many times. It didn't embarrass me. I could have spoken to him on the phone, I guess, but the big diference is that he invited me to take a cup of tea in the house of a so-called friend. I saw him many times and I was presented to him by Mr Zihavi, who I have known since I was Manager of Benfica and he was involved in business with two Russian players I had. As Pini lives in London, when I came to England we have eaten together now and then, and one occasion was with Mr Abramovich. Of course, we talked football, but if I meet Arsene or Ferguson, we talk about players. That is normal. What do you expect me to talk to Abramovich about? The weather? Or cards? I have been to David Dein's house many times, but I don't think I will be the Manager of Arsenal. It shouldn't be difficult to have friends in football without people assuming things.

'That he bought Chelsea was a big surprise. All I knew was that he was going into football or maybe Formula One, which he told me a while ago. We were not going to discuss a contract. We are trying to qualify for Euro 2004 and then have a good championship. I can see myself being England Manager until 2006. I stopped trying to convince you years ago that I am staying. I don't worry about it because then you have even more grey hairs.'

Had he spoken to Ranieri about the speculation? 'I talked to Ranieri.' Had he apologised to the Italian? 'I didn't say anything because there's nothing to say.' A close associate of the Italian told me, 'I spoke with Claudio and he told me that, yes, Eriksson had called, but it was not to reassure him about anything. He rang him before the opening game of the season to tell him he would be calling up Terry, Joe Cole and Bridge, and to say that he would be at the game at Liverpool.'

Had Abramovich asked him, either during their rendezvous or at another time, to be the Manager of Chelsea in the future? 'No, no. You are invited to take a cup of tea in the house of a friend, and you are not going there to discuss making a contract with the club.'

Asked later by a Sky TV reporter if he thought that meeting had been a mistake he said 'no', but then modified his response to 'maybe'.

Asked what he planned to do to silence the speculation about his intentions, he said, 'Nothing. I have no intention of doing anything about it. Let's try to beat Croatia, then qualify, and then have a good Euro. Then we'll see what's happening.'

David Mellor wrote in his *Evening Standard* column, 'The new owners of Chelsea need to decide whether they want Claudio Ranieri to continue as Manager or not. What isn't acceptable is this sense that he's half in and half out − still in the job but not enjoying their full confidence. He's expected to produce results while not-so-secret talks go on with Sven-Goran Eriksson, and to receive players into his squad nobody thinks he himself has chosen.

'There is a problem with Ranieri picking new players because legend has it he doesn't go to many matches himself, so he wouldn't know about some of them. But Ranieri has always impressed me with his steadiness under fire, while his work at places such as Valencia testifies to an ability to turn a sow's ear into something of a silk purse. But if you start off with not just a silk purse but a solid gold one, is he really the man you would choose to get the best out of a diamond-studded squad? Frankly, I doubt it, and so, too, I suspect, does Mr Abramovich, doubtless egged on by the egregious Mr Pini Zahavi. I don't believe a word of Eriksson's explanation that his visit to Abramovich's pad was just a social call. As I know from my own experience as a Foreign Office minister, it's nigh on impossible to build friendships through an interpreter.

'And frankly, it's an insult to our intelligence for Eriksson to pretend it was anything other than a business trip. And I also believe, to keep the place warm, Eriksson is indeed supplying information that has led to some worthwhile additions to Chelsea's squad.

'Far from being a troupe of greedy, over-the-hill foreigners, the first four likely signings are all in their prime and three of them − Glen Johnson, Damien Duff and Wayne Bridge − have grown up with English football. The fourth, Geremi, had a great season with Middlesbrough and has nothing to prove about hacking it in the Premiership. And as a dead-ball specialist, he should be invaluable. But if Chelsea are to do what a lot of us have advocated and build success on a British spine with foreign add-ons, again the question that won't go away is: is Ranieri the fellow you would pick to manage such a squad? Or wouldn't you rather make Martin O'Neill an offer he can't refuse, or take a punt on David Moyes? The new owners give the impression with Ranieri that they're willing to wound but afraid to strike. And I'm not sure that's fair on anybody.'

As for Eriksson, Mellor was not impressed. 'We all know Sven-Goran Eriksson manages England, but none of us know who manages Sven. Or maybe nobody does, a situation new Football Association Chief Executive Mark Palios – about whom I hear nothing but good – needs to do something about. Sven must stop giving the impression he's having an each-way bet on England. He is paid a king's ransom for total commitment and it's about time he showed it. No more ads. No more meetings with club *prominente* that lead to the obvious conclusion that he's planning to jump ship. Sven isn't actually doing us that big a favour by staying on. And Palios has nothing to lose in making clear that any more inopportune expeditions to places like Château Abramovich will lead to a quick exit. Far better, as well as more dignified, for the FA to fire the bullet in the event of further provocation. What they shouldn't do is sit around waiting for the inevitable letter of resignation.'

Eriksson wanted to become Manchester United Manager until Sir Alex's incredible U-turn. That came as a complete shock to then Chief Executive Adam Crozier who made the mistake of issuing a denial when it was later shown to be true. Now his successor Mark Palios has an identical problem.

Ranieri will need to be tough as he lives under the shadow of Eriksson. Add Sir Alex Ferguson and Graeme Souness to the list of potential new coaches and Ranieri started the season knowing that this will be the most important in his entire career.

Sir Alex's inference that he had rejected an approach from Chelsea immediately after Abramovich's takeover was leaked just two days after the announcement of Manchester United's Chief Executive Peter Kenyon's defection to the Blues. Was it designed to reassure United fans of his loyalty compared to that of Kenyon? Or was it the opening shot in his contract negotiations to increase his value?

Zahavi was quoted as saying that it was 'not true' that Ferguson had been offered the job, and he had not been. However, Ferguson is fully aware that he would be offered it when it was appropriate, but for the time being Ranieri was being given his chance.

But if it raised further doubts over the future of Ranieri, the Manager famous for indulging in mind games knows it won't do any harm to destabilise one of his main challengers.

The truth of the matter, however, was that Ferguson was not actually made an offer, although he was made aware that he would be a top target should the club decide to change their Manager if Ranieri was not successful.

Sources involved made it clear that any 'approach' to the United Manager would have been tentative, preliminary and no more than a sounding about timing of availability should it be necessary, very similar to the talks with Eriksson. There has been much discussion as to whether the position was offered to either of the two coaches, but I can reveal that an official source states categorically that neither were offered the job. Yet it all adds to the evidence that there are contingency plans should Ranieri fail.

Ranieri has received assurances over his future, having been given £111m to spend on new players since Abramovich's takeover, but he knows he has to deliver.

Ranieri has been looking over his shoulder, with Graeme Souness, the Blackburn Rovers Manager, another rumoured to be in the frame, although Souness would not be in the top six of coaches who would feature on any shortlist with the prerequisite being success and experience in the Champions League.

When Ferguson was initially sounded out, he made it clear, as did Eriksson, that they would wait to see how it developed in their present employment and how Abramovich's new regime would work. 'It would take something catastrophic for me to leave this club,' Ferguson told the *Manchester Evening News*. 'My whole life is Manchester United. When you become Manager of this club, you get woven into the fabric of the place.'

Cynics suggested that the story was leaked by Ferguson, either to undermine Chelsea or, more feasibly, to raise the stakes before contract negotiations with David Gill, Kenyon's successor. Gill said that he hoped to secure the 61-year-old Manager's services beyond his present contract, which expires at the end of the 2003/04 season, and he was confident that talks would 'move ahead soon'. His message, after Kenyon's departure, was centred on continuity.

Given the extent of Abramovich's investment and his seemingly limitless ambitions, landing the club's first title since 1955 might not be good enough. The Champions League is where Abramovich will judge the new order at Chelsea.

Ranieri said, 'I do not know how long my chance at Chelsea will be. No coach can put a time limit on his job. But how can I not enjoy what is happening here? I have waited all my life for this kind of opportunity, I must not be worried about it.'

But when he was asked at the pre-season Asia Cup press conference in Kuala Lumpur which managers in Italy had made the most impact on his career, he said, 'Capello, Sacchi, Trapattoni ... and Eriksson ... ha, ha, ha.'

One Italian whose future looks secure at Chelsea, however, is the goalkeeper Carlo Cudicini. 'I really like Cudicini,' Abramovich said. 'He is a great goalkeeper ...' and he also happens to be one of Ranieri's shrewdest buys, as Cudicini cost a bargain £160,000 from Castel di Sangro.

Ranieri, in a managerial career stretching back 15 years, has proved himself to be a builder, rather than a buyer, of teams. Now the Italian Coach is being asked to succeed as both.

Personally assured his job is safe – for the time being – by Tenebaum and Creitzman, there was a public declaration of support from John Mann: 'Mr Abramovich wants to express explicitly his support for Claudio Ranieri as manager. He thinks he's doing a great job and has made sure Claudio knows that.'

9

THE FIRST STARS APPEAR

ROMAN ABRAMOVICH OVERSEES EVERY purchase, whether he discusses the transfer transactions from his offices in Chukotka, Moscow, his Knightsbridge home or on his private yacht. He says, 'I have videos sent to me of the players we want to buy before I agree to go ahead with it. Of course, there is no point having money if you can't spend it, but I don't throw my money away either.'

Ken Bates insists Chelsea won't be suckered into paying over the odds for transfer fees. He said, 'There are a lot of agents who were going to get worthwhile jobs like lavatory attendants before we came along, but we won't get taken for a ride. We won't be pushed around on transfers just because people think we have got loads of money. They might think that Christmas has come early, but it hasn't.' The signings of Damien Duff and the final player to arrive, Claude Mekelele, however, came at inflated prices compared to the rest.

Oddly enough, a little-known teenage talent from the East End marked the start of the Russian Revolution. England Under-21 international Glen Johnson jetted off to the Blues' pre-season training camp in Italy after signing a five-year contract following his surprise £6m move from West

Ham. The 18-year-old was 'gobsmacked' to be the first of many new arrivals. 'I just want to get out there and to get to know everybody. They are a great club. There are lots of internationals here and I can't wait to play with all the players,' was his initial reaction.

The promising right-back became the most expensive teenager in Chelsea's history. 'I have not paid it much attention, to be honest,' he said, referring to the hype surrounding his move. 'I have been taking everything as it comes and just getting on with it. This is a massive step for me, a big learning curve. It was hard for me to leave West Ham but I couldn't let this chance slip. I was sad to be leaving the club I had been with all my football life. This time last year I was still in West Ham's reserve team and now I'm looking at playing in the Champions League. It's hard to take in how quickly everything has happened. My only target this season is to secure a first-team place.'

There's time for a change of lifestyle as well. 'I'm at Dartford at the moment and I'm buying another place not far away with my mum,' said the young man from south of the river. Mrs Johnson will, no doubt, keep an eye on him.

A year earlier, Johnson was looking forward to playing in West Ham's youth team and maybe a few games in the reserves. He then spent two months on loan at Millwall before January 2003 when Glenn Roeder, with his team deep into a relegation fight, turned to Johnson and West Ham won their first home Premiership match that night.

Johnson rates his assets as both attacking and defending but he confessed, 'When I was younger, I was a striker, and then when I changed to defender, I had a bit of both in me then. I was in the Under-14s and my Manager said he was going to try me out as a centre-back, and that was it, I never played centre-forward again for a few years.' He signed for the Hammers as a centre-forward and he knows Carlton Cole from the Under-21s.

As he prepared to make his Blues début in the friendly against Lazio, he recalled it was only two years earlier that he was shaken by the sudden death of Hammers Assistant Coach Les Sealey. Former Manchester United keeper Sealey, who suffered a heart attack at the age of 43, was the guiding light behind Johnson's meteoric rise. Johnson said, 'I'd like to think that Les is looking down on me from somewhere and able to see all these good things that are happening now.'

It was Johnson's friendship with Sealey's sons Joe and George which led to the quietly spoken youngster moving into the goalkeeping guru's home.

Roman Abramovich, the benefactor at the centre of the Chelski Revolution.
His wealth is estimated to be £8.2 billion.

Top: Damien Duff – Sir Alex Ferguson considered that he was overpriced at £17m.

Bottom: Hernan Crespo. £16.8m for a world-class striker.

Adrian Mutu. £15.8m for the striker who was already a big hit with the fans as the new Zola.

Top: Juan Sebastian Veron. £15m for the former Manchester United and Lazio star who helped Eriksson win the Scudetto.

Bottom: Claudio Ranieri with two new signings: Spurs keeper Neil Sullivan and Claude Makelele, whose £16.8m capture from Real Madrid caught the imagination of the world of football.

Joe Cole – a secret deal for the West Ham midfielder was set up by Ken Bates, but Chelsea couldn't afford him until Abramovich arrived with £6.6m for the young player.

Top: Glen Johnson – £6m for the surprise first signing in the summer spending spree.

Bottom: Wayne Bridge – the £7m move to Chelsea, which took Graeme Le Saux to Southampton, will enhance his England chances.

Top: The old Chelsea tried to sign the Cameroonian Geremi a year before Abramovich arrived, but couldn't afford the £6.9m it eventually cost to poach him from Real Madrid.

Bottom: Ken Bates – the man who sold his shares for £17.5m and bought himself a new Bentley – celebrates a goal with Roman Abramovich on the opening day of the Premiership season at Liverpool.

Claudio Ranieri, the coach who lived in the shadow of constant speculation about Sven-Goran Eriksson.

'Les has been the biggest influence on my career, without any doubt. He was more than just a coach – he was like a dad. He took me under his wing when I went to West Ham as a schoolboy and looked after me all the time. He was an unbelievable character – a top guy. When I joined the club as an apprentice, I lived in Les's home in Loughton. He had an extension built on his house for me to sleep in. It was an arrangement that suited everyone because my mum lived in Kent and it was much easier for me to get to the West Ham training ground from Les's home. So I stayed with him during the week. Mum was happy for me to move there because she knew it was such an important time of my life and it was vital for me to knuckle down. I'd been living with Les for about six months when he suffered a heart attack and passed away. It was just awful – absolutely unbelievable. I was only 16 at the time and it was terribly difficult for me to deal with. I still stay in touch with Joe and George, who were both trainee keepers at West Ham. And my mum is very close friends with Les's widow, Elaine. I spoke to Elaine about my move to Chelsea the other day and she was so happy for me. But I'd just like her to know how much I owe to Les.'

Roeder suffered a brain tumour earlier this year. Johnson added, 'I couldn't believe it when I heard the news. It was Easter Monday and we'd just beaten Middlesbrough at Upton Park to keep our survival chances alive. He was fine in the dressing room after the game and there was no sign of any problem. I'd just got home when Jermain Defoe called to say that the boss had collapsed in his office and been rushed to hospital.' Roeder made a full recovery following his life-saving operation. Johnson confirmed, 'Glenn's fine now ... he is much better. We had a good chat when Chelsea made their offer. He didn't want to sell me but wasn't in a position to turn the money down. He just said that I'm a good lad and he knows that I'll keep my feet on the ground. He told me to go on and achieve bigger things with Chelsea. I went to the Chadwell Heath training ground to say goodbye to everyone and they were all so happy for me. I'd asked quite a few of the guys for advice before accepting Chelsea's offer. They told me that it was a great chance which I couldn't turn down because it might never come again.'

Chelsea next agreed a fee with Real Madrid for Geremi. He believes that the Blues have the ambition to rival the likes of Manchester United, who were also interested in signing him, as well as Real. He said, 'We are trying to build a team. Little by little, we can do things. We are trying to sign a lot of players so why can't we be like Real Madrid? Chelsea are one of the big clubs in Europe and have a lot of ambition. The Chairman has shown how far he will go and now we have to try to win something on the pitch. Last year, I really enjoyed playing in England and many people told me that my football suited English football. I am an ambitious player and I wanted to play in a big team in the Champions League. I had the opportunity to play at Chelsea and I took it. They had been interested in signing me before, but it didn't work out. Now I want to achieve with them everything that they want to achieve. I wasn't playing regularly at Real Madrid and I prefer to be at a club where I'm going to play. It was not because of Luis Figo or David Beckham. It is just that every player likes to play regularly. I have left a very important club but the potential is here for Chelsea to become just as big. Madrid have already reached the very top, but the ambition of the new owner here shows how far he wants this team to go.

'I think we could win the Premier League and even the Champions League this season. For me, I'm very happy to come to one of the bigger teams in the Premier League. I have a lot of ambition, I'd like to win a lot of titles if possible, it's why I'm here. I know that Chelsea have and are going to sign big players, that's good for us, let's see what happens.'

Geremi is one of the prime candidates to succeed free-kick specialist Zola. He said, 'I know that Franco was one of the best to deliver the set-piece, but I know I'll try to do the same. But that's football, you have to work hard and try to improve every day. That's what I'm going to try to do here at Chelsea.'

Blackburn finally were forced to accept a £17m offer for the 24-year-old Republic of Ireland winger after three bids for Damien Duff had been rejected. The fee triggered a get-out clause in his contract. Duff and his adviser Pat Devlin negotiated terms, but the player needed time to think it over. 'It's down to Damien now – no one's going to pressurise him,' explained Delvin.

Devlin denied the player was holding out for a move to Manchester United after Sir Alex Ferguson missed out on Barcelona-bound Ronaldinho. 'It's very simple – he either stays at Blackburn or he goes to Chelsea. It's one or the other,' Devlin said. 'There's been no interest from Manchester United that I'm aware of. If there was, I'm sure Blackburn would have alerted not only ourselves but Chelsea as well.'

Duff, who arrived at the Bridge in a black cab, admitted he had thought long and hard for days over the deal. He said, 'This was probably the biggest decision of my life and I didn't want to rush it. I had seven great years at Blackburn and there was no big reason to move. It was just a matter of thinking everything through.'

Duff, capped 36 times by the Republic, scored 35 goals in 190 appearances for Rovers. His pace down the flank will give Chelsea an added dimension. He said, 'It looks as though great things are going to happen at Chelsea. It just feels right. It is a big, big chance and I can't wait. I won't know what fitness level I am at until I join my new team-mates in Malaysia. I have been training with Blackburn reserves and keeping myself ticking over, but I just can't wait to meet up with the lads and start kicking a ball again.'

Duff carries the highest price tag ever attached to an Irishman. But he is determined not to let it weigh him down. 'It is a great honour for myself and my family. But the most important thing is to do it on the pitch now and, hopefully, I can do it all for Chelsea. But I'm trying not to think about the transfer fee. All the talk about money doesn't really bother me at all. All I like to do is to get on with my football. Of course, people are expecting high things from us, especially after the money that has been spent. Every year, Chelsea are expected to do well and even more so now. So we hope that we can do it. But we won't feel that extra pressure down at the training ground or, hopefully, on match days. We are just worried about playing football and getting the right results.'

Before the Abramovich takeover, Liverpool were always regarded as favourites to sign Duff, but Gérard Houllier was told that £10m did not come close to activating the release clause. The Anfield club's withdrawal was confirmed when they signed Harry Kewell from Leeds for a cut-price £5m.

Duff made a name for himself in the World Cup and got a liking for the big stage. He admitted, 'I know I'm more than capable of holding my own among the best players in the world. I've always been confident in the ability and talent I have.'

Duff arrived at Rovers' youth academy as a slight 15-year-old with bags of potential. Former Ewood Park boss Kenny Dalglish said, 'You still get a great source of pleasure when a young kid comes good. Not all of them fulfil their potential, but we knew he was something special before he arrived and he has certainly lived up to expectations. Damien has developed into one of the most entertaining players in the game. He is a smashing lad off the pitch and I'm sure a high-profile move won't affect him in any way. Certainly, I have seen no change in him as his career has developed from an unknown into one of the most famous names in the Premier League.'

As they left Heathrow for Kuala Lumpur for the pre-season tournament,

Duff said, 'I didn't really want to leave Blackburn because I was very happy there and it is a wonderful club. But it is time for a change. Chelsea are on the up. They are a huge club already and are only going to get bigger. So I want to be part of it. I really don't give a fuck about money, I just want to be happy. Yes, making the move down here, to all the unknown, is nerve-wracking. But it was a challenge I couldn't turn down, and with the young signings we've made this summer we can definitely challenge the likes of Manchester United and Arsenal for the Premiership title.'

Asked what had finally made up his mind, he added, 'I suppose it was the gut feeling I had when I came down here. In the past week, I've flown down about three times. It just feels right. It's time to move on to a big new challenge for me. Chelsea are one of the biggest clubs in England and I want to be part of making them one of Europe's biggest. The new owner is throwing money at the club but he's doing it wisely and is building a squad to win things. The easy thing would have been to have stayed at Blackburn where I was happy and played every week. Here I'm not guaranteed my place but it's a big challenge that I couldn't turn down.'

Duff was just ten minutes away from taking off on Blackburn's flight to the United States for a pre-season training camp when the call came through that a fee had been agreed with Chelsea. Having decided that he could not turn down the chance at least to speak to the Blues, he then took a further week finally to make up his mind after consulting friends, family and colleagues. Graeme Souness told him in the departure lounge at Manchester Airport that Chelsea had raised their offer to meet the £17m buy-out clause. 'I'd heard snippets all week but I was getting on the plane when the gaffer said that Blackburn had accepted an offer and, with ten minutes to go, I'd better make my mind up! After I missed the flight, it took me about a week to make the final decision as I rang everybody I knew. I wasn't going to make a snap decision as it was the biggest decision of my life. But I think I've made the right decision and, hopefully, that will show on the pitch. Who knows who we'll be bringing in over the next couple of weeks but the squad already looks strong and we're just looking forward to the season starting.

'The lure of playing in the Champions League was definitely a big reason behind my decision to come here – but so was challenging for the title. I've realised there are world-class players here. I'm looking forward to working with them and I hope they can help me improve as a player.'

As far as his long-term future was concerned, Duff admitted that he could be tempted to return to Blackburn before the end of his career. 'I'm grateful to everyone at Blackburn for making me, over the last eight years, the player and the person I am today. And you never know ... in a few years, I could be back as a Rovers player again – please God.'

Duff was still surprised at how quickly the move went through. 'It came as big a shock to me as it did to Blackburn because it all happened so quickly.' And the speed of his rise to become one of the most highly prized footballers of his generation has naturally meant that he's had to cope with an intense interest in his professional and private life. In the 2002 World Cup, he was mortified when his mother Mary revealed to the Irish nation that her son played with a Padre Pio medal stitched inside his sock.

Now installed in a luxury apartment in the Chelsea Harbour complex while he searches for a house, he still calls home to Dublin every day, talks regularly to his four brothers and sisters, and delights at the prospect of his 'ma' coming to London to do 'the shopping and the shows'. He now drives a Mercedes sports coupé with a Celtic emblem hanging from the rear-view mirror.

Having exchanged a country cottage in the Ribble Valley for the frenzy and noise of the King's Road, 'People seem to think that I'm some kind of country hick who spent all my time in the hills above Blackburn. That's just rubbish. I'm an Irishman and I enjoy a good night out and what have you ... but only at the right time. I've come here to play football. Everything else can wait its turn, can't it now?'

His hero is George Best and he traces his affection for Manchester United and Celtic to his father Gerry. 'I'm reading George Best's life story at the minute. I'm trying to stay relaxed about the whole thing. It's been a hell of a month for me.'

Duffer, as he's known throughout Ireland, is famous for his easy-going outlook on life. Brian Kerr, the Republic of Ireland Manager, claims that he suffers from Adhesive Mattress Syndrome because he can sleep anywhere, any time, and generally looks as if he's just got out of bed. Duffer takes it all in good spirit. 'Yes, I sleep a lot, but I read a bit, have the odd night out, a game of golf or snooker or what have you.'

Much time has been spent in bed recently recharging batteries drained by twice-daily training sessions. 'It's an important part of a footballers' life,' he says. 'You need to get your rest, to do the business on the Saturday and train. Once the season starts, I'm just fascinated about keeping my energy levels high, so I'll probably do fuck-all! I'm sure I'll be kept busy at concerts and shows and what have you, but hopefully I won't be getting myself into trouble. I've definitely grown up as a player. I've been at

Blackburn since I was 16, something like eight years. Coming to London, it's just a totally different world – it's at the opposite end of the scale, but I'm sure I'll get used to it. In Blackburn, it was a happy country life but coming down here it's just pure madness. But I won't let it bother me.'

Ranieri and his medical staff have devoted time and energy to strengthening the hamstrings that have caused Duff such problems. Despite this, in his last season for Blackburn he scored 9 goals in 26 Premiership matches.

His favourite players are Luis Figo and Robert Pires. 'They play in similar positions to me, do similar jobs and what have you. I like to study both and learn from them. That Pires is a class act, to be sure. Pace, goals, everything ... he's got everything, hasn't he?

'My friends back home in Ireland don't envy me. To be honest, I'm envious of the things that they can do rather than the other way round. They can go out to the pub, to clubs, do what they like whenever they like ... I can't. I wish I could go back home more. I miss my friends and family, I miss my mum's cooking.'

Duff will look for a house in the country, like he had up north. 'Hopefully, I'll find a place a bit more chilled. That's what I was used to in Blackburn, but it won't bother me. It'll only be a distraction if I make it one, and I won't, I'll only worry about the football side.

'I may appear laid back, but I'm not all the time. Maybe at times in the season if things don't go well it might get on top of me. Obviously, it is a lot of money but, hopefully, I'll keep working hard and I can prove I'm worth it. There's no point in getting uptight about it and letting it affect your football.

'A couple of years ago, I wouldn't have been able to hack this at all, I'd have been in the toilet or something else. But in the past couple of years, on and off the pitch, I suppose I've just become a better person and a better player, going to the World Cup. I've certainly grown up.'

And despite his comments about being ready for 'the pure madness' of the capital, he admits, 'I am a bit of a country boy up there in Blackburn. My home is out in the hills. I just live for my football and go home to bed, but it is a new challenge down here. It's a different life and I am ready for it.'

Duff spoke to Ranieri and the conversation had been 'interesting'. He said, 'I didn't really understand a lot. He is just football mad. All he wants to do is talk about football. It is what he lives for.'

Devlin, the Dubliner who advised Duff on the move, observed, 'Dealing with Chelsea and listening to their ambitions reminded me of Blackburn when Jack Walker took over. I was the Irish scout there and very close to Kenny Dalglish. He backed Kenny on everything he wanted and Kenny delivered the title. Mr Abramovich clearly wants to build a team to win the Premiership and the Champions League and he is not going to stop until he gets it. The big thing when you want to sign anyone is to impress the player and that's exactly what Chelsea did with Damien. They made it clear to him from the word go how much they wanted him and that they would do whatever to get him.'

The mystery for Devlin is Manchester United's non-involvement in the final chapter of the saga. Devlin added, 'Speaking as an Irish soccer man, I can't understand why United didn't come in. They upped their offer for Ronaldinho to £21m and lost him, yet they had a better player under their noses at Blackburn for less money. But they missed their chance. I'll never understand why.'

Well, if Devlin was seeking an answer, Fergie didn't disappoint as he explained, 'I wasn't interested at the price. Duff's only 23 and he's an excellent footballer. But £17m? A lot of money. A lot of money.'

Duff's personal terms are £20m from his move, a five-year deal worth a basic £70,000 a week, then there's signing-on extras in the region of £1.5m. Despite the riches on offer, Duff only accepted a move when it became clear Manchester United were not interested.

He took five days to mull it over and, despite all the denials from Old Trafford that an interest was declared behind the scenes that the player knew about, the suspicion was that the Manager knew of the player's preference through skipper Roy Keane. United asked to be kept informed but they were not going to match Chelsea. Keane rang his fellow Irishman to ask him to consider the idea and raise his hopes, but the final word was down to Ferguson who rejected the price tag.

Devlin's commission was reputed to be £2m, raising questions again about inflated fees to agents after Harry Kewell's £5m move to Liverpool when his agent Bernie Mandic, who is not a registered agent, pocketed around £2m. More than £8m was eventually paid to around a dozen agents as the final transfer bill reached £110m for ten new stars. Sometimes two or even three agents were involved in any one deal, so the man credited for masterminding the majority of the deals, Pini Zahavi, collected far less than the £6m he was often reported as receiving. But the players tried to remain aloof from the activities of their representatives.

How did Duff feel about the opening game of the season against

Liverpool? 'Hopefully, I will play against Liverpool. They have big Irish connections. I have friends and family who support Liverpool. I've always enjoyed playing against them.'

Will he go to church before the match at Anfield on Sunday? 'I'll try,' he smiled. 'I try to go to Mass every week. I'm a believer. I try to keep my feet on the ground. My best mates are all my old friends from home. I value things like that. Compared to some people, I've been very fortunate. Some mornings when I'm driving into training I think, "Damien Duff, you're a lucky lad and all." That's the kind of feeling I never want to lose.'

Meanwhile, over at Southampton, Chairman Rupert Lowe wrote in one of the Southampton fans' websites, 'I regret to inform our supporters that we have today given Wayne Bridge permission to speak to Chelsea Football Club with a view to signing for them ... Wayne has quickly achieved great footballing success in his time with our club and has served us well. He has, however, made it known to both Gordon Strachan and me that he believes a move to Chelsea to be a career progression and an opportunity he cannot turn down.

'He is grateful for the tremendous support he has received from our club, from both staff and supporters, which has undoubtedly contributed to his success. He has, however, made it clear that he wants to play Champions League football, which he believes will give him a better chance of making him first choice for England. He will enjoy greater financial rewards at Chelsea and the club is geographically well placed for him to visit his family regularly. In the past, we have rejected offers for Wayne Bridge from clubs to which he was not attracted. He has now handed us a transfer request thereby making it difficult for us to retain him, despite the fact that he still has three years remaining on his contract. We subscribe to the view that sporting success is achieved by people who want to play together, share a common goal and are committed to the club and their team-mates.'

Southampton-born Bridge signed for the Saints in January 1998. His league début followed on the first day of the 1998/99 season in a home clash with Liverpool. Bridge was ever-present in the 2000/01 season and was voted the club's Player of the Year. He made his England début in a friendly against Holland in February 2002 and was part of Sven-Goran Eriksson's squad for the World Cup in Japan and South Korea. Bridge said, 'It still feels a bit strange but I'm sure it's something I'll get used to. I'm just looking forward to meeting up with the rest of the lads. I'd been at the club so long and everyone's treated me so well. I discussed it with my family and we all thought it was a great move for me, so hopefully people at Southampton will understand that. A few factors influenced my decision but the prospect of playing Champions League football was a big one. This is a very exciting time for everyone at Chelsea. When they came in with an offer for me it seemed like too good an opportunity to turn down.'

Although losing Bridge, Southampton did, however, pick up Graeme Le Saux, whose move in the opposite direction breaks a 12-year association with the Blues. Portsmouth, Manchester City and Fulham were also interested, but the only destination was St Mary's if the Bridge transaction was to be successful and Chelsea clearly made it worth his while.

Bridge's move will boost his battle to win the England number 3 shirt from Ashley Cole, something that Cole himself is acutely aware of. Bridge reckons he is now on a level playing field with his friend and Arsenal rival who has been playing regularly in Europe's premier club competition for the past two years.

The 22-year-old Bridge, capped 12 times by Sven-Goran Eriksson, said, 'I know it will help my international chances to be playing in the Champions League. It gives you the experience of playing against top foreign opposition week in and week out. I was surprised and delighted when Mr Eriksson first called me up last year and I know I'm the sort of player he likes. But when you've made the squad, you want to become first choice in your position and this will help. Ashley has been playing in the Champions League with Arsenal for a couple of years and it has improved him. I just want to test myself against the best as well.

'Ashley and I get on very well. We have the same agent – David Manasseh – and it's a friendly competition between us. He's a very good player. We've even played together for England with me in the left-midfield position. It was the toughest decision I've ever had to make to leave Southampton. It hurts because I've supported them since I was a boy. But joining Chelsea is a challenge I felt I couldn't turn down.'

With Duff and Bridge signing within hours of each other, Abramovich took his summer spending spree to £36.5m in just 21 days, and Ranieri continued to deliver on his pledge to have a British backbone in his team. Bridge said, 'You need a certain number of British players if you are going to succeed in the Premiership and Chelsea now have more than they have had for quite a few years. You hear talk of the new owner coming in and drawing up lists of players, but the players Chelsea have brought in are clearly people that Claudio Ranieri has spotted and liked the look of. I've played quite a bit alongside John Terry with the England Under-21s and he is a real leader. He is so composed on the ball, he always seems to have time and he is the sort of player you want to play alongside. Like most people, I haven't seen much of Glen Johnson – but I have seen enough to know he is a very promising player. I played against him at St Mary's last season and he's a player who gets up and down well and seems comfortable when he is going forward as well as being a strong tackler. Both are players I would like to play alongside for England as well as Chelsea, although you don't like to look too far ahead.'

The left-back was ribbed by his former Southampton team-mates ever since Abramovich's arrival when his name was first linked with the impending spending spree. Bridge, whose hobbies include games of Scalextric with his old Saints pals, acquired a new Russian nickname as well as enquiries about whether he would be changing his middle name to Stamford. 'As soon as Mr Abramovich came in, it was obvious that Chelsea were going to be able to buy the sort of players they could only have dreamed of in the past. Since the rumours started about me, my Southampton team-mates have given me a few new nicknames. James Beattie has called me "Stamford" and "Bridgeovski". And he also reckons I'm going to have a daughter called "Chelsea".'

Bridge and Duff jetted out to Malaysia to join the Blues in the pre-season tournament. Bridge said, 'I just can't wait to get over there to meet my new team-mates. I know John Terry and Frank Lampard through England, of course, but there are so many quality players at the club who can improve my game. I've already enjoyed playing at Stamford Bridge so far. It was a great result to win 4-2 there 18 months ago, when James Beattie scored a couple. Then, last season, Saints got a draw off them. I hope Southampton's good run against Chelsea comes to an end now! And I hope the supporters at the Bridge take to me like the Southampton fans did when I first got into the team.'

Tony Dorigo, former Chelsea star left-back, backed Bridge to win his battle with Cole. 'Wayne is looking to go into the spotlight. Playing for Chelsea will help him do that. It will give him a chance to show his stuff. Going from Southampton to Chelsea is a big step up and he will be able to really test himself by playing against the best in the Champions League. Ashley Cole has already done that with Arsenal so, by moving to a bigger club like Chelsea, Wayne will put himself on a level playing field and in a great position to be first choice for England.'

Although Bridge made his England début over 18 months ago, and was included in the World Cup squad, Cole, who is four months younger, is out in front with 19 caps and started every game in Japan . Aussie-born Dorigo, 37, experienced a similar rivalry for the England left-back role with Stuart Pearce ... and Psycho came out on top as he amassed 78 caps. Dorigo added, 'I'm very impressed with Bridge. He is still young and has done extremely well in an up-and-coming side. I like Cole as well. He has a slightly quicker turn of pace. He has had the edge over Wayne, but a move can change that. Chelsea will play a much more attacking style than Southampton and Wayne will get forward lots more. It'll be very difficult for Sven-Goran Eriksson to ignore him.'

Cole said, 'It is scary Chelsea are throwing all this money about and buying people willy-nilly. It is a little bit frustrating knowing other clubs are spending and we are not. It is not just Manchester Untied this time; Chelsea are chucking money around and Liverpool are buying some players, so we know it is going to be harder than last season. I think Chelsea could change the balance at the top. I hope so, it will be better for everyone. Liverpool, Chelsea and Newcastle have bought players and they are going to be up there. But they have a lot to prove. The more players they buy, the more pressure they put on. We are confident in our squad and believe we can stay up there despite Chelsea buying all these players. It will be hard for us, I know. Chelsea have brought in world-class players but they must work together and gel and that will be difficult in the first season. But, for us, there is now less expectation from many fans. Hopefully, that will be an advantage. Maybe we will be up the top of the table without too many people talking about us. All eyes will be on Chelsea. Also, the pressure will still be as high for United, and all this could work in our favour.'

Cole expects tougher competition from Bridge. 'I don't care with what happens with England. A good season with Arsenal is my main aim. As for Wayne, he had to get out of Southampton if he wanted a chance with England and winning things. Hopefully, it will be a good move for him ... but not too good!'

Bridge begged Southampton fans not to abuse him when he returns to St Mary's. He fears a stormy reception, as many Saints fans criticised him for putting in a transfer request. Bridge said, 'The decision to leave was the most difficult decision I have made. It hurts to leave your hometown club, who you have supported since you were a boy, and where you have played since you were 13 or 14.

'My dad, Mick, was a season-ticket holder at the Dell and he always came to watch me play for the club. But I sat down with him and my mum and we decided this was a big move, it was Champions League football and that I couldn't turn it down. Many of my friends are Saints fans and they know why I have left. I didn't want to have to hand in a transfer request but that was the only way I could talk to Chelsea. I understand why I might get stick when I go back there but I hope the fans realise why I made this decision. I know most players get it when they go to their old club but Alan Shearer always gets a fantastic reception when he goes back to Southampton or Blackburn because everyone realises what a great servant he was. If I got anything like that reaction from the crowd, I would be happy. Since I got into the Southampton team, things have gone brilliantly for me and the club. They have a new stadium and qualified for Europe.'

The first four signings were in place, but the transfer acquisitions kept coming as Ranieri sought 'champions' next, the stars who had already experienced at the highest level and proved themselves successful.

10

A VIEW OF THE BRIDGE

FROM THE BERNABEU TO Old Trafford, the powerhouses of world
football, the shock waves were unsurpassed.

Manchester United and Arsenal might fear for their Premiership pre-
eminence, but Real Madrid were concerned that the new Chelsea might
challenge their European domination.

Real's Director Emilio Butragueno observed, 'We have been watching
Chelsea with interest and they could turn out major contenders for the
European Cup. They seem willing to spend a lot on acquiring top players
and, with that sort of money, anything is possible in football.'

Chelsea must win the title or they will have wasted Roman Abramovich's
millions, maintained Sir Alex Ferguson, the Manager with the reputation for
mind games and who didn't disappoint on that score. His usual
brainstorming target has been Arsene Wenger since dispensing with Kevin
Keegan, but now he has turned on Chelski, a back-handed compliment,
having spotted the new threat to the old order of supremacy being
maintained by Manchester United and Arsenal.

Fergie's barbed comments have often been aimed at the Arsenal boss,
but now he has Claudio Ranieri and his sugar daddy firmly in his sights.

Ferguson turned up the heat by insisting that Chelsea's huge outlay must bring immediate results for the Russian Revolution, or 'Red Rom' will be regarded as a failure.

'It depends on how well they do in their first season,' said Ferguson. 'That might activate a lot of things. There has been a lot of money spent and clubs expect results.'

Ferguson tipped a five-horse race for one of the most open chamionships for years, but when it comes to the final hurdle, he believes it will once again come down to a straight fight between his United side and their old rivals Arsenal. 'Every year, we say there'll be four or five teams challenging for the title,' said Fergie as United prepared to fly home after their two-week pre-season tour of the United States. 'But every season it comes down to two clubs – ourselves and Arsenal. I don't know how Arsenal will respond, because I don't know the character of all their players. But I do know they will want to do their best because of what happened last season and because they have some fantastic players in their squad. Newcastle played a really important part in the title race last season, right up until the last few games. Liverpool were doing great until December, and I thought Chelsea showed more consistency. So you expect these teams to be knocking on the door. But when it comes to the run-in, there's usually only two involved. And if you look at the League over the past decade, it's been dominated by ourselves and Arsenal. So we expect a real challenge from Arsenal once again. And it's one myself and the players are really looking forward to.'

Fergie was fascinated by the unfolding revolution at Chelsea but believed it would take another season for the impact of their new-found spending power to turn the club into genuine title contenders. Yet he believed the decision to buy young, emerging players rather than established stars is ultimately the right one and will see Chelsea challenge for the title in the coming years. 'They've bought an interesting choice of players. Young players to build a team for the future. That represents a clear statement of intent. Glen Johnson, Damien Duff, Wayne Bridge ... they're all young. And the players already there, the likes of Frank Lampard, William Gallas, John Terry and Eidur Gudjohnsen, they're all young too. They have a good basis in those players, but it may take them longer to challenge for the title. When it comes to experience, ourselves and Arsenal maybe have the edge on them. It's going to be a fantastic season and we relish the challenge ahead. The players are hungrier than ever and so am I. The team spirit is great and we can't wait to get going.

'I'm not sure they will win the League this season but they could do, because they must have the biggest squad in the division. It's been a great summer for Chelsea and I would imagine their supporters are really buoyed by it all. All the signs are good for the club long-term because they have got some very good footballers. But I think they have got a lot to prove this season and I don't believe they will win the League. You can buy the title if you've got good judgement, though the situation I see there is they've bought young players and maybe they need experience and time. I don't think they'll do it this year but the long term looks good.

'I always say to myself when clubs make players available, "Why do they want to sell him?" Geremi? You have to ask why Real Madrid were so keen to get rid of him. They sent him on loan for a year. They were negotiating a fee with Middlesbrough. They were trying to sell him and nobody else was coming in. In the cases of Glen Johnson and Duff, it's more straightforward – their clubs wanted the money. With Johnson, West Ham were skint and anybody who came in with that sort of money would have got any of their players, whether it was Jermain Defoe, Michael Carrick or Joe Cole ... £6m was a lot for a 19-year-old boy [Johnson], but you can see a future for him. He'll probably be in the England set-up soon.'

How ironic that Manchester United Chief Executive Peter Kenyon should express his views that he was unsure whether the millions being splashed out at Stamford Bridge are the kind of thing the game needs just as transfer fees and wages were starting to be controlled. United will refuse to be drawn into spending huge money just because of Chelsea's activity. Kenyon observed, 'What has happened at Chelsea has certainly ignited the transfer market. It has been pretty depressed for the past 18 months and prices have fallen along with salaries, and I think that's good for the industry. The worry is that this will again lead to inflated transfer prices and salaries. One positive is at least there are millions going into the game. But I don't see us paying £30m for one player again for some time.'

Ferguson showed his temperamental side had not deserted him when he articulated his challenge to Chelsea. The Premiership champions missed out on Duff, a long-standing target, as Ferguson opted not to compete with Chelsea's bid as he believed the player to be grossly over priced. After the disappointments of Ronaldinho, Kewell and Duff, as well as Newcastle refusing to sell Kieron Dyer for £20m, Ferguson said, 'We need to draw breath. The problem for our club is that as soon as someone wants to sell a player, they attach our name to it. We are not doing any business at the moment and are analysing the situation. There are probably two or three players we will be interested in over the next few weeks but we are not going to rush out after what has happened over the last few months. We want a break.'

London rivals Arsenal endured an even more torturous summer. The club's financial crisis left Wenger trying to offload Francis Jeffers, Giovanni van Bronkhurst, Kanu, Ray Parlour, record signing Sylvain Wiltord and Jermaine Pennant to cut his wage bill and furnish him with some finances to speculate seriously in the transfer market. Wenger has been left juggling Arsenal's finances and desperately trying to balance the need to maintain a successful team with building a new £400m stadium at Ashburton Grove, which had been put on hold with the club's debts mounting up to £60m. It left him casting envious glances at Chelsea, and Wenger even entered the mind games himself by branding Abramovich's rejuvenation of the stagnating transfer market as 'dangerous' for the game. 'Chelsea's transfer dealings are inflating an otherwise deflated transfer market,' said Wenger. 'That could be a dangerous thing for football. Chelsea have won the lottery. They have always spent in the transfer market – usually as much as Arsenal – but now they are in Manchester United's bracket. Chelsea will be even more competitive next season because they will buy and have the potential to buy, but it doesn't always guarantee success. In recent years, the competition has come from United, but now I think we can add Chelsea as well.

'Chelsea buy a player a day – we buy no player a month. To write us off just because we haven't spent £100m is too easy ... I think we have got enough to compete at the top again. At the moment, the newspapers have already removed us from being favourites for the title, but I don't mind that. What's important is what's happening on the pitch and I know this team has a great potential.'

Wenger remained unperturbed by Abramovich's millions even though Thierry Henry and Patrick Vieira had initially been top of the Wish List, until it was clear the Gunners wouldn't sell at any price. Wenger was adamant, 'They are not for sale at any price. It is that simple. Patrick has not signed his new contract yet but we are close. When he returns to pre-season training, we expect him to sign.'

Wenger added, 'It was a huge surprise to me that the change was made so quickly at Chelsea, because Ken Bates looked quite confident to manage the financial situation down there. What will the new resources do to Chelsea? I don't think it is a concern of ours, because we do not want to sell our good players to anyone. We want to maintain the stability here that we have developed in recent years. To build a great team is not all about money. First, you have to create the spirit and togetherness within a squad and that is not easy. Of course, it's not all down to money. But if you want to be successful, it's better you have it.'

Peter Hill-Wood, the Old Etonian Chairman, reminded Chelsea – and mega-rivals Manchester United – that Arsenal are still a Premiership force to be reckoned with. 'I've been involved in the game for a long time and I have seen lots of people spending a lot of money and not winning a damn thing.'

The £400m-plus being spent on a new stadium led some to believe that Arsenal might find it difficult to turn down huge offers for the likes of Henry and Vieira. Hill-Wood insisted, 'No! We wouldn't consider selling. For any price? Well, I mean, basically, no price that anybody could possibly think of. They are absolutely not for sale, to anyone – end of story.'

Is the fact that Vieira is out of contract in a year and has yet to put pen to paper an immediate cause for concern? 'No, we're very relaxed about that too. I'm sure it's going to be OK.'

Even rumours of player unrest because of Vieira's £110,000-a-week wage demands – and comments from Dennis Bergkamp's agent that Arsenal's new offer to him was 'embarrassing' – failed to weaken Hill-Wood's resolve. 'It's a good story to build up, but it's not true,' he says. 'I think everybody, by and large, is extremely happy. If somebody doesn't get exactly what he thinks he wants, it's not surprising his agent talks out and says he doesn't like the offer. But the idea there's general unrest is complete nonsense. There is absolutely no crisis at Arsenal.'

Hill-Wood, 67, remains optimistic that stars like Vieira, Bergkamp and Robert Pires will follow Henry in signing new deals. But he admits, 'It's out of my hands. However, I'm confident we're going to have a very good squad next year.'

What about claims that Wenger had to persuade the directors to break up the pay structure to accommodate Vieira? Hill-Wood says, 'That's an invention from somewhere, I know not where. We don't work like that. It's always a consensus view. We pay the maximum we can possibly afford to pay, and we take advice from Mr Wenger as to his assessment of the value. You have to run a business with the amount of money you have available.

'Yes, he [Wenger] has got money at his disposal for signings. Not billions, but he's got a little bit of a war chest and he's looking at spending it wisely. And he's got a pretty good track record in that department over the years.'

Wenger remained confident that Arsenal are in the frame for honours this season, despite working in a financial straitjacket. 'When I open the newspapers, it looks like we are a sinking boat, but I don't share that view. The competition will be a better level next year but we have always been the most consistent. If everybody wants to write us off, that's up to them but I wouldn't do that if I was them. I'm a strong believer that we are getting stronger every year. And I'm convinced we will be competitive in the title race. Chelsea have always spent a lot of money, maybe more than Arsenal. But they look now that they are in the bracket of Manchester United, spending-wise. I don't know if it will bring them trophies but the competition is open. In the past, it was just Manchester United and us in the title race but now there are others. Chelsea have the potential to do it. I welcome it, but I would say it looks like the competition is getting harder every year and it looks like next season will be even tougher. We have eight to nine midfielders, five strikers and nine defenders at the club and adding people to people is not always the key to success. Sometimes it creates a bigger problem than you have already.

'It has been a difficult summer and, despite what people say, our best players are not for sale.'

David Seaman was also offered disappointing terms before he quit for Manchester City, while Chelsea target Vieira hinted he wouldn't sign a new deal until the club invests in the transfer market. Wenger has so far failed to sign a keeper and missed out on Harry Kewell to Liverpool – and Arsenal's competitiveness in the market has sunk to a new low. Wenger admitted that his £10m budget is shrinking by the day. He said, 'I do have a budget but I wouldn't like to talk about the number because we are a bit more cautious than we usually are. We have never been big spenders but this season we'll be smaller spenders than ever. At the moment, the financing of the stadium hasn't been sorted out and, as a result, we have to be more cautious.'

Abramovich and Chelsea rapidly became the team that the rest of the Premiership loves to see fail. That used to be the preserve of Manchester United, and to a lesser extent Arsenal, but Chelsea is now confronting the sort of pressure that Arsenal and United have become used to.

Arsenal's Swedish star Freddie Ljungberg was alarmed at Chelsea's spending power but knew it would make the Premiership a better spectacle. Ljungberg argued, 'Of course, you worry about other teams getting an advantage, but what has happened at Chelsea is good for football. They are from London, like us, so it is going to make for some nice derbies. They will have a strong squad and they will be better than last season. In the last couple of seasons, they have been brilliant against the good teams but not so consistent against the poorer ones. That may change. If they sort that out they will become really dangerous. We still have the same players as last season so, hopefully, we will do better this time. We've played well the last couple of seasons but, when you look at other teams, they are strengthening their squads.'

Ljungberg knows that spending millions improves the chances of success – but it does not guarantee it. Arsenal have all the experience when it comes to fighting for honours, while Chelsea will take time to become a cohesive unit. As Ljungberg pointed out, 'We've won the Premiership before and the FA Cup, so we will keep on working. I'm sure the Chelsea fans are happy someone has come along and put a lot of money into the club and they will be hoping they can make a strong bid for the championship.'

The spending spree has sparked concern within the game and Birmingham City's David Gold voiced fears about the impact on other clubs. The days leading up to the opening match of the competition, when Birmingham faced Newcastle, were dominated by Chelsea transfer talk. While Chelsea spent £34m on four players, Birmingham thought they had pushed the boat out with the £5.5m capture of David Dunn earlier in the summer. 'We have spent all our money, and that is the difference,' said Gold. 'We are relatively new members of the Premiership and it takes a number of years to build up the squad, so £5m doesn't go very far. At Chelsea, this new principal has come in with huge sums of money and it does cause clubs like ourselves a problem. We spent £5.5m on David Dunn and our fans were ecstatic because they felt we had gone the extra mile. But when clubs are talking about billionaires coming in, your fan-base then becomes dissatisfied. While what has happened to Ken is fantastic and very exciting for football, it does create problems in that we cannot satisfy the expectations of the fans in spending five or six million. It's not enough. There are bigger people and bigger amounts of money out there, so it is difficult for the smaller clubs. There seemed to be a bit of common sense coming back into the game but Chelsea's spending has given us a problem.'

Birmingham, Chelsea and Newcastle represented English football in the inaugural Asia Cup in Malaysia, affording plenty of opportunity to discuss these issues around the dinner table.

During Freddy Shepherd's time in the Boardroom, Newcastle forked out nearly £200m on transfers and still don't have a single trophy to show for it. Shepherd said, 'Roman Abramovich may be the new kid on the block in English football, but he will quickly learn that money is no guarantee to success. We've been down that route and the evidence that big transfer fees don't necessarily bring in trophies is shown by the spaces in our trophy cabinet.'

Current Toon boss Sir Bobby Robson has spent £64m since his arrival at St James's Park in September 1999 and predecessors Ruud Gullit (£33.4m), Kenny Dalglish (£37.3m) and Kevin Keegan (£61m) all failed to bring a trophy to the north-east.

Abramovich is threatening to make those figures look like small change, but Shepherd believes Abramovich will have to show patience as he bids to take over the mantle of Arsenal and Manchester United. And he points to the repercussions of the Keegan era at St James's Park as the downside of trying to buy overnight success.

Under Keegan, Newcastle lashed out a staggering £61m between 1992 and 1997 and got to within an ace of claiming the Premiership title in 1996. Shepherd admits Newcastle's spectacular spending policy probably cost them the title when they blew a 12-point lead to let in Manchester United. Shepherd added, 'Ever since the excitement and entertainment of the Kevin Keegan era, we have been known as the Board that couldn't say "No". Whenever a manager came in and asked for transfer funds, he got them. Only Manchester United have spent more than us over the last decade.

Our ambition was exactly the same as Abramovich's. We wanted the title and we wanted it quickly. Money was no object. First Kevin wanted £1.75m to buy Andy Cole to get us out of Division One and he got it. Then he wanted more to buy Peter Beardsley, Les Ferdinand and, finally, the summer after we missed out on the title, a world-record £15m to land Alan Shearer. And we went damned close to knocking Manchester United off their pedestal. Two seasons in a row we were runners-up in the Premiership. But we never quite got the big-name players to gel or got the right balance in the team. We were fabulous going forward but, despite the huge outlay, we never quite mastered the defensive side of things. It was a case of so near and yet so far.

'Abramovich clearly has the cash to bring in a host of world-class stars and it looks as if he is determined to make an immediate impact. But he could learn a lot from what happened at Newcastle. You should never spend money for the sake of spending it. We learned that in 1996 when we blew that 12-point lead. We were romping away with the championship and had plenty of money in the bank.

'Kevin said he wanted £7.5m to bring in Tino Asprilla as the final piece in the jigsaw. In retrospect, it was money we shouldn't have spent. It was no fault of Tino's, but he just didn't fit into the team. We changed our pattern to accommodate him and the balance was never really right. Abramovich will face a problem if he tries to integrate too many new players into the side at one go. We have learned that building a team takes time. Manchester United are probably the best example of how it should be done. Sir Alex Ferguson built a solid core of players from his youth team and has gradually added a couple of new faces each season.'

Shepherd believes that Abramovich's arrival will give the Premiership a massive fillip. 'I think Abramovich will be good for the game. The transfer market has been stagnant for some time and his arrival has re-created interest. It looks like a lot of his money will go out of England to La Liga and Serie A, but the fact that he will be importing world-class stars to the Premiership can only improve the status of our league. Some of his cash will almost certainly end up in English coffers and that will help stimulate more transfer activity in the Premiership. It's amazing to think that our £8m deal for Jonathan Woodgate is the biggest deal in England this year. I said at the time that fee would probably prove to be too high in retrospect. When you see players of international standard like Harry Kewell and Robbie Fowler going for £5m and £3m respectively you know the domestic market is seriously depressed. But it remains to be seen whether Abramovich's millions can provide a stimulus. The problem is that if he forks out £70m or so for players like Christian Vieri and Andrei Shevchenko, he is unlikely ever to get his money back. He may start out as a benefactor, but like any hard-headed businessman he will want to see a return on his investment. To justify that sort of outlay, Chelsea would have to win the Champions League – and even after a decade at the top, Manchester United can testify how difficult that feat is.'

The Newcastle Chairman is confident that the Magpies have finally got their transfer policy right. 'The days when we bought ageing foreign players are gone,' he said. 'Sir Bobby Robson has adopted a policy of buying young British players of quality. We haven't ruled out foreign players altogether, as shown by our £8.5m signing of Hugo Viana, but we definitely think British is best. Mr Abramovich can go down the Continental route, but our experience shows we are better off with players who are schooled in the English game.'

Ken Bates defended the club's new policy when he said, 'We haven't spent that much. Up to now, we've bought four players for a total of £34m, which is only £4m more than Manchester United spent on Rio Ferdinand. Last season, Claudio Ranieri didn't spend a penny and we improved from sixth to fourth place in the Premiership. Because of players released at the end of last season, we're a bit thin in certain areas.'

Bates insisted there was no added pressure on Ranieri. 'He has a proven track record at Chelsea and before.'

Abramovich's takeover gained tacit approval from the Football Association's new Chief Executive, Mark Palios, who, when asked if he had any concerns over the Russian oil magnate, said, 'Not of his arrival. If you were to say that the Premiership would become the playground of ten Russian or other ethnic billionaires, then I might have a concern as it might distort the level playing field. But for one or two guys coming in and doing this, then I think it just adds to the competition and I'm pretty pleased to see it happening. My personal view is that it is has provided a fillip to a pretty moribund transfer market.'

Premier League Chairman Richard Scudamore was equally non-committal but would not be raising any objections.

Scudamore observed, 'We live in such times of heightened awareness,' he said, shortly after arriving in Malaysia to promote the FA Premier League Asia Cup. Chelsea can't afford to go on doing this and there will be a point fairly soon when it will all settle down. I believe, though, that the uncertainty in the wake of Chelsea's activities has been good for us. As Chief Executive of the Premier League, I would like to have different clubs winning it every year. It's the nature of the game that everyone tries to steal a march on the opposition. If you look at the press clippings, there was similar concern when Everton paid £300 for a player and the same thing happened when the 'mercenaries' arrived from Scotland. The important thing is that clubs act responsibly and operate within their means. It's important Chelsea's actions do not prompt another hyper-inflationary period with other clubs overstretching themselves.

'There is also no indication that more money guarantees you success. These days you are dealing with the thin end of the market because there is so much talent now in the Premier League that improving your squad significantly is becoming more difficult. As long as it doesn't lead to certain clubs winning every match. One of the attractions of the Premier League is that, in the past few years, the champion clubs have lost more and more matches. Bolton can beat Manchester United and Blackburn can do the double over Arsenal. As long as that continues, we'll be OK.'

Glenn Hoddle is among a number of Premiership managers to have voiced his concerns in public. 'As far as Chelsea are concerned, the [transfer] market is inflationary. I'm not sure the game can afford it,' he said.

Elsewhere in north London, Arsene Wenger goes further. While money being invested in football is, in principle, a good thing, the Arsenal manager says the Russian's riches could force other clubs to return to the bad old days of relentless overspending. 'The interesting thing is that, at the moment, Chelsea are an inflated part of a deflated market,' says Wenger. 'They can push that up artificially because of their financial power, and that's dangerous.'

At west London rivals Fulham, 33-year-old Manager Chris Coleman is grateful that events at Stamford Bridge may stop people expecting too much of him in his first full season in charge. 'Chelsea may take the pressure off me a bit,' he says. 'They have blown the transfer market wide open. They look like they are going to spend a lot of money and there will be a lot of pressure on them to succeed.'

Jim Smith, the veteran managerial hand who is now Harry Redknapp's assistant at promoted Portsmouth, is more forthright. 'It could be a disaster for football if the financial wheel turns again. It's scary. The timing, just when football was starting to follow more sensible housekeeping, is unfortunate.'

There are parallels in what is happening in west London with how King Kenny steered Blackburn to the title in '95 when the late Jack Walker bankrolled Blackburn's bid. The former Chairman poured £60m into his beloved club to achieve championship glory, just three years after Rovers were promoted via the play-offs. But Dalglish does not accept these similarities. 'Chelsea are in a much stronger starting position than we were at Blackburn. They have a Champions League place and finished fourth last season. At Blackburn, we needed to get promotion before we could even start thinking of winning the championship. What is happening now can only make the next title race even more exciting. Apart from United, Arsenal and Chelsea, Liverpool and Newcastle will also look to make a push.'

Dalglish's Blackburn stormed to the title with the likes of Shearer, Sutton, Le Saux and Batty as Walker backed Dalglish's judgement in the market. 'Money alone won't win you the title – it's the players who will do that. I am sure Ranieri is comfortable with the situation. He has worked in Spain and Italy where the president buys the players and now someone else is providing the money to bring in the new faces. From his point of view, that is a great position to be in. He has already demonstrated he is one of the best-equipped coaches in the game. He is shrewd and knowledgeable and, when you look at who they have signed so far, you have to say they are all good investments. Now it's a question of everyone gelling and, until we see the outcome of that, you cannot predict just how quickly Chelsea will rise to the top. They were a good side last season and will certainly be an even better one this time. By having so much cash at his disposal it is inevitable standards will rise and that is good for the game as a whole. That is why I am looking forward so much to the new season. These are exciting times for the Premier League and not just for the Chelsea fans.'

Dalglish is the only other boss apart from Ferguson and Wenger to have won the Premiership title. Dalglish insisted, 'I thought Chelsea were in with a shout of winning it even before they started signing new players. In recent years, United and Arsenal have set tremendously high standards but now Chelsea are just as powerful as those two.

'How can it be a problem for the game if someone is investing in the Premier League? Don't forget, £30m of the £37m Chelsea have spent so far is invested in our league. Only the money for Geremi has gone out of this country. You have to take your hat off to Chelsea because they are creating so much excitement, not only for their own fans but increasing the competition and standards for the rest of the country.'

Former Blackburn stars Tim Flowers and Tony Gale insist that money can, indeed, buy you glory. Ex-England keeper Flowers, 37, now retired and coaching at Leicester, said, 'You only have to look at Real Madrid to see that you can buy success. They have spent more than anyone else on players like David Beckham, Zinedine Zidane, Ronaldo and Luis Figo and what have they got to show for it? Two European Cups in the last four years. Jack Walker spent millions to win the Premiership for Blackburn, with £3.6m for Alan Shearer and then £5m on Chris Sutton. At the time, those sums were unbelievable. And now Chelsea have a new owner willing to put his money into the club in the same way. Of course Chelsea can do it. The money is available and they are already a very good side as well. If Chelsea get the sort of players they are being linked to, then – Bang! – they are in business.'

A decade ago, Walker's big spending was the catalyst for Blackburn's first title triumph in 81 years. Chelsea last won the league crown 48 years ago. Former Rovers centre-back Gale, 43, argued, 'Jack Walker started the boom in football with his big signings and big wages. But it paid off. Now Chelsea have the money behind them to spend big on star players and are going to try to do the same. The bid for Veron is another sign of their intent and he will further improve the squad. They have the financial clout and finance is everything if you are aiming for success – as long as you spend the money on the right players and you have the right balance at the club.

'At Blackburn, we had the right management team in Kenny Dalglish and Ray Harford, who commanded total respect from the players. Yet I think it will take Chelsea more than one season to get it right. It is vital they get the correct players and forge a great team spirit, like Blackburn had. If they do, they can achieve what they have always wanted to achieve.'

Sir Jack Haywood, like Walker, has backed his local team. The Wolves supremo was cautious. 'I don't know if this fellow quite has his heart in it because Chelsea is not his local club, like it is with me at Wolves or the late Jack Walker with Blackburn. There's also Lionel Pickering, who did so much at Derby, and I often said that the three of us should get to know each other because one day the men in white coats might come along and put us all in the same padded cell. The man at Chelsea is not a local boy, is he? I'm delighted for Chelsea, though, it's great for them. Abramovich currently needs a straitjacket more than I do. It's nice to know it's not just a mad English thing. But the Chelsea spending has inflated the transfer market again. I didn't ever think I would see the day when someone would come in and throw more money around like he has.'

Gary Lineker predicted that Newcastle will pose the biggest threat to the established order, but he observed, 'It must be great to be a Chelsea fan at the moment.' But he added, 'It is impossible to predict how Roman Abramovich's purchase of Chelsea will work out since it will depend on how many players he can bring in, what stature they are and how quickly they can gel into a team … As rosy as things look at present for Chelsea, they should remember what put them in a position where they needed to be rescued so dramatically.

'However they do, it is going to be fascinating following their progress this season and to see just how committed new owner Roman Arbamovich is and how much he is willing to spend to get success. Whoever else is brought in, perhaps his most exciting purchase was his first – Glen Johnson. Trevor Brooking tells me he is going to be sensational.'

Peter Osgood backed the big-buy policy to deliver major success, but not this season. The former Chelsea great is excited by the presence of so many top-class young stars. He is concerned that Abramovich may want to see instant glory in exchange for his massive spending. Ossie said, 'Success will be demanded, but he has to understand you cannot wave a magic wand and deliver the Premiership title just because you have spent a fortune on the squad. Yet success will come. I am convinced of that when I look at the quality brought in by Claudio Ranieri. He is buying for the future as well as for this season and that has to be good for Chelsea. Plus he has four young England talents on board, including Wayne Bridge, Joe Cole, John Terry and Frank Lampard. That is also a major plus.'

Osgood will be intrigued to see how the club keeps such a massive stable of midfield egos happy. 'It will be very interesting to see how things pan out.'

11

GOING ... GOING ... GONE!

KEN BATES WAS IN the departure lounge at Heathrow when he spotted his old mates from Anfield, Manager Gérard Houllier, Chairman David Moores and Chief Executive Rick Parry.

The Chelsea squad were heading for Kaula Lumpur for the inaugural Premiership Asia Cup, while the Liverpool party were on their way to their own Far East tour. Bates couldn't resist the opportunity to show off his unique brand of humour as he shouted across the lounge, 'Hello, boys, anyone want to come and play for Chelsea? We'll double your money!'

Now, of course, given the fact that the Roman Abramovich empire had Steven Gerrard and Michael Owen on its 'futures' list of potential signings, probably unbeknown to the outgoing owner, the joke was not one of Bates's best. Bates felt the joke was taken in good spirit at the time, but a small item in a national newspaper about the incident caused him a certain amount of embarrassment. Added to Bates's comments about Sven-Goran Eriksson, that made huge headlines, there was a degree of disquiet within the Abramovich camp and, although it had been agreed that he'd stay on until 2005, mutterings began over whether his term of office might be shortened as a consequence of his indiscretions.

Bates put the Heathrow incident into perspective when he told me, 'It was an innocent remark made to some dear old friends; no malice intended and they took it the way it was intended. There was absolutely no nastiness in it at all. There is such thing as camaraderie in the Boardroom, you know, and David Moores took it in the spirit it was intended when he shouted back, "Fuck off!"

'I also told them, as they were passing through security, that we would see them on the seventeenth for the opening game of the new season and they wound me up by saying, "Are you going to come this year, after bottling it last season?"

'I couldn't get up to Anfield for some reason but I always enjoy going there and, likewise, when they come to the Bridge. We always have a good time together, and when Gérard was in hospital, Suzannah sent flowers and our good wishes for a speedy recovery.'

Eye-witness Jamie Carragher thought it was amusing. He observed, 'It was quite funny at the airport. As we were queuing up Ken Bates walked past us and shouted, 'All right, lads, come and join us and we will double your wages.' It was all in good humour, everyone was laughing about it. I thought the whole thing was just funny really.'

But while the new Chelsea were engaged in a massive recruitment campaign, and Liverpool publicly had to rebuff the speculation that Chelsea would offer £50m for Gerrard, there was no doubt that, behind the scenes, the Abramovich regime was indeed courting the Liverpool and England midfielder.

Carragher added, 'Chelsea are going to have a stronger team. But I thought it was interesting when Frank Lampard said a few lads were feeling a bit unsettled as so many players are being linked with their positions. I know it can be a bit upsetting. If you think you're going to be sold, it plays on your mind. It hurts to say it, but Manchester United have proved over the years continuity is the key to being successful, not just buying players.'

As well as the incredible recruitment drive – many, indeed, via Heathrow – there was also a steady flow of departures. Gianfranco Zola, Enrique de Lucas, Jody Morris, Albert Ferrer and Ed De Goey were already on their way out before the takeover, but youngsters like Leon Knight left for regular first-team football. Others were farmed out on loan for the same reason, like Carlton Cole to Charlton for the season, and Mikeal Forsell to Birmingham. Some experienced internationals such as Zendon went to Middlesbrough on loan. New boy Alexei Smertin was loaned for the season to Portsmouth. Hasslebaink and Petit were rumoured to be on their way, but they somehow survived.

Claudio Ranieri won't stand in any unhappy player's way if they want to find another club. He said, 'Of course, we can't play everyone, how can you? But when we signed the players, we made our position clear and offered no guarantees. I expect heart, commitment and passion from my players and if they can't give me that, if they don't like the situation, I will let them go. We are building for the future, success will not come overnight. It's like building a house. At the moment, we have put down the foundations and now we must build upwards. I know that every player wants to be involved in every game. That will not be possible at Chelsea because we have 26 here and only 11 can play. It is not a difficult decision. We can only have players here who are intelligent and know what the situation is.'

Le Saux, the veteran left-back, was the first big-name casualty of the takeover. He was shipped off to Southampton as Gordon Strachan made it clear that no deal for Bridge would have taken place otherwise. The Saints Manager said, 'We may have lost one of the best young full-backs in the country but we have one of the most experienced around as a replacement. Le Saux falls into the category immediately behind Bridge and Ashley Cole, and I thought he might even have forced his way back into the England team last season. There would certainly have not been a deal with Chelsea if Le Saux had not been part of it. He might be 34, but age does not bother me. He is fit and ready, excited at joining us and he will be my first choice.'

As wage levels were a drawback, Le Saux moved on a free transfer; he was on £30,000 a week at the Bridge. Le Saux received a 'leaving present' from Chelsea, rather than the reported solution that Chelsea would continue to pay half of his salary. It probably amounted to the same sum! Chelsea also paid the fees of Le Saux's agent and those of Bridge to raise the costs by a further £1m.

Le Saux reacted as positively as he could when he said, 'I am very excited about this move. It is a great time to be joining the club. Southampton had a fantastic season last time around, reaching the FA Cup Final and getting into Europe.'

After signing a two-year deal, he added, 'There is some sadness in leaving Chelsea after 11 years but the flip side is the buzz of joining a club where I have always felt at home. I used to come over from Jersey for soccer camps here when I was a teenager. The club is probably in better shape than at any time since then. The move happened quickly but these things often do.' Le Saux made more than 300 appearances for Chelsea in two spells and won the Premiership title with Blackburn in between. He has also played 36 times for England.

Saints Chairman Rupert Lowe, who beat off competition from rivals Portsmouth to nab Le Saux, believes the player's immense experience can make up for the loss of Bridge. Lowe said, 'We made it clear we wanted Graeme because he will add great experience and know-how to what is a young team. He has played for England and in Europe and is a very intelligent footballer and person. Of course, we are sorry to lose Bridge, whom we have groomed from a teenager to the full England side but we were able to hold him only while he wanted to be here. If someone insists on going and hands in a transfer request, we have to decide what is in the best interests of the club.

'You can't make someone play if they don't want to be here – but if Roman Abramovich had not taken over at Chelsea, Bridge would still be a Southampton player.'

Despite being almost an automatic first choice at Chelsea last season, conversations with the hierarchy there seem to have left Le Saux in no doubt that he needed to leave. Even before Abramovich arrived, Le Saux was deep in contract talks that were not progressing very well. He had a year to run and the club were in no mood for improved terms to keep him.

'It didn't come as a shock at all,' Le Saux said. 'I realised it was time to move on. I was never in a position to leave myself open to regret. I don't make decisions lightly.'

Like Zola, he conducted his departure with dignity. 'I have good friends who are Chelsea supporters and I still speak to some of the players. Like everyone who's interested in the sport, I'm looking at what's happening there from a general perspective – whether they are going to gel or not, whether it's a risk – although when a man's that wealthy, it's not really a risk. Chelsea have suddenly inherited huge wealth and are spending at an excessive rate. But it's taken Manchester United, and other teams like Arsenal and Newcastle, a long time to build a successful team, a team not just of expensive players but of quality and based on camaraderie. It undervalues what United have achieved over the past few years just to say that success is based on being a wealthy club. There's far more to it than that. You need a spirit and money can't buy you that.'

Yet Le Saux should know how money can help to construct a championship side, having been part of the Blackburn Rovers team which won the Premiership in 1995 with the assistance of Sir Jack Walker's millions. Like Dalglish, he dismisses direct parallels, pointing out that the investment at Blackburn was less sudden and that some of the buys – himself included – were hardly expensive. His hope is that Abramovich's wealth does not harm the game. 'That's something we will have to find out. It is potentially a concern for football in England when the sport is going through a difficult time financially. We all hope that it doesn't destabilise an already fragile market. It is naïve to say money brings success, because football has a nasty habit of disproving that philosophy. It will be interesting to see what happens but there is no tinge of regret that I am not in there.'

Conversations with Strachan and Lowe left him with 'no second thoughts' about the transfer. 'With the timing of me leaving Chelsea, it was important for me to come somewhere that had the quality and ambition and the stability of a club like Southampton. The environment that I'm in down here in terms of the stadium, the training facilities and the opportunity for my family all helped me to make this decision.'

Strachan was delighted to obtain Le Saux's services. He said, 'There's a stature about him. He's been good for the players. When we watched him playing last year, [my assistant] Garry [Pendrey] and myself thought he must have a chance of playing for England again. We never thought by any stretch of the imagination that he would be playing for us this year.' Le Saux probably never imagined he would be at Southampton, either!

The next player who seemed destined to leave appeared to be Hasselbaink, who emerged as a transfer target for Spanish side Real Betis. Chelsea were originally keen to offload the Dutch striker, who will earn £80,000 a week in the final year of his contract. 'We need a goal-scorer,' said the Betis Coach Victor Fernandez. 'Jimmy knows the language and the Spanish League. I'm sure he will come to Seville if we can arrange the financial terms of the deal.'

An early indication that the 31-year-old Hasselbaink was on his way came from David Mellor and his inside knowledge because of his close friendship with Bates. He wrote in his *Evening Standard* column, 'After being thrilled by Jimmy Hasselbaink's first two seasons at the Bridge, I hoped for some evidence against Lazio that the old divine spark had been rekindled. It hasn't been. Jimmy looked as out of sorts as he did last term. Claudio Ranieri apparently believes Hasselbaink's got another great season in him. I disagree. Chelsea need a world-class striker in the Owen, Henry, van Nistelrooy mould. Without one, the next campaign could still be iffy, despite the strengthening of the defence and midfield. Seeing Jimmy waste a stream of chances almost ruined last season for me. I don't want to go through that again, but I might have to.'

Before the opening Champions League tie against Zilina, Ranieri suggested Hasselbaink could stay. Ranieri said, 'Does Jimmy have a future at Chelsea? Why not? All my players have a Chelsea future.' Mutu was unavailable; even so, Hasselbaink was left out so he wouldn't be cup-tied for another club. Ranieri added, 'I have 26 champions. When I pick 11 and there are five on the bench, the other 10 will have to sit in the stand or at home. But we are aiming to build a strong squad here.'

Hasselbaink remained on the bench, but after the 2-0 win he said, 'I want to stay at Chelsea and fight for my place, which I am going to do. Of course I am disappointed not to play. I want to stay at Chelsea, not Real Betis. They might be interested in me but am I interested in Real Betis? Even if they were in the Champions League, I would not want to go.'

It was a major turn around when Hasselbaink came off the bench in the opening game at Anfield and scored the winner, helping Chelsea cement their best start since 1994 with two Premiership wins in a row and, despite the signing of Crespo, and an embarrassment of attacking riches, Ranieri wanted Hasselbaink to stay.

After renewed interest from Barcelona, Ranieri insisted, 'Hasselbaink is not going anywhere. I want him here. If we get Crespo, I will be very pleased – but Jimmy stays with me. I enjoy his football. He works hard, is focused and played well when he was alone up front and when alongside Adrian Mutu.'

Hasselbaink's record of 71 goals in 119 starts for the club stands up to any scorer in Europe and, to emphasis Ranieri's determination to keep him, the Manager selected him for the return leg thereby killing off any move as he was then cup-tied in Europe.

The 19-year-old Carlton Cole departed instead. Cole will spend the rest of the season with Charlton Athletic. The England Under-21 striker, who scored 3 goals in 13 Premiership appearances last season, went on loan to gain valuable experience in south-east London. Chief Executive Trevor Birch explained, 'Carlton has a big future at Chelsea and this is a wonderful opportunity for him to improve his education and give him some regular Premier League football. We are sure he'll come back a better player.'

Cole said, 'I just want to get goals and prove I can score in the Premiership. Hopefully, this will work out for me – and I think it will. I was training with Paolo di Canio and we were linking up well, so, hopefully, he'll help me in my game. He's like Zola in that they are both magicians on the ground.

'At the beginning of the season, the Manager told me I would need to be playing more games and I agreed that's what I needed. I thought that would be at Stamford Bridge but the Manager had other ideas. I'm the youngest striker so I knew it would be me to go out before anybody else did. There are so many strikers at Chelsea and we're going to buy another one, so it's important for me to go away somewhere and learn my trade first and come back to the club better and stronger. I was worried when I read that all these players were coming but the Manager assured me I am still in his plans. He continues to believe in me and he wants me to show what I can do.'

Cole believes his long-term future remains at Chelsea. 'It's the perfect move for me. I'm dead chuffed that I can stay at home with my family and play football in London. I don't see it as a step down at all. Charlton are a Premiership team and should have a good season, but my future is at Chelsea. I spoke to Curbishley and he was very positive. I had several other clubs after me but Alan was the most positive of all the managers I spoke to. I'm hungry to show I should be starting, but there's plenty of things to work on. I'm not going to go there and walk into the team.'

Yet it was only months earlier that Cole was being talked about as the very future of the club. That raises the inevitable questions about young talent coming through at the big clubs. However much Manchester United spend on big-name stars, no one points a similar accusing finger at them, and they have managed to develop plenty of promising youngsters, like Beckham, Scholes and the Nevilles. John Terry apart, the youth academy at Chelsea has hardly been productive.

Ranieri said of Cole before the Russian Revolution, 'He has a very long contract and a very big future at Chelsea. He's strong, quick, has two good feet and is a good header of the ball. In fact, I've never coached a young player like Carlton. He has everything he needs to explode.'

Now Ranieri explains, 'Carlton is a player I like, but how many games would he play this season if he was here? He's young and learning, and I will always play Adrian or the other strikers ahead of him at this stage. I would rather give Carlton the chance of playing every Saturday for Charlton, so that when he comes back here next summer he has improved.'

Another young striker, Leon Knight, just 20, was sold for £100,000 to Brighton. He was far from happy. He scored four goals in Brighton's first two league games after initially joining them on a two-month loan spell, having started just one game for Chelsea. He also spent the last two seasons on loan at Huddersfield and Sheffield Wednesday. Knight said, 'I want to get out of Chelsea because they've been holding me back. Steve Coppell and Brighton are the right combination for me. I have been at Chelsea since I was 13 and have started one game. It's a relief to know I will be in a place where they want me.'

Forssell was wanted by German side Borussia Münchengladbach where he was on loan from January to May in the 2002/03 season. He returned to Stamford Bridge hoping to break into the first team but the capture of Mutu and Crespo again limited his chances. Borussia director Christian Hochstatter said, 'We are doing everything to get him to return. I've chatted to Mikael and he would love to come back, but there are other clubs that might have something to say about it. I can only hope his heart will decide.' He was also linked to Lazio, but he chose Birmingham for an initial four months that was likely to be extended for the rest of the season. That angered Bayer Leverkusen as Reiner Calmund, the Managing Director, claimed, 'We reached agreement with both Forssell and Chelsea.'

Ranieri just wanted a suitable club to give a promising youngster the chance to sharpen his game, as he said, 'It's good for him as he can play more often and good for me as I can watch him easily.'

Steve Bruce beat off 14 clubs and said, 'He is just our type – young, hungry and desperate for success. I've admired Mikael since Gianluca Vialli described him as Finland's Michael Owen. We are all trying to analyse what is happening at Chelsea. We told them that if they were ever going to let Forssell go they should tell us, and I think they only decided after signing Hernan Crespo that we could have him. If they want to get rid of Petit, Mutu, Hasselbaink or any of the others, I hope they will tell us first.'

Emmanuel Petit attracted interest from Tottenham and Manchester City as it became clear Chelsea were tying up a deal for Makelele, but the 32-year-old Petit, with just one year left on his existing contract, remarked, 'I have the trust of my Chairman and the Coach at Chelsea. I have seen the rumours, but it is nothing. I won't be going to Manchester City. If other defensive midfielders arrive at Chelsea, I would be delighted. As it stands at the moment, we are starting the season with just two defensive midfielders.' Petit, who joined Chelsea from Barcelona, also said he has no interest in a move across London to Tottenham and intended to stay and fight for his place. He came off the bench in the second leg of the Champions League qualifier at the Bridge and made a goal from a corner.

Glenn Hoddle thought he could snap up a bargain for around £1m with the World Cup-winning Frenchman. Hoddle was told the Blues want to keep Petit and said, 'It's a pity, but the plan doesn't seem to be going anywhere at the moment.' Hoddle added that rumours of reserve goalkeeper Neil Sullivan being offered to Chelsea in a part-exchange deal for Petit were wide of the mark, confirming, 'That's not something we are thinking of doing.' Sullivan did move to the Bridge, but not as a makeweight in any Petit deal.

Boudewijn Zenden was another of the once big-name stars seeking an exit, and the Dutch international was linked with clubs as diverse as Charlton, Inter Milan, Ajax, Lazio, PSV Eindhoven and Hamburg. Zenden felt his style of play didn't suit Ranieri as he explained, 'He has an Italian mentality; I have a Dutch one. He only plays not to lose and I always go on to the pitch looking for a victory. At PSV, Barcelona or in the Dutch national side I have always been used to spending 20 per cent of my time defending and 80 per cent attacking. But with Chelsea, I spend 60 per cent of my time in my own half. Ranieri does not like attacking football, and he prefers to see his team wait in their own area and then break out on the counter instead of taking a game to teams. He always draws up his tactics in accordance to the personnel of the opponent's team and there have been times when he changes his system in one game as many as four times, which is difficult. For a player it is difficult to be on form if you never play five or six games in a row. But for some reason Ranieri thinks that I can be on top of my game playing 20 minutes from time to time.' Such comments hardly endeared Zenden to his Coach!

His agent, Chiel Dekker, confirmed Charlton's interest in a loan deal for the whole of the season, as Zenden was anxious for first-team football to protect his international status with the European Championships coming up. The 26-year-old Zenden said, 'I have been reading everything in the newspapers about Roman Abramovich and that got me thinking. When I see how many new faces are coming to Stamford Bridge, I have to realise there's not much of a future for me there. I have played 45 international games for Holland and I want to play a lot more. But I know I have to play every week for my club otherwise Dick Advocaat won't pick me. He only picks players who play on a regular basis. I have to find a club where I can play every week. That's why I phoned my agent and why I had talks with Ajax and PSV Eindhoven.'

Zenden turned out not to be interested in Charlton, though, with Dekker saying, 'Boudewijn only wants to go to a club where he plays for the big prizes and a club that plays European football. We will have more talks with clubs and we hope that Chelsea will understand our position.' Zenden, though, would have to take half of his £35,000-a-week Chelsea pay cheque. Then Middlesbrough made a late move and they were in a position to ensure that his salary wasn't significantly slashed.

Meanwhile, Zenden expressed an interest in joining Paris St Germain. Coach Vahid Halilhodzic wanted him and Zenden said, 'PSG are a great team. A lot of work needs to be done but, for me, it would be a great solution to help them.' But he turned up at the Riverside in a beat-the-deadline loan deal to be introduced to the Boro fans before their home defeat by Leeds. He said, 'I'm sad to leave Chelsea; there were a lot of magnificent people there, but it is important for me to play regularly. It'll be a relief to be able to play. Everybody knows my situation at Chelsea. Nobody is guaranteed a first-team place, but it's important for me to be playing with Euro 2004 coming up. I've had a lot of offers and talking to Steve McClaren really helped make up my mind. He has been persistent for two or three weeks. He gave me a good impression of the place and everything is here to perform well.'

The club ensured that the 'loan' stars farmed out for the season don't come back to haunt them. But that only adds to the growing disquiet over the newly adopted loan system in the Premiership designed to help ailing clubs offload players from the wage bill; it has become an art form at the Bridge. Gordon Taylor, the players' union leader, has expressed his worries that the fans will be questioning the loyalty of certain players when they are confronted with certain contentious situations. Should there be a relegation decider or a final place for the Champions League up for grabs, and a loan player is up against a club that owns him but could profit, there are sure to be concerns. It could be worse if the loan player is playing against his own club. Chelsea shut that loophole with their own contract clauses, but the Premiership as a whole is going to have to look very closely at this new policy. However, Smertin has requested that he should be allowed to play against Chelsea because the Russian wanted to use that as a shop window to prove to the club he is good enough for their squad.

The number of long-term loan deals has not pleased the Professional Footballers' Association. 'Apart from losing the identity of your team,' Mick McGuire, the PFA Deputy Chief Executive, said, 'we could have a situation where a senior player could score a goal or give away a goal at the end of the season that affects the team that he has come from. That does not sit comfortably with us.'

Winston Bogarde officially became a Chelsea outcast without a squad number. Unable to sell Bogarde for the best part of two years, the former Dutch international has been on £40,000-a-week wages despite hardly playing first-team football since his arrival on a free transfer in August 2000. He retained his number 7 shirt last season but that has now been taken away from him and not replaced with another spot in the first-team squad. Bogarde didn't seem all that bothered. 'Not being given a number doesn't upset me. All I can do is carry on working as hard as I possibly can in training and see what happens. I won't give up.'

Record buy Duff assumes the number 11 shirt previously worn by Zenden, who realised he was well down the pecking order when given the number 24 shirt, even though numbers 4, 5, 7 and 10 had not yet been taken until more players arrived. Johnson took the number 2 shirt left vacant by Albert Ferrer, Geremi takes on Graeme Le Saux's number 14, while Bridge is 18 and Ambrosio is number 31 previously worn by Mark Bosnich. Cole took the number 10 shirt with Veron number 22.

Enrique and 24-year-old Jody Morris left before the takeover. Morris said, 'I am delighted to be joining Leeds, it's a great move for me.' But he got a rasping farewell from David Mellor in his *Evening Standard* column: 'Jody Morris wants to put an end to his bad-boy image at Leeds, and jolly good luck to him. Morris implies bad behaviour was to blame for his departure from Chelsea, but that's not so. He was released because, despite being given every chance in the second half of the season, he just wasn't good enough against top opposition. Maybe a change of lifestyle will allow him to remedy some of the faults in his game on the training ground. But I'm not holding my breath.'

Many long-departed former Chelsea players had shares in Chelsea Village, including Mark Hughes. So, too, did *Fantasy Football* presenter David Baddiel, a lifelong fan. Roberto di Matteo caused great sorrow inside the camp when the Italian was forced to retire from football last year after failing to recover from a broken leg suffered during a UEFA Cup tie against St Gallen. Chelsea's financial problems meant they were unable to pay the 33-year-old his £1.5m compensation package – so di Matteo agreed a share issue instead. At the time, the 7.5 million shares awarded to the midfielder were worth around 15p–17p each, but Abramovich's takeover is worth double that. Under the terms of the deal, the Russian will pay 35p for each share – with di Matteo raking in £2.6m. Bates says, 'I sold 7.5m to di Matteo. We owed him £1.5m compensation, and could not afford to pay him. "Don't worry, Mr Bates, you pay me when you can," he said. Then last September, he phoned and said, "If you can't pay me, why don't I take shares?" He's now got 35p a share and it could not happen to a nicer person.'

Similarly, the captain at the time, Dennis Wise, was reaching the stage where he had failed to hold down a guaranteed place under Ranieri and wanted out. Wise had always been very close to Bates, and the Chelsea Chairman tells me, 'Wise said, "Come on, Chairman, give me shares." I agreed and he bought 7.5m shares at 20p, and now has made a handsome profit.' Just under £1.2m ... not bad for the veteran midfielder now with Millwall in the Nationwide League.

12

THE FIRST FULL CUP

CLAUDIO RANIERI PROMISED THAT the new Roman empire will stretch [across the whole of Europe; it will not stop until Chelsea have conquered the Continent.

Instead of fearing the sack as he took the Blues to his home city for Chelsea's first match under new ownership, Ranieri believed the meeting with Lazio in Rome was simply the first step en route to winning the Champions League. The Italian Coach knows only total success will keep Russian billionaire Roman Abramovich happy.

Speaking at their training camp in southern Italy, Ranieri said, 'Throughout my career, I've had to fight on my feet at clubs where the situations have been tough, really tough. But at Chelsea with Mr Abramovich, the expectations are now very different and we have to start winning big trophies very soon before getting to the top of European football. I started in football management 15 years ago at the very bottom, but now I think we have the chance to go right to the summit. He told me and the players he wants to be the top club in Europe.

'In my opinion, Mr Abramovich represents a gigantic opportunity for this club and Chelsea have to make the very most of it. I can even say if

Roma offered me the Manager's job today, I'd tell them, "No, I want to win every trophy possible with Chelsea and then we will talk about it!"'

Ranieri is no fool. His ability to charm Ken Bates, learn decent English and lift an underperforming squad into a Champions League place has already proved his doubters wrong, those who mocked his pidgin English when he first arrived until he banned himself from giving press conferences.

The Italian knows Sven-Goran Eriksson's shadow hangs over Stamford Bridge, but Ranieri was concentrating all his efforts on turning Abramovich's millions into a cabinet full of trophies.

After meeting the Russian entrepreneur, Ranieri believes he is another Silvio Berlusconi, who bought a bankrupt AC Milan in Italy's Second Division and turned them into the club which dominated Europe for a decade. Ranieri beamed, 'I met Mr Abramovich only a day or two after he bought the club and, the truth is, everything I see of him reminds me of Berlusconi when he arrived in football and decided to make Milan great. Our meeting was in Chelsea's offices and, although there was an interpreter, Mr Abramovich told me to speak in English because he could understand me well enough. He spoke in Russian and the meeting lasted about one hour during which I told him straight, I saw no reason for him to get rid of me. I simply told him the truth, that last season people called us no-hopers but we made it to the Champions League and that, like us, he should be proud of that.

'But I also told the new owner it was already in my plans we should do much better this season. The thing was, he knows everything in real detail and was obviously well informed before he bought the club.

'I don't know how he made his millions and it doesn't matter to me compared to the knowledge he wants great things for Chelsea.'

In the knowledge Abramovich moves in circles which enabled him to loan a personal Lear jet to Ronaldo so he could attend Christian Vieri's thirtieth birthday party in Italy, Ranieri suggested a star-studded shopping list. The Chelsea boss could hardly believe that, one by one, the Wish List came true.

He observed, 'How much better is it this summer compared to the last one? I can tell you last summer I put my list to the club and not one of the players ended up joining because Chelsea had financial problems. For sure we'll do better in the market this time. In fact, I think it will be totally different. Mr Abramovich has already signed Geremi and I think that is fantastic for Chelsea. I've tried to get him for two seasons without success. I want his power and ability, plus he can play comfortably in right midfield, centre midfield, right-back and centre defence. As for young Glen Johnson, I think he is a phenomenon, fast and skilful.

'I cannot talk about Juan Veron or Edgar Davids, but I will confirm we need a great player in midfield because the Champions League qualifier is right around the corner in August.'

Ranieri had one lingering regret – Gianfranco Zola. He explained, 'We were talking about his new deal and told him the 'old' Chelsea couldn't afford the extra money he wanted. I had no idea the new owner was coming because it was a secret until the very last moment. Franco had agreed terms and, even though Chelsea made such a good offer under Mr Abramovich, Franco came back and said, "People like us are born to sell dreams and, in Cagliari, they really need me in order to start dreaming great dreams once more."'

Roman's new empire most certainly looked, on its first public outing in Rome, that it was never going to be built in a day. Abramovich watched his Chelsea side for the first time on a Friday night as they were battered 2-0 by Lazio and quickly saw why Ranieri needed so many new faces. Abramovich was in the capital with his wife and children to see just what he was getting for his investment. Seated just behind Ken Bates in the Directors' Box of the Stadio Flaminio, Abramovich politely refused all interview requests as he sweltered in the evening heat. Lazio's directors – even more desperate for cash than Bates had been a month earlier – queued up deferentially to shake his hand.

More than 25,000 fanatical Lazio fans turned out at Italy's national rugby stadium to see a Chelsea team they could face in this season's Champions League.

Most seemed to be there just to boo Giuseppe Favali, the only black player in Lazio's line-up. But Brazilian winger Cesar was the first to lose his calm, clashing with Jesper Gronkjaer after the Dane's innocuous challenge.

Frank Lampard intervened and was met with a hail of empty plastic bottles from behind the high fences which keep Lazio's infamous 'Ultras' away from the pitch.

For both teams, this was the first game of their pre-season preparations, yet there was an unusually competitive edge – although Chelsea's eagerness to impress was understandable.

Every other top player in Europe was being linked with a move to Stamford Bridge, and those already in possession of the shirts were keen to show they did not need replacing.

Full-back Glen Johnson, the first recruit to Abramovich's revolution, was given a chance to show his pedigree on the right side of a makeshift Chelsea defence.

Marcel Desailly and William Gallas were not back in training after their Confederations Cup exertions for France, John Terry was rested to protect a strain and Graeme Le Saux flew back to London for talks to join Southampton.

So it was hardly surprising that Johnson, 18, had his work cut out containing superstar strikers Simone Inzaghi and Claudio Lopez. The youngster impressed with one last-ditch tackle on Inzaghi, but ruined his good work by then losing the ball to Lopez whose 25-yard drive was well saved by Carlo Cudicini.

A minute later, Chelsea went behind when Lazio full-back Massimo Oddo crossed low from the right and Inzaghi shook off Mario Melchiot to score from close range.

The Italians should have doubled their lead just before half-time. Celestine Babayaro went missing as Stefano Fiore delivered another ball which Inzaghi drilled wide. No wonder Ranieri wanted Wayne Bridge to strengthen the left side of his dodgy defence.

Not that Chelsea were much better up front, where stand-in skipper Jimmy Floyd Hasselbaink looked as though he had spent the summer eating his way through his £80,000-a-week pay packet.

The visitors did not manage a shot of note in the first half and Mario Stanic even managed to miss the target with an unchallenged header from Gronkjaer's cross.

Three half-time changes by Ranieri failed to turn the tide and Cudicini saved from Fiore and Inzaghi again.

Rome-born Cudicini, who played one game for Lazio nearly ten years ago, was given a standing ovation by the fans who unfurled a huge banner proclaiming 'Welcome, Carlo, you will always be one of us'.

It was better support than the keeper received from his team-mates. And he was left stranded again after 52 minutes when unmarked Yugoslav defender Dejan Stankovic headed home from Lopez's free-kick. Abramovich did not look happy while Bates shifted uncomfortably in his seat.

Chelsea's team that night comprised Cudicini, Johnson (Kitamirike), Melchiot, Huth, Babayaro (Keenan), Gronkjaer, Lampard, Zenden, Stanic (Forssell), Gudjohnsen (Cole), Hasselbaink (Kneissl). The unused substitutes were Ambrosio and Di Cesare.

After the match, the defiant Italian Coach brushed aside talk that he would be shown the door and claimed that he was relishing the chance of creating his own multi- million pound superteam. As he good-naturedly breezed past the waiting media throng minutes after the defeat by Lazio, Ranieri quipped, 'I know the bookies have stopped taking bets on me.'

When asked by a media inquisitor if he found that situation funny, Ranieri quickly retorted, 'Of course I do. Very funny.'

And he made all the right noises about Mr Abramovich, dropping several hints about being given time to blend the new Chelsea with the old. 'I feel good,' said Ranieri. 'I feel it is important to continue to build the squad. We have been working now for 15 days. The owner is working very hard to give me the best team possible. Now it is my job to fit together the old team with the new. I'm confident I will get it right but I need some more months.'

He added, ' I've been waiting all my life to get this opportunity. I've been working very hard for the last 15 years and, finally, I have this chance. It's a great opportunity. And I'm confident I'm not going to waste it.'

Ranieri insisted he had been given the green light to go out and buy any player he wanted in a bid to create the biggest team in the world. Instead of fretting about his future, Ranieri was convinced his clear-the-air meeting with Abramovich was far more than simply a stay of execution.

He added, 'This is the biggest challenge of my career. It's the first time in my career that I can look for the greatest players and I can choose which ones I want. I am interested in everybody. We are looking in every nation. For now, for us it's important to listen to everybody and then we'll pick up what we need. We're asking clubs to see which players are available and then we will close the deals. I feel excited about the whole prospect. Our philosophy is to try to put together a squad of young, good players and some champions – the same plan as last season.'

Although the situation Ranieri found himself in the previous season was a bit different, with the then debt-ridden Chelsea getting just one player in on loan – Spaniard Enrique De Lucas.

After signing Johnson, Geremi and Bridge, and with a move for Duff agreed, Ranieri revealed he wanted to sign another two or three top-class players. He continued, 'I don't want to talk specifically, but I can say that, apart from Bridge and Duff, we will still look for two or three others.'

A deal with Manchester United for Juan Veron was still on the cards, while Chelsea refused to give up on Arsenal's dream duo of Patrick Vieira and Thierry Henry.

Deportivo La Coruna's £12m-rated Roy Makaay was mooted as a top target, but Pini Zahavi told me at the time, 'He is not on our list.'

Ranieri added, 'I feel good about the choice of players we can buy, but it's important to continue to build the squad. The owner has been trying very hard to give me the best team possible. But it's important to combine the old team with the new players. For now we're building a big team. Give me some more months and then I can tell you about our goals.'

Complications set in over Veron as United's chance of landing Ronaldinho collapsed. Ronaldinho jetted out from Paris to Barcelona, who had agreed a £21m fee with Paris St Germain.

Chelsea agreed a £17m fee with Blackburn for Duff but a source close to the winger insisted, 'Manchester United are the team Damien is going to join next season. It's imminent – it's happening.'

Ranieri was extremely keen to sign the Argentinian. Zahavi said, 'Roman wants Veron very much – but the man who is insisting on having him is Ranieri. He wants to make him the King of Chelsea.'

Manchester United targeted Newcastle's England international Kieron Dyer and Chelsea were also interested if the Duff deal broke down. When Abramovich asked Eriksson to recommend talented youngsters, both Dyer and Jenas received glowing references from the Swede. Two years ago, Newcastle valued Dyer at £20m. The market may have slumped since but Chelsea would still have to top that figure to tempt them. Manchester United, long-term admirers of Dyer, are also keeping tabs on the situation.

Ranieri added, 'I don't really want to talk about Bridge and Duff, but I am happy now and I am sure I will be happy in a month's time. And after them I want to make three more signings. This is the dawn of a new era, I am sure about that. It is very exciting for me to look and to choose.'

Ranieri doesn't fear the sack but has warned his players they must be up for the task. 'I think it's normal because in all my experience I have seen chairmen with the same sort of targets as Mr Abramovich. The Chairman chooses the Manager, he chooses the players and then wants results. If you give results you are fine, if not the Chairman will change things at the club. Every time it's the same. I have a chance and very intelligent players and now there will be more competition for them. Players who want to win will come here and I think all my players like to win. Those who don't accept competition will not last.'

Bates added, 'Don't forget, Claudio took us sixth in the first season, fourth last season with only free transfer players. He's now obviously getting better players – and the players he's bought so far are the ones he wanted last summer. All this thing about money. Did you know we've actually spent less money than Manchester United spent two summers ago? How much more money are we willing to spend? It's not a question of money, it's a question of getting the right team – you can't buy success. Mr Abramovich isn't a multi-millionaire because he's a fool with his money.'

Speaking in Malaysia, where Chelsea were preparing for the Premier League Asia Cup, Ranieri said, 'I am used to not spending much money but now that has changed. For me, it is very important to pick up the best players. We have very good players but, of course, we need something more to compete with the top teams like Manchester United, Arsenal, Juventus and Real Madrid. When I made the list, I just put the names. I am not the Manager, I am a coach. For me, signing the right players is more important than the cost. Of course, the 'big champions' cost a lot. I think if my players want to win something, there must be good competition for places. There are a lot of competitions in England and we are playing every three days. The players have to be ready to play whenever they are asked. All the major teams have 23 or 24 'big champions.

'It is important to build a good team and it takes time. United and Arsenal spent years doing it and now they are very good. I have a strong team and I am sure at the end of the league we will be very, very close to the big teams.

'I want to win things. I am an ambitious coach, I have ambitious players. I like the pressure. In Italy, the pressure was crazy. I am used to working under pressure. It is OK and I am ready for it.'

Prior to Chelsea's opening game against Malaysia, managed by former Chelsea player Alan Harris, young John Terry told Chelsea fans to expect 'exciting times'. Terry, who signed a new contract a month earlier, believed the established stars will also be given their chance before the squad is totally revamped. He said, 'It's exciting times for Chelsea at the moment. All the players have spoken to Mr Abramovich and he says he is happy with the current squad, but if he can add to the side then he will do so. This is going to be a very good season for Chelsea.'

He believed victory in the Premier League Asia Cup would be the perfect way to kick-start Chelsea's challenge for major honours. 'We are looking forward to the game. It is a fantastic stadium and the Malaysian fans are very passionate about football. Hopefully, we can take the Cup home because winning a trophy would be a good way to start the season.'

Terry denied there was any apprehension among the players about the number of high-profile new arrivals at the club. 'We've made four good signings so far and there's no problem as far as the lads are concerned. We will be playing a lot of games next season and, with players coming into the squad, it means the Manager can rotate things. Damien Duff and

Wayne Bridge had their first training session with us yesterday and it went well. I'm looking forward to playing with them in the team. The atmosphere has been good. We were all tired the first day but now we're over the jet-lag and looking forward to the game.'

Ranieri warned his players about the conditions when he said, 'We will have to be very careful about the weather as regards to training. The humidity is going to be a problem here.'

Veron and Vieri remained top of Chelsea's lengthy shopping list, but Chelsea balked at the £25m price tag for Dyer. Abramovich and his advisers felt that Veron had never been given an opportunity to express his talents at Old Trafford and were confident that he could be their playmaker. Veron was with United on their US tour, but the Old Trafford club discreetly touted him to other clubs in Italy and were delighted at Chelsea's interest.

Sir Alex Ferguson claimed he had the strongest midfield throughout his time at the club yet, tellingly, did not mention Veron when running through a list of those who allow him to make such a boast.

Meanwhile, William Gallas signed a one-year extension to his contract, tying him to Stamford Bridge until 2007. The French defender already had three years remaining on his previous deal but has further committed himself to the club he joined from Marseille two years ago. Gallas had not travelled with the rest of the Chelsea squad to the FA Premiership Asia Cup, having been excused the trip because he played for his country in the Confederations Cup.

Gallas said, 'Somebody told me, I said that, or they read that. I was very surprised because I just said I want to stay with Chelsea because I like this club. And I said I want to see which players will come, because I want to win one trophy with Chelsea.' The advent of the spending spree played a part, as he added, 'Now I see that Chelsea want to win things, and that's why I signed a new deal with them.'

Behind the scenes, the bid and negotiations continued. Chelsea tabled a bid of £14.5m for Emerson but would have to pay £20m-plus. Roma were desperate to keep him. The 27-year-old has 51 caps but missed the World Cup after breaking an arm in training. Emerson has two years left on his contract and demanded showdown talks with the club. He said, 'I need to know what the club's aims are regarding my position. Eventually, I will talk to other clubs.'

Ranieri said, 'We're still waiting to sign what I call a "big champion". I am waiting for a champion because it is important to have a big name. Of course, we have already bought good players who are champions in their own right, but you know the kind I mean.' Chelsea also offered £14m for Veron and were still pursuing the Argentinian midfielder despite his original insistence that he did not want to leave Old Trafford.

Ranieri wanted the new players as quickly as possible because he reckoned he'd have problems bedding so many new stars into his team. Ranieri threw down the gauntlet to Sir Alex Ferguson and Arsene Wenger by saying it is possible to cut the 20-point gap in the Premiership between their clubs. Ranieri's priority was a commanding central midfielder and admitted Veron was a 'champion player'; in addition, he wanted a striker or maybe two, with Vieri also regarded as his favourite at that time. He said, 'I am not the kind of manager who sits back with a big cigar and the brandy out thinking, "This is the life." I love to get on with it and get out coaching the best players. I would like all the players we want in soon. The deadline for the Champions League qualifier is 7 August and that is a very important game. You can try things now, but players are arriving one by one. This is my difficulty. It is true we need a central midfielder because we only have Frank Lampard and had to play Zenden there against Lazio the other day. Petit has also had injury troubles. Veron? I don't like to say whether this is the one or not. I need big champions and he is one, but there are others, too. The earlier these champions arrive, the more time I have to build a team. We have a big gap between Manchester United, Arsenal and where Chelsea finished last season. It is a gap that is 20 points, and we need to be getting up to the 87 mark. That is a big gap. Me saying it can be closed is no good; it is what happens on the pitch that speaks the most. It is going to be difficult for us because the others like Manchester, Arsenal and Newcastle are already strong. Their squads have been constructed. We are just building now. We are working hard to catch those at the top and that is our aim. To close 20 points in just one season is a lot, maybe too much, but why not have a go? That is our philosophy. It is easy for the clubs who are at the top ahead of us. They just need to pick up one or two and their squad is done.

'We will be going to win every competition – the Premiership, FA Cup, Champions League. But, for now, the preliminaries for the Champions League are very important and my team is not yet ready. We must be ready. I want players to show great motivation to get there to show how that gap can be bridged. I cannot put the new owner under pressure because he is the one who has to choose the right moment to buy the new players.

'People say I am the luckiest coach in world football because of the backing I am getting from the new owner. I would say yes, that is right. I am a pitch manager and love coaching. Ken Bates has said the pressure is on to be successful and I would have to agree with him. But I am used to it.'

Malaysia 1-4 Chelsea

Well, it was only Malaysia's fledgling national side that was on the end of a demolition but the architects of the win were Russian-bought, and proof that Chelsea will have to be taken seriously. Ranieri watched three of his new boys – Damien Duff, goal-scorer Glen Johnson and Wayne Bridge – play an important role in a highly impressive and efficient victory. Also making his Chelsea début was goalkeeper Marco Ambrosio, in for Carlo Cudicini who, although suffering from a virus, was fit enough to start on the bench. Ranieri, often criticised for over tinkering with his teams, had to make an enforced change after 25 minutes when big German central defender Robert Huth suffered a cut over his eye following a collision with Malaysia's Hairuddin Omar. Huth went off to have stitches inserted in the gash to be replaced by former West Ham defender Johnson, also making his début. Johnson went to his favoured position of right-back with Mario Melchiot switching to the centre of defence.

Ranieri was in the mood to crack jokes afterwards. 'Maybe I'll just have to buy another 22 players,' he quipped in response to a question about whether his stars fancied playing Maccabi Tel Aviv in the Champions League after six players refused to play in Israel two seasons ago. Ranieri had one eye on the Champions League draw, which decided Chelsea will face either Maccabi Tel Aviv or MSK Zilina of Slovakia in a qualifying round. 'It is not important who we play but it is important that we win and get into the Champions League group stages,' he said.

The Chelsea boss was in daily contact with Abramovich and Chief Executive Trevor Birch and, when asked about the club's approach for Real Madrid star Raul, he said, 'Raul ... 100m euros? Only? Maybe tomorrow Rivaldo.'

Ranieri is the first to point out that it is no use assembling a galaxy of stars if they do not gel on the pitch. 'Only the pitch speaks,' he said. In Kuala Lumpur, Lampard opened their account before Malaysia pulled one back thanks to a horrendous blunder by third-choice keeper Marco Ambrosio, who let a tame header slip through his hands. But Hasselbaink, Gudjohnsen and Johnson finished the locals off in an excellent last 20-minute spell. Duff, ably backed up by the impressive Johnson and Bridge, showed that Chelsea are moving in the right direction. Duff made his début in the second half and ran the Malaysians ragged with several jinking runs,

Top: Trevor Birch, whose shock sacking as chief executive came after he helped to purchase all the new stars. He is shown here with the first of the new signings Glen Johnson.

Bottom: David Mellor held secret talks with Ken Bates to pull off a deal for Paul Taylor before Abramovich arrived.

Top left: Thierry Henry – one of Abramovich's favourite players, and Ranieri's too…

Top right: Chelsea would sign the French midfield star Patrick Vieira if they could.

Bottom left: Abramovich tried to buy Cagliari to get Gianfranco Zola, the crowd's favourite, back.

Bottom right: Alex Ferguson let it be known that he could move to Chelsea if he wanted.

Sven-Goran Eriksson met with Roman Abramovich four days before Ranieri did.

If ever Steven Gerrard's contract talks with Liverpool broke down, Chelsea would pounce…

Wayne Rooney, the young superstar who is on the future 'hit-list'.

Pini Zahavi has become the best known Mr Fix-It in world football. *Inset:* Jonathan Barnett represents some of the country's leading players, and is highly influential in some of the big transfers and player contracts.

Chelsea are now the only club in the Premiership who could afford David Beckham.

Top left: Keith Harris, of Chelsea's financial advisers Seymour Pierce.

Top right: Peter Kenyon was poached from Manchester United with a £3m 'signing-on' fee.

Bottom left: Stephen Schechter knows the inside track on how the police and fire-fighters' pension funds in California nearly bought Chelsea instead of Abramovich.

Bottom right: Mel Goldberg, the man who reveals the secrets of the 1920 German bond.

eventually setting up Gudjohnsen for a headed goal with a superb cross. Johnson even got in on the act with a headed goal on his second appearance, while Bridge lasted the full 90 minutes and looked solid. Ranieri rang the changes after 61 minutes with Duff coming on for Zenden; the striking partnership of Eidur Gudjohnsen and Jimmy Floyd Hasselbaink replaced Cole and Forssell; and Sebastian Kneissl replaced Jesper Gronkjaer on the right.

'Glen, Damien and Wayne did very well for me ... that is all of the new ones, isn't it?' Ranieri asked his interpreter, clearly losing track of how many he has actually bought and how many were on the way!

The only new boy absent was Geremi, who had yet to resume training after an extended summer break.

If Ranieri had lost track, then captain Terry insisted the rest of the old guard had not. He was asked how it felt to be a fixture of the Stamford Bridge line-up only to hear of so many illustrious new additions heading his way. 'Are we worried or excited? I can honestly say the players are fine about it,' said Terry. 'We are happy and the team spirit is still good. These are among the most exciting times Chelsea has seen in terms of what could happen in the future. No one knows how far it will go. What is certain is that we're assembling a great squad. Everyone knows how many games there are, what with Europe and the Premiership. The Manager will pick his players and he has good options in every position.'

Among the crowd in the stadium were Sir Bobby Robson, whose Newcastle team awaited the winners in Sunday's final. Ranieri observed, 'Newcastle will be a challenge for us on Sunday. At the moment, they are slightly better than us because we don't yet have Gallas or Desailly and Petit is injured. But this win makes for a good start to the season for us and is very encouraging.'

Harris, the Malaysian national Coach, said he was expecting a near sell-out crowd in the 70,000-capacity National Stadium, so it was a big disappointment to see so many empty seats. The opening match between Birmingham and Newcastle attracted only 13,000 spectators. The Premier League were keen for this experiment to work as they sought to raise their profile in Asia, but the disappointing attendances at the first two matches may make them consider seriously whether to continue with the competition next year.

Chelsea were in their new away strip of white shirts with a central, vertical blue stripe. Ranieri said, 'It was very hard, I wanted to preserve my strikers but we needed the victory and the last half-hour was very good for us. It was a very good victory, the first half was hard and we found the humidity difficult. I really appreciated the football played by the Malaysian team. Both Damien and Wayne Bridge need to work more because it is only their first match and they have only had a few days' training, it was a very important fitness test. I need another midfielder because I am playing just Frank Lampard and other young players.'

David Mellor was enjoying the first chance to lord it over Manchester United. He wrote in his *Evening Standard* column, 'What a funny fellow Alex Ferguson is. Funny peculiar, I mean, not funny ha-ha. "We won't be drawn into a transfer fight with Chelsea," he said this week, for all the world as if United are in danger of being dwarfed by the free-spending Russian now in charge at the Bridge. Very droll, but pull the other one, Alex. Chelsea have so far spent £34m. In one 12-month period, Ferguson spent £77m on three players, one of whom, Ruud van Nistelrooy, has been a triumph, and another, Juan Sebastian Veron, a disaster. As for Rio Ferdinand, the jury is still out.

'So it's Ferguson who's the last of the big spenders, not Roman Abramovich. And it's Ferguson who proves buying players is only the start. Getting them to perform is quite a different matter ... Ferguson is retiring hurt from the transfer market, or so he says, not because of the Russian invasion, but because he failed to sign Ronaldinho. PSG were apparently offended by various Fergie-like ultimatums, and the player himself wasn't keen on Manchester anyway.'

The Asia Cup Final
Chelsea 0-0 Newcastle United (Chelsea won 5-4 on penalties)

Ranieri was caught on camera answering his mobile phone as the players gathered to collect their first trophy under the Russian Revolution and their Manager's first piece of silverware since he joined the club. Surely it wasn't Roman calling him? 'No,' smiled Ranieri, 'it was Trevor Birch congratulating us.'

The Chelsea boss saw three of his new recruits dispose of Newcastle thanks to a penalty shoot-out after a tight match ended in a goalless draw. The Chelsea team on this occasion comprised Cudicini, Johnson, Terry, Huth, Bridge, Gronkjaer (Forssell), Lampard, Nicolas (Keenan), Zenden (Duff), Hasselbaink and Gudjohnsen. Ranieri said, 'I have received congratulations from the Chairman and the Chief Executive, so maybe Abramovich will call later. This is just the fuel we need for the new season. We created chances, so we deserved to win, even if the scores ended level.'

Sir Bobby Robson described the first half as like an old English cup tie, but in 90-degree heat.

Chelsea's heroes were centre-backs Robert Huth, 19, and captain John Terry, with Terry scoring the clinching penalty.

Newcastle fell behind in the shoot-out, which the local crowd of 47,500 loved, with Alan Shearer hitting the bar and Laurent Robert also missing the second kick. Shay Given hauled the Magpies back with two great saves from Duff and Hasselbaink. At 3-2 in the shoot-out, Hasselbaink had the chance to win it but Given guessed right and, though the ball spilled out of his grasp, it hit the post and rolled out. Robson, a victim of famous penalty shoot-outs when England boss, lost his cool with Jenas after an atrocious spot-kick. With Newcastle trailing 5-4 in the shoot-out, the baby-faced midfielder strolled casually forward to deliver the most shocking chip. Robson made no attempt to hide his disgust, waving his arms in anger and launching into a four-letter tirade from the sideline. Jenas simply covered his face in embarrassment while Jonathan Woodgate tried to hide a snigger as his team-mate slunk off to face the wrath of his boss.

Gronkjaer was man of the match after winning an enthralling duel down his right wing with Olivier Bernard. 'Robert Huth was fantastic,' said Ranieri. 'I am very pleased with our performance. I was eager to see how they would shape up against a good Newcastle side. And they came off brilliantly. This sets a good pattern for us to follow. We have come through two very hard games in three days and played some fantastic football against a very strong Newcastle team, with many great champions.'

13

FOUR NEWCOMERS GET THEIR CHANCE

CLAUDIO RANIERI CONTRIBUTED TO a book entitled *England, Their England*, supplying the names of the best foreigners ever to perform in English football as part of a study of their impact on the domestic game.

Little did he know when he filled in the names of his choices it would come back to haunt him as it revealed the players he really did admire the most.

He sent off his selection at the end of the 2002/03 season when Franco Zola was still deciding his future, and he had doubts over whether he should offload Hasselbaink and Gudjohnson, and was looking at a modest player acquisition of Joe Cole and Scott Parker.

At the head of Ranieri's 'Fantasy Team' of foreign imports was Henry and van Nistelrooy and, with the arrival of Roman Abramovich, the Italian Coach would have loved them both, but they were without price.

In defence he chose Cudicini, Stam, Blanc, Desailly and Silvestre, two of whom he already had in his team. Central midfield was a giveaway, where he selected Gullit, Vieira, Petit and Pires – no Zola! Vieira was another target, but again out of reach.

Interesting, of course, that he chose Petit ahead of Veron, a player he was later to sign and describe as the 'best in the world' in his position!

Ranieri also knew the arrival of new stars, no matter how many and how much they cost, would be enough on its own to dethrone even Manchester United, let alone Real Madrid.

He said, 'When I first became Head Coach three years ago, my target was to win the Premier League, but first we had to reconstruct. Reconstruction has now gone well and we have some great players at Chelsea. Last season we didn't lose many games, but we had far too many draws. We must improve again this year and all the time look to our young players for the future. John Terry has shown the way but these players have achieved nothing yet. They have achieved nothing for themselves and nothing for Chelsea, so together we must fight, fight, fight for that to happen.'

Ranieri urged his squad to follow the example set by Zola. 'When they have won what Gianfranco has won and are still working and playing like him at his age, then they can say they have achieved. It is necessary with young players to be patient but it is also important that we keep an eye on our targets. We want to improve on last season, whoever is in the team. If we do the best we can, then I know we'll have a good season.'

The inevitable first signs of discontent emerged virtually from the moment the new arrivals walked through the door, when Danish star Jesper Gronkjaer was worried whether Geremi might play on the right rather than in the holding midfield role. Gronkjaer said, 'It is unsettling because we read the newspaper as well. I know I have to perform consistently and I have been working hard. It is having an effect on the players. We are all just trying to concentrate on playing football. I am keeping my head down. It is going to be harder to get into the team but we cannot complain because it will be an advantage to Chelsea in the long run. It is not a problem for me because there are so many games this season, the Manager will pick a team that is best for the day. I won't have a problem with new players coming here because it is good for Chelsea and the fans.'

Well, nothing wrong with that from Chelsea's point of view. Ranieri made it clear he wanted a 22-, maybe 23-man squad, with at least two players for each position. Some player egos would be dented, but that's what happens at the really big clubs.

Lampard confessed that all the speculation surrounding new signings was disturbing some of the players. No doubt he was affected more than anyone with the impending arrival of Makelele. Lampard said, 'It is unsettling for the players. Most of the positions in the team have been mentioned in connection with a new player coming in and that does have an effect. Of course, it's good to have quality players connected with moves to Chelsea and I know central midfield is one of the areas of priority. We're a bit short there at the moment and I'm looking forward to having someone come in and play alongside me. It will be good when everything is settled and the squad is finalised. There have been plenty of names mentioned. Veron is one and he is certainly a top-quality player and Emerson is another who has been mentioned. Personally, all the speculation just spurs me on. I only had about three weeks off during the summer and I've never felt so fit at this stage. Competition for places can affect different players in different ways but I enjoy the challenge.'

Winston Bogarde, however, had a contrasting point of view. Despite playing only four games in three years, he wondered whether the change of owner might precipitate a change in his chances. The Dutchman faced a tough task, having failed to convince Ranieri to pick him even before Abramovich's investment in new signings. Bogarde, who has a year left on his £42,000-a-week contract, said, 'It was like coming back to a different club when I returned from vacation this year. I have no idea whether the radical changes are going to be good or bad for me. I still want to play first-team football for Chelsea. There have already been several new signings and it looks like there may be more to come, so getting a place in the team will be harder than ever, but I won't give up hope. I really want to play for this club and I only have this year to achieve that. Competition will be tough, but I will fight for my place like everybody else. This looks to be an exciting season for Chelsea and I would love to be a part of it.' Bogarde had little chance to impress Ranieri on the pre-season tour to Malaysia as he was forced to fly home early due to a family emergency.

The first pre-season friendly on English soil saw the first four players making their débuts for Chelsea. Such was the the attraction of the new Chelsea, that the start was held up for 15 minutes. It was worth waiting to see Geremi's stunning free-kick – à la Zola – that ensured the Russian Revolution kicked off in winning style. Ranieri said of Geremi, 'He's like a horse – he can run, run, run and scored an amazing free-kick. He was practising them in training earlier today. He's used to scoring from these free-kicks. Also this morning when we trained, he started and scored from his first shot and continued to shoot very well. It's important for us because a lot of the matches you can score from the free-kicks, these balls are very important.'

Geremi's delightful 44th-minute effort proved there is life after Zola in the specialist free-kick department. Geremi, back after Confederations Cup duty, made sure Ranieri's side just edged it. Geremi said, 'I don't know if I can take free-kicks like Zola, but I'll try to do them the best I can.'

Ranieri played Geremi in the centre of midfield and explained, 'Geremi is used to playing on the right, in the middle, in defence, he's a universal player, it's very important for me because I can change the situation when we need to. Now it's not important to say Geremi will play in this position or that, it's important that Chelsea has another good champion player, this is what's important for me.'

Geremi was happy in central midfield as he explained, 'I used to play there and the Manager knows I can play there and so what I do is work hard and wait for the Manager. If he makes me play anywhere, I am going to do my best. I am used to playing anywhere. It might be good or it might be bad, I don't know. But if the Manager likes that, you are happy because every time you are going to play.' After the first half in the centre, he switched to right-side midfield, and concluded the match at right-back. 'It's an advantage to play many positions and to try to help the team.'

Ranieri's other new signings – Bridge, Johnson, Duff, and free-signing sub keeper Ambrosio – did well but can obviously do better. Ranieri said, 'This was a good match for us, we needed a workout. We're not as fast as I would like, but we are trying. I saw some good things in the first half and some not so good in the second. Several of them played very well but sometimes it was too much as individuals, especially the young ones – we didn't play as a team, they wanted to impress on their own. We will have to change that before the start of the season. I thought Geremi played very well and Johnson did some fantastic things.'

Chelsea surged into a fourth-minute lead after Palace centre-back Symons headed the ball against team-mate Hughes. The ball rebounded to Forssell, who buried a low volley. A 37th-minute error from Bridge, when he passed straight to Johnson, almost let in Palace, but Cudicini's reflexes saved them. But he had no chance two minutes later when the defence was undone down the left from a quick Hughes free-kick, and unmarked Freedman coolly lobbed home. Chelsea regained the lead a minute before the break when Geremi, fouled by Hughes, took instant revenge by curling home a 30-yard free-kick.

Chelsea made three changes at half-time, substituting Cudicini, Desailly and Duff, and then Hasselbaink came on for Gronkjaer just before the hour.

Gallas was doubtful for the first leg of their vital Champions League qualifier, with a slight groin strain, and failed to make the squad for the friendly at Palace. Gallas was left out of the club's tour to Malaysia – along with Desailly, Geremi and Petit – so they could begin training at the club's training ground in Harlington. Ranieri said, 'If William is not ready to play against Watford, then I won't risk him in our Champions League qualifier. He has a slight injury. It's not serious but we are being cautious. It is important for him to get games. I'm not worried about his overall fitness as he only stopped playing a month ago.'

Ranieri started with Hasselbaink and Carlton Cole up front at Vicarage Road after leaving them on the bench against Palace. Forssell impressed on his return to Selhurst Park, having had two loan spells at Crystal Palace earlier in his career. He made the most of starting alongside Gudjohnsen. The Finland international, who was loaned out to Borussia Münchengladbach the previous season after recovering from a serious knee injury, scored a fine goal to put Chelsea ahead after five minutes. Forssell had started only six Premiership games in five years at the club, but Ranieri insists he will get more opportunities this season. Ranieri said, 'Mikael scored a fantastic goal and he will definitely get his chance to play for Chelsea this year. I knew Borussia wanted to sign Mikael, but I wanted him here. I wanted him to stay because I need a couple of players for every position. In front, I have good players with Jimmy, Eidur, Carlton, as well as Mikael, and I am happy with them. But I have mixed my strikers during the pre-season and I will do so again for the next match. Jimmy and Carlton will start against Watford.'

Forssell insisted he is not concerned at the prospect of Vieri joining the club, even if he agrees to a £25m move. He said, 'I have seen the reports over Vieri, but I am not worried about Chelsea bringing in another striker. Ranieri wanted me back here so that is a sign I have a future at Chelsea. I want to prove myself to Chelsea and show what I can do. If I'm getting games, I don't want to play for anyone else. I have two years left on my contract, but I hope to stay longer. I have to thank Crystal Palace for a lot; I got to play a lot of games, I got goals, I got everything, confidence, I developed as a player and when you go through the school of the first division you are ready for anything.' Of course, as it turned out, Crespo signed along with Mutu and Forssell was packed off on loan to Birmingham.

Ranieri was pleased with the pre-season programme. 'We've trained very hard in these days after the Malaysia tour because in Malaysia we didn't work because the humidity was very, very high and now we had to work in these days (since being back from Malaysia), and I am happy also because the players wanted to do a lot.'

There was one more game before the Champions League qualifier and still the Manager was without Gallas and Petit. He said, 'Manu won't be playing because yesterday he started with us to touch the ball but I don't think he's ready yet. But Gallas, I think so because today was only a precaution and I think next match against Watford he'll be ready.'

Joe Cole emerged as a transfer target as Ranieri made it his priority to find a 'link' player. Chelsea were also interested in striker Roy McKaay, but they were too late as Bayern Munich were days away from completing the signing of the Dutch striker. But a deal for the Hammers star was tied up before Thursday's deadline for the European Championship qualifiers.

Cole thought his chance of moving to Chelsea had ended with the Abramovich takeover. Cole was lined up for a £6m move but the new regime moved for Edgar Davids, Emerson, Veron and Makelele. Cole dropped back in the England pecking order after promising so much, but a move across London will reignite Sven-Goran Eriksson's interest.

The Blues ripped Watford apart at Vicarage Road as, behind the scenes, the spending continued. Ranieri's men strolled to a 4-1 success against their Division One opponents, originally agreeing to travel to the cash-stapped club on condition they received 50 per cent of the gate money, so they would have been pleased with the attendance of 18,500 paying around £20 each ... not that the new regime were actually in need of the money! The team for the match was Cudicini (Ambrosio), Johnson, Bridge, Terry (Keenan), Desailly (Huth), Gronkjaer (Hasselbaink), Geremi, Lampard, Duff (Nicolas), Forssell, Gudjohnsen (Cole).

Afterwards, the Italian boss gave his glowing verdict on Cole, but again claimed to be in the dark about Veron. 'I know Joe Cole is very, very near, but I don't know anything about Veron,' Ranieri said. 'Without Gianfranco, I need a player who can dribble – and I think Joe Cole is that kind of player. Cole will bring some fantasy to our team. In my opinion, he can play in any midfield position from the left to the right, or behind the front two. He's not signed yet but I hope he arrives. He's fantastic one on one. He's very clever and passes the ball very well. I like him when a match is close. He can dribble, pass and score a goal. He's strong and an Englishman. When I arrived, I said I'd like a blend of young English players and experienced players. Slowly, slowly, that way is possible.'

His first quartet of signings – Johnson, Geremi, Bridge, and Duff – all featured as Chelsea produced a super-confident performance in their final pre-season friendly before the Champions League qualifier and their Premiership opener the following weekend.

Bates and Birch were at the game but afterwards refused to discuss Cole and Veron. Bates's only comment was, 'Watford gave us a very good game and I think they'll be a real force this season.'

Forssell, Hasselbaink, Duff and Neal Ardley (own-goal) netted for the Blues, with Helguson replying for the Hornets in front of a decent 18,629 crowd. Ranieri added, 'We were fresh tonight and the first half was fantastic. We passed and moved very fast and I like that kind of football. I saw Damien Duff grow and it's important that he and Jesper Gronkjaer played very well.'

Watford boss Ray Lewington said, 'People talk about the gap between Division One and the Premiership, but what about the gap between Division One and the top of the Premiership. It scared me after 20 minutes tonight. At that point, I thought the game was a slight mistake.'

14

BIG SPENDER

ROMAN ABRAMOVICH REAFFIRMED HIS pledge to spend as much as it takes to secure major trophies, and one day he will even be bidding for David Beckham.

While he was enjoying the thrill of buying new, expensive players, there was a downside as he was taken by surprise over the amount of publicity his takeover attracted.

Abramovich said, 'I haven't thought about how much money I'm prepared to spend. I suppose that depends on how well we play – and how determined we are to win. If I feel we need to buy any particular player to get the results we want, I'll just spend more money.'

The next day, Chelsea signed Joe Cole for £6.6m and 24 hours later it was Seba Veron for £15m. From his office overlooking Anadyr Bay, in the remote peninsula of Chukotka, with paintings of polar bears on the walls, he was being kept informed of all developments.

After hearing that the deals for Cole and Veron had been tied up for £22m, to add to his outlay of £37m for the first four arrivals, Abramovich relaxed in Anadyr's only nightclub, sipping chilled mineral water on an enormous black leather sofa in a back room. Abramovich became Governor of Chukotka two years ago. The republic is accessible only by plane and has a population of just 72,000, many of them indigenous tribes such as Chukchi, Eveni and Inuit. The oligarch has his own private Boeing Business Jet 737, painted mustard-yellow, and was using video conferencing to mastermind his latest transfer raids.

As for buying the England captain, who was at the time scoring his first goal for new club Real Madrid in Tokyo, he mused, 'I have never met him, but if he ever considers the possibility of returning to England, if he doesn't make it in Spain ... I like him.'

Ken Bates would talk Abramovich out of any move for Beckham, but then again, the Chairman wasn't all that keen on Veron, as he thought it not to be a wise move to finance Sir Alex with more transfer kitty that could be used to strengthen the opposition to Chelsea's new ambitions. Bates argues, 'I don't think Beckham would have been a contender for Chelsea, because of the baggage. You know, Prince and Princess Beckham, Beckingham Palace and all that kind of crap. If Roman had been here a couple of weeks earlier, I don't know if we'd have tried to sign Beckham. He'd become bigger than his club and I'm guessing that's why Ferguson got rid of him. Roman wants a team, not a personality. The team is bigger than anybody. That's Roman's philosophy, Claudio Ranieri's view – and mine, too. When Eriksson said that if Beckham had gone for the England bonding trip to Spain he would have had a private villa of his own, that was disgraceful – where's the bonding in that?'

How much clout Bates now has with the new owner is debatable, but it is reasonable to assume that if Abramovich wants Beckham, then he will do his best to get him, irrespective of the cost. The suggestion that Beckham's long-term plan is to return to the Premiership with a London club would only encourage Abramovich. However, there are those close to him who would actually subscribe to the Bates caution.

Abramovich admitted he has been stunned by the publicity generated by his takeover. Despite his disappointment at the response in his homeland, where many are outraged that he has invested so heavily in foreign sport, he has been welcomed by the Chelsea fans.

And he has been overwhelmed by the welter of words written about him. 'I didn't realise they'd write so much about me in the British newspapers. It's incredible. But I did know that, in England, football is a kind of religion. So there was always going to be a lot of interest.

'Some people in Russia, who call themselves patriots, said I should have put money into Russian sport, not into a foreign team. The problem is that we don't live in a free country. We're not used to people being allowed to spend their own money how they want to.'

But plans are under way for a stadium in Moscow for three local teams, funded by Abramovich. In the long term, he would like to bring Chelsea over for a 'friendly'.

And still he realistically refused to demand that Chelsea excel in their first season under his stewardship. 'I would love to think it will, but we have made many acquisitions and so it is hard to say if it will be the most successful season in the history of the team. Even the best players don't immediately make a team. The internal structure of the team has been destroyed and time is needed for the players to play together and only then can you hope for a result.' That demonstrated a knowledge of the game on his part that few were aware of.

Meanwhile, the pursuit of new talent continued unabated. Birch admitted, 'Prior to the company being sold, we were pursuing one plan but the arrival of Mr Abramovich allowed us to pursue another plan. And long may it continue, it's been a terribly exciting time.'

Joe Cole and Scott Parker were originally the midfield option deals at £6m a piece that Bates admitted to me that the club could not afford to pursue, but hoped at the time the new owners would take up. Once Abramovich was installed, instead of a young England fringe player still aiming to fulfil his potential, and another also of great promise, Chelsea moved to buy some of the world's most respected and gifted midfield stars. But eventually they returned to Ranieri's Plan A, and bought Cole!

Chelsea had already spent a record £17m on Duff and Birch observed, 'He's a great player and I think the more people you speak to who tell you that, you realise what a good buy it has been. Claudio has been interested in him for some time but we didn't have the wherewithal to buy him at that stage so he was one of our top priorities.'

Duff was impressed by the strength of the squad and expected further arrivals as he said, 'We looked strong in Asia and God knows who we will be bringing in over the next two weeks.'

Veron was the first of the 'champions' Ranieri spoke of, rekindling all the suggestions that he had come highly recommended by Eriksson, who, of course, built his team around the player at Lazio.

'We have good midfield players like Emmanuel Petit and Frank Lampard, but they are only two,' Ranieri said. 'A big team needs three or four. We are working on it.'

Veron decided to join Chelsea after an incredible U-turn. First, he wanted to stay at Old Trafford, then it became clear to him his Manager wanted him out. Sir Alex indicated publicly during his club's tour of the States that Veron would stay, but a £20m contract offered at Chelsea, plus the growing fear he was going to be frozen out by his Manager, in the way Beckham had suffered, persuaded Veron to change his mind.

Veron was allowed to make up his own mind about the move by Sir Alex and, more than a fortnight after he had initially turned down the opportunity, his agent was at the Bridge negotiating his move while the player was training along with the rest of the United squad at the New York Giants stadium. Manchester United eventually accepted the £15m bid and Veron was ready to end his sorry two years at Old Trafford.

Yet the player made a special effort to impress Ferguson during United's tour in a last-ditch attempt to persuade Sir Alex to change his mind. According to eye-witnesses, Sir Alex smiled and shook his head in disbelief during one training session when Veron scored what the Manager admitted was one of the most amazing goals he had seen. Chesting the ball down 20 yards out, the Argentine then crossed one leg behind the other and stabbed the ball with incredible power into the top right-hand corner. His team-mates spontaneously applauded the audacious display of skill.

Privately, Ferguson had been disappointed with the return he got from the player after shelling out such a massive fee to Lazio; he'd made 82 appearances, and scored just 11 goals. Although the Manager often defended his big-money acquisition, the player was brilliant in one game, and weak in others. Some United fans called for Veron, who has cost a staggering £76.2m in five moves, to be sold earlier in the season. But during the 2002/03 campaign, the Manager insisted that Veron would still end up being a success at Old Trafford. Now he had had a change of heart. The alternative was that Veron faced the bleak prospect of being turned into a Premiership outcast if he stayed, as Sir Alex admitted that Veron's reluctance to move to Stamford Bridge had left the United boss with no option but to consider the Argentinian no more than a squad player ahead of the new season. It all pointed to Veron suffering the same fate as Dwight Yorke, who had been frozen out after initially rejecting a move to Blackburn Rovers. Yorke eventually made the move to Rovers but endured a year of torment and humiliation on the sidelines at United.

Veron was aware that Fergie had brought in Eric Djemba-Djemba and Kleberson into a midfield unit already containing Roy Keane, Paul Scholes, Nicky Butt and Ryan Giggs.

Yet Ferguson publicly insisted at the start of the tour, 'You can't dismiss the class of the boy, the work-rate, the desire to play. They are all great. Nothing has changed as far as I am concerned. There was an opportunity for Seba to go to another club but that has not happened. He will be an important squad player.'

Then United lost out on Ronaldinho and were told they had no chance of landing Kieron Dyer. Veron had some glimmer of hope. And the rumour mill was kick-started again when Newcastle Chairman Freddie Shepherd, in Los Angeles on company business, suggested that a deal for Dyer or striker Craig Bellamy was on. It was not.

After helping United to a 3-1 win over Club America in the second of United's US tour games, Veron said, 'By no means do I plan to leave. I feel comfortable and happy with United. But if the club is planning to transfer me, that's another matter.'

Sir Alex insisted Veron would stay as his side faced Juventus at the Giants Stadium. Ferguson claimed to know nothing of speculation suggesting a fee had been agreed with Chelsea. Instead, Ferguson suggested the player's agent was acting without authority and repeated his assertion that Veron would still be at the club when United begin the defence of their Premiership title. 'Seba is a terrific player and I want him to stay,' said Ferguson. 'I don't know anything about the speculation. Agents talk to a lot of people, they have a lot of power and sometimes they can think different things to the player. But Seba is a mature man. He is very experienced and he knows what he wants. If there was a situation arising, I'm sure he would talk to me. He hasn't done so and I'm quite happy about that. My impression was that he had settled down, everything had gone quiet and there was no problem. Seba is a marvellous player and he is contracted to us. It is going to be difficult for a deal to be done tomorrow. He will be playing for us.'

Just as Ferguson reiterated that the deal was over, Veron's agent, Fernando Hidalgo, was quoted as saying, 'The meeting with Chelsea on Wednesday is very important. Everything is OK at the moment but we will need to confirm what he discussed on Tuesday. If Seba is very happy with what Chelsea offer, then we will close the contract with Manchester United.'

Sir Alex watched Veron lead a 4-1 rout of Juve and again insisted that the Argentinian would still be at Old Trafford at the start of the season. Veron collected the Man of the Match honours in front of 79,005 delirious fans, capping a superb United performance with two outstanding assists which led to goals for Scholes and van Nistelrooy at the start of the second half.

Ferguson maintained his stance that the midfielder was going nowhere. 'I don't know what the hell is going on in England. People keep seeing him on this tour and people still keep saying he is going,' said Ferguson. 'Unless he is going to be whisked from right under my nose, they are wrong. Seba is a marvellous player. He has wonderful imagination, he always wants the ball and has a great engine. He was outstanding tonight.'

Ferguson admitted he thought Veron might have taken the first-half free-kick from which Giggs curled home his side's opener but, after standing aside for the Welshman on that occasion, Veron was in no mood to relinquish centre stage for the remainder of the evening. It was his pass which allowed Solskjaer to set up Scholes for United's second and it was also Veron who provided the perfectly weighted pass for van Nistelrooy, which the Dutchman took on his chest before lashing a first-time volley into the net. 'It was a magnificent goal,' admitted Ferguson. 'I have seen him do that many times in training. He hits the ball with such power. It is a real feature of his game.'

The reaction of Veron's team-mates was to beg Veron to stay. 'Seba was the best player on the pitch,' enthused van Nistelrooy. 'He didn't lose the ball once, all his passes came off and the assist for my goal was absolutely brilliant. When he got the ball in the build-up to my goal, I knew he was going to pass to me because he can play passes like that with the outside of his foot. There aren't many players capable of lifting the ball the way he did. Probably nobody expected it but me.'

Van Nistelrooy's comments were echoed by Phil Neville, who watched in awe as Veron played in the Dutch striker with a delicately chipped pass which was then superbly volleyed into the Juventus net. 'That pass was out of this world,' said the England international. 'I think winning the league last season has really helped Seba. He has been one of our best players on tour and that bodes well for the future.'

Van Nistelrooy revealed how the dressing room rallied round Veron in a bid to keep him out of Chelsea's clutches. He said, 'I am really glad for him because now he is staying. All the players have spoken about the situation with Juan over the past few weeks and it looks like it is all in the past now. If you asked every player in the dressing room, none of us would be happy if he were to leave. We all want him to stay and I think he will. He sees this as a second chance.'

Chelsea initially offered £13m, then raised it to £15m ... United were holding out for £17.5m. But it finally emerged that United agreed in principle that Veron could leave. Chief Executive Peter Kenyon confessed,

'We have had a Chelsea offer now and, at this stage, it's not been accepted although it will be under review. It'll be the middle of next week when we'll decide what we need to do. It appears they have reached agreement on personal terms with Veron's people but he's our player and we'll decide what's best for the club.'

Kenyon admitted if United do sell they'll take a hefty hit on the money they paid out to Lazio two years ago. 'We write down players values over the length of their contract anyway, so it's not as though he is in the books at what we paid for him. There have been no other firm bids for Seba, although there was initially interest from Italy.'

Finally, even Fergie back tracked. 'We had an offer from Chelsea and have put it to the lad because the feeling we got was they had been talking to him. I put it to him to see if he wanted to go and he never gave me an answer.'

After the first four signings played for the first time in the 2-1 win at Palace, the inevitable question for Ranieri was: what about Veron? Ranieri laughed, 'I don't know anything – you like to stir.' But when asked again about Veron, Ranieri did an exaggerated Pinnochio-style motion with his hand on his nose, suggesting he knows a lot more than he's letting on.

Ferguson left Veron on the bench for the 3-1 win over Barcelona in Philadelphia. Sir Alex insisted, 'You can't read anything into that. We have a quota of midfield players who need a number of games. It was Roy Keane's second full game, Paul Scholes has played two, Seba has had two and now Nicky Butt has had two matches. I wanted to spread the load around and that is why I played the team I did. There is absolutely nothing whatsoever concerning Seba Veron in terms of him being left out of the team.' When asked outright whether Veron would be part of the Red Devils' squad when United open the defence of their Premiership title, Ferguson replied, 'I can't answer that.' Quite a turnaround since his earlier definitive answer that he most definitely would be!

Kenyon confirmed that United had received a bid but it had been well below their valuation. Hidalgo continued to make public statements claiming the transfer was still on.

Fergie's observation that with the signings of Djemba-Djemba and Kleberson he was a little 'overloaded' in central midfield reflected a belief that Veron's time as a United player was over.

Ferguson eventually explained why he was ready to let Veron go; he was keen to get some younger legs in midfield. Ferguson said, 'I felt if we could get Kleberson we could start negotiations for Veron after that. It gives me a collection of very good midfielders. Kleberson is 23 and Djemba-Djemba 22, both young midfielders who could serve us well in the years to come. That's the reason we finally let Seba go.'

Ferguson was still conciliatory at this stage, and despite Veron's inconsistency, he added, 'You always miss the sort of top-quality he can give you, he's done it in a lot of games for us. There is no question he has been a terrific player for Manchester United but we have also played without him lots of times before. We have a collection of midfielders and I'm sure we will be able to compensate now he has left us.'

Veron's agent confirmed that his client was ready to sign for Chelsea; the main reason that the player opted to go was that he would have had to play wide on the right if he had stayed at Old Trafford ... if he had played at all. His father, Juan Ramon Veron, said, 'Ferguson didn't understand that Sebastian didn't want to play out wide on the wing. It's not his position. He moves a lot better in the middle. He's always wanted to play in the centre, like he did in Italy. That's the position he'll play in at Chelsea and I know they'll get the best out of him. He's excited about the new season, he'll prove he's OK and reaffirm all the good work he's done in Europe.'

Manchester United accepted a loss of £13m. Hidalgo said, 'The player will arrive in London at midday. He's going to take his medical.'

United made the announcement via the Stock Exchange. United stated that £2.5m of the £15m fee was 'conditional on the performance of the Chelsea team over the next four seasons'. One of the secret reasons for the hold-up was the cunning plot by Ferguson to attempt to sign right-back Glen Johnson as part of the Veron deal. Johnson had not made a competitive appearance for his new club when Sir Alex made it clear that Veron would not be going unless he got the player destined for the England team. Chelsea resisted, but one of the quirks of the request is that Zahavi, who has been representing Chelsea, is also a close confidant of the Manchester United Manager, and also has a role in the representation of Veron. But Zahavi would not countenance Chelsea losing Johnson and Sir Alex relented and sold Veron in a straight cash deal.

Veron became Abramovich's sixth signing. Hidalgo said, 'He is happy. It has been a club decision, and he has accepted it. He is ready to do the best he can with this new opportunity at Chelsea.' Alluding to initial doubts, Hidalgo added, 'When decisions are made, everyone has to follow the consequences. Seba is proud to join Chelsea – but it was not his intention to leave the club [United].'

When Veron arrived in London to seal his deal, he admitted that he felt he had been forced out. Chelsea provided wages of £100,000 a week and the guarantee of regular first-team football. Veron vowed to prove he is no Premiership misfit, believing the different culture at Chelsea under Ranieri could see him get a second lease of life in English football. He said, 'Ferguson trusted me when I first arrived. But later on, it seemed we didn't understand each other as well. There were times when I felt he preferred some of my team-mates. I think I'll understand Claudio Ranieri better because of the language. I can do a job in English football – and in London that will be reaffirmed.'

Ferguson responded, 'The overall package in terms of what we save on his salary and what we get from Chelsea made it difficult to turn down.' Kenyon added, 'It was a footballing decision. We got an offer and the price was eventually acceptable. In the light of the other players we have got, we felt we should take the offer from Chelsea and do other things. The transfer was started by an approach from Chelsea. We didn't put him up for sale. We have got Kleberson coming, subject to a work permit, who will fill in that role'

Ranieri also scotched speculation that Vieri was about to join the stampede of players heading to Stamford Bridge, saying, 'I think Christian will stay at Inter.' He warned, 'Rome wasn't built in a day. I think Alex Ferguson had seven years to win his first title and for me now it is important to build a team and secondly a group. I want to build a spirit for the group because you can have all the best players in the world but if you do not have a group you cannot win. They must be a group, then maybe you can win. This is my target and then I want to see if we can close the gap between us and Manchester United, Arsenal and Liverpool.'

Celebrating the arrival of Veron and Joe Cole, Ranieri enthused, 'I think Veron is the best midfielder in the world and I'm very happy to have him at the club. When Veron comes to Chelsea, pure gold comes to Chelsea.'

Ranieri refused to be drawn into discussing whether he was surprised that United had been willing to let him go. 'I don't think about it,' he said. 'I don't think about what Manchester United are thinking. I think about Chelsea, I think positive and I feel very happy because our midfield is stronger now. They are both fantastic players and they can play together. I did not see Sebastian in all the matches [for Manchester United] but for me he is a top-class player and I am sure he will play better with us.' The Italian then felt it necessary to add, 'I gamble,' immediately retracting his comment by saying, 'I'm not a gambler, I don't bet. So when I sign a player like Veron, I know it's not a gamble. He is a sure-fire winner and I know I am going to win with him even though everyone is saying I will be the first coach to be sacked this season. I don't believe that.'

Responding to the Manager's claims that he had signed the best midfielder in the world, the Argentina international said through an interpreter, 'It's exaggerating a little, but it's a very big motivation and I'll prove that to the boss.'

Asked whether Veron and Cole can play in the same side, Ranieri said, 'If you can speak football fluently, you can talk in every position and both Juan and Joe are fantastic with and without the ball. But Veron can play wherever he wants to play. He is the chief.'

Veron intended to repay the faith shown in him by Ranieri. 'I had good games, bad games and exceptional games [at United],' Veron said. 'Italian football and English football are very different and perhaps that's what caused a change in my game but I hope I can do better. I was a bit surprised United were willing to let me go. Two or three months ago when a lot of clubs wanted me, the Manager insisted I stayed, but over the last few weeks his attitude changed. That didn't change my relationship with him. I didn't feel as if I'd been misled by him. Despite him saying in America how much he valued me, the decision to let me go had already been taken.'

Veron insisted, 'There's much more to come from me at Chelsea. I would say my performances have been no more than ordinary, average. I don't know if I really gave my best at United. I've had some good games, some excellent games, some bad games, but there's been no continuity. Maybe that's because there is a lot of difference between English and Italian football. Making that switch wasn't easy and it cost me. But I feel motivated to respond to all the people at Chelsea who have shown so much confidence in me.'

But what if Veron could not command a regular place, as happened at Manchester United? 'It could be one of the problems, but as I have said before, what I lacked was the continuity in the team throughout the season. Of course, I spoke to the Manager, but in a big club like that, with so many good players, I had to take advantage of the time and places I could play. In Italy, I had five brilliant years. What I aspire to do here is to create the same image of myself that I had there.'

Will he achieve such an image by, in effect, taking a step down from the champions? 'There are very few clubs like United in the world, but Chelsea have also become as big, if not bigger, than Manchester United.'

The Argentinian is delighted to be joining Chelsea at the same time as

Cole. He said, 'I'm not just saying this because he is sitting next to me, but he is a great player and for me he is the best player in England.'

Veron's best performances have come for Argentina and Lazio, when he has had Diego Simeone alongside him. At United, he was best with Phil Neville, Quinton Fortune or Nicky Butt alongside him. Veron's likely partner at Chelsea is Frank Lampard. 'Nobody works harder,' said Gary Neville of his England team-mate. 'His energy levels are unbelievable. I bet he does more running than any other player.'

After so many contradictory statements, Veron admitted that he had confronted Sir Alex about his future as he expected another chance at United this season. 'I would say he [Ferguson] wasn't sincere with me. Two months ago, a couple of clubs expressed an interest and he said I wasn't for sale. He gave me the impression that I was wanted. But when there was more money on the table, his conversation changed. That's a hard one for me. Two months ago, it was a different situation ... it was very clear that he wanted me. But when I spoke recently with Ferguson, he said nothing, he just told me I was sold and that was it.'

Veron realised Chelsea's approach was being taken seriously towards the end of United's recent tour of America. He was told Abramovich's offer was too good to turn down. Veron said, 'The story was running and running and nobody in Manchester was denying it, so I asked Ferguson, "Do you want me in the squad?" He gave me a rather convoluted explanation about the tactics of his midfield, saying in a very roundabout way that he would find it difficult to play me from the start if this and that and the other happened. So eventually I just confronted him and said, "I'm not asking you if I will start every game, I am asking: do you want me in your squad?" Then he came out with the line about Chelsea's offer being very good, financially interesting, tempting. I realised it was all about money. I said I'm not interested in money, but if that's what this is about ... I guess that was the turning point for me.'

As one might expect, Fergie didn't take too kindly to being branded two-faced. 'Seba knew all along what was happening, so to say I was two-faced about it is a disgrace. I spoke to him a few days after we started pre-season training and explained that we had accepted a bid from Chelsea and I explained it was because of the midfield players we had. At the time, I knew Kleberson was coming and we'd have an embarrassment of midfield players. I explained all of this to him, we shook hands and everything was fine. But the day before we left on tour, Chelsea changed their mind, said they couldn't pay £15m and wouldn't follow through with the offer. By then, Veron had taken all of his stuff from our Carrington training ground and his agent was talking to Chelsea. We had to phone him to tell him he was still a United player.'

Veron claimed he never wanted to leave Old Trafford and was sold against his will. But Fergie disagreed, as you would expect him to do, insisting Veron was fully aware of the transfer bid every step of the way and that he wanted to quit United. He asserts, 'He didn't not want to go. His agent was speaking to Chelsea and he knew it was happening.'

The contradictions surrounding Ferguson's true feelings about his star midfielder were evident in the way Ferguson had vehemently defended his star in the face of some tough questioning. Fergie even stormed out of one press conference when asked if he thought Veron was struggling. 'People are always going on about fucking Veron. You tell me, what's wrong with Veron? He's a fucking great player. You are fucking idiots.' Prior to the Community Shield clash with Arsenal, however, Ferguson seemed to have a change of heart. 'Juan Veron was capable of exceptional football and was talented. But, at times, he found the Premiership a bit difficult. He was a European player and that was where we got our best form from him.'

In reality, United jumped at the chance to sell despite a transfer loss of £13m. Fergie says, 'We had to look at the long-term view and, overall, the package we received was too good to turn down.' He also insisted United will not be any weaker for the loss of Veron and Beckham after some fans expressed their anger. But Ferguson claims the duo's departure will make little difference as neither player took part in the key games that won United the Premiership last season. He said, 'The team that won at Newcastle, drew at Arsenal and beat Liverpool is still here. And I am not necessarily looking to change that team, either. The team that operated at the end of last season is fully ready to go out at the beginning of this season.'

In addition to his comments about his treatment at the hands of his former Manager, Veron also slammed the lifestyle in Manchester. 'It's just in the provinces, not a capital city like London is. I know my life in London is going to be much better and very different. At least in London the rhythm is similar to Buenos Aires.'

Veron refutes claims that leaving Manchester United for Chelsea is a step down. 'They are working to turn this into the best club in the world.' And the knock-on effect of his signing seems to have sparked renewed interest in Chelsea from other 'champions' worldwide. Zahavi told me, 'Now many more players are taking notice and want to come to the club.'

Joe Cole became the latest recruit from Chelsea's relegated east-London rivals. The Hammers decided to cash in on one of their most valuable assets rather than lose him for next to nothing when his contract expires at the end of the 2003/04 season. A West Ham statement said, 'Everyone at the club is extremely sorry to see Joe leave Upton Park. Following 18 months of very amicable discussions between Joe, the club, his father and his agents, it was made clear that Joe would not consider extending his contract past its expiry, believing that his international career would be enhanced by regular European club competition experience.'

Cole needed little persuasion that he was better off in the Premiership than in the Nationwide. West Ham were rapidly becoming a club in deep trouble after the sales of Trevor Sinclair, Glen Johnson, Frédéric Kanouté and now Cole.

Cole turned up at the Chadwell Heath training ground but quickly disappeared when he was informed that the two clubs were in talks. Since giving Cole his international début two years ago, Eriksson has been faint in his praise, even though he did take him to the World Cup finals. Cole will have the chance to prove that he is more than just a bag of tricks and that he can transform matches on the big stage. Cole's versatility – he played on both flanks and through the middle for West Ham – will be needed as he tries to find a regular place at the new Chelsea where even established internationals such as Petit, Gronkjaer and Zenden must be wondering if they will even make it to the substitutes' bench, while Mario Stanic will be checking the dates for the Carling Cup.

Cole insisted, 'It was a difficult decision, but I feel now is the time to make a break from West Ham. The club will always be an important part of my career and I still have great affection for the club and the fans. More than 18 months ago, I was asked by West Ham to sign an extension to my contract. The club had just finished seventh in the Premier League but I felt that, to further my international career, I would need to move on to a club that was playing regularly in Europe. For all my belief in West Ham, I could not see them competing at that level. I made this known to West Ham and said that I would see out my contract with them if they wanted me to, but I would understand if they would look to sell me.

'Last season, I felt that I demonstrated to everyone my commitment to the club and the commitment to the cause of keeping West Ham in the Premier League. It hurt like mad when we were relegated. Now I wish the club and all its great supporters the very best for the forthcoming season and the future. I hope they follow my career and appreciate the effort that I have given to them.'

Cole might have been the captain and icon at West Ham, but at Chelsea he is just another midfield craftsman; this could be the making of him after a period in which his progress stalled. 'All last season, apart from perhaps the first few games, I was playing out of position,' he said. 'I didn't get forward as much as I'd have liked. But because the team seemed to gain better results when I played that way, I tried to do it every week. Now I'm here I'd like to get further forward, though you can't expect it automatically when you come to somewhere like this, because every player is quality. It's going to be a challenge.'

Ironically, Cole watched Chelsea as a youngster. 'I used to come to Chelsea and watch from the Shed a lot. I used to love watching Dennis Wise and, before that, Kerry Dixon. I settled at West Ham because I felt most comfortable there. I had an enjoyable time but my career has come full turn and I'm back at Chelsea. It's such a great club. There are great things going on at this club. To leave West Ham was very hard, it was very emotional for me. I'd been there since I was a baby, really. I spoke to Glenn [Roeder] and John Terry about it and they were full of praise for the club. I just want to get on with my football here now and try and win things at Chelsea. I will learn my trade playing with some of the best players in the world, but also I want to play. No player wants to sit on the bench. I just want to play as many games as I can.'

Cole was quick to reassure Ranieri he would have no problems dealing with the pressure. 'I've been dealing with expectations since I was 17. People expect me to do amazing things every time I get the ball so I don't think there will be much difference now I am here. In all honesty, I don't think I'd have stayed even if we'd not been relegated. My first reaction when I heard Chelsea wanted me was "Great". It's a big club and there weren't any second thoughts, really, although I had to speak to my friends and family first. There's so much opportunity for a player here and I think it's a good move.'

Cole, who scored 13 goals in 150 appearances for West Ham, added, 'When I first came here I spoke to the boss about where he sees me playing and he was very positive, but you understand there is competition when you come to a club like this. Coming here and having the opportunity to play in the Champions League can only make me better, for Chelsea and for England. I've seen it already. I trained for the first time and it was so much faster than what I was used to. You have to think about things so much more and that will definitely make me a better player.'

Ranieri had been tracking the 21-year-old for the past two seasons. The Chelsea Coach said, 'Joe is a fantastic young player. I first watched him properly two years ago and since then I've always been speaking with John Terry, Frank Lampard and Paolo di Canio about him. They all told me Joe is ready for Chelsea.'

Cole, who will wear the number 10 shirt – 'only because I came the day before Juan did' – added, 'I think I can bring a lot of quality to Chelsea and I promise that I'll always give 100 per cent and fight. I've always been there for a challenge. England is very important to me. I was falling out of England contention last year, even though I felt it was one of my better seasons. It's down to me now. I've got the stage where I can play and show Sven-Goran Eriksson what I can do. If I get the chance to play, then he'll see me.'

The FA has levelled three misconduct charges at the young midfielder, one of which involved a brawl with Bolton's Rufus Brevett in West Ham's crucial 1-0 away defeat in April 2003. They are accused of damaging the tunnel canopy after a skirmish following the final whistle. Both faced the threat of prosecution and were quizzed by police. But no criminal charges followed because the matter was referred to the FA. Cole is also accused of taking part in a massed confrontation that saw him square up to and apparently push Bolton defender Bernard Mendy, and he is alleged to have verbally abused the fourth official at the game. Each guilty verdict for misconduct normally brings a three-match ban, which could see Cole ruled out for up to nine games.

Part of the confidential internal discussions involving the purchase of Cole was one possibility that he could be loaned out to Moscow Torpedo as a favour from Abramovich to his close friend and one time banker Alexander Mamut. As Mamut's purchase of Torpedo fell through long before Cole was bought by Chelsea the idea was quickly dropped. When Chelsea eventually opted to buy Cole, there was no need to raise with him the loan to Moscow.

Frank Lampard was delighted to link up with his former West Ham and England colleague. 'I know Joe well and he is a great player,' said Lampard. 'So far, the club has done well to bring in a mix of top English players as well as foreigners. I am sure Joe will improve the team and himself by coming here. It is amazing what has happened since May. Then everyone was talking about the club's debts. Now, everyone is saying we could win the Champions League. It has meant a complete change in the expectancy level and it is up to us to live up to that.

'There's obviously pressure from everyone. People outside Chelsea will be wanting us to fail. I can understand that, but we don't want to be failures. One of our aims at the start of the season is to win the League. It may be true that people would like to see another club apart from Manchester United and Arsenal win the title, but a lot of my mates are Spurs, West Ham and Arsenal fans and I know they want us to fail. As soon as money gets spent in the way it has, then you get a bit of jealousy. That is normal. The fans are expecting us to do good things with the squad we have got and, considering the players we are bringing in, we should be fighting to win the League. If we miss out, just, it won't be a failure.'

Lampard, an £11m buy from Upton Park, added, 'Last season was very good for me, so I feel as if I am on top of my game, and playing as I have been, I would like to think I will be in the team. I am pretty confident of that. People talk about this name and that name, but I want to be in there whoever comes. It is amazing.'

Lampard has no doubts that the arrival of both Cole and Veron will benefit the team. 'I know Joe well. He is a great, skilful player – a great talent. A lot of people expected us to go and buy foreign players with the takeover but we have bought well. Joe is another great signing.'

Terry was also in a positive frame of mind. 'No, I don't have any worries over losing my place. Last season, the players did great to get us into the Champions League and the Manager appreciates that. The players are happy there is competition for places. Everyone is waiting for us to get turned over but that's part of it. We are the talk of the town and it's good pressure to have. Winning the Premiership was the ambition of the club when I first broke into the team. But we now believe we have a great chance. The Manager has made some great signings and we have heard there are going to be a couple more. I can't wait for the season to start.'

Trevor Brooking insisted the club had no option but to take Chelsea's cash for Cole. The club is in debt to the tune of an estimated £60m. Brooking said, 'The sum we had to recoup was £20m. We were lucky that certain players were out of contract – that enabled us to reduce the wage bill. Without the sales of the four – Johnson, Sinclair, Kanouté and Cole – we would have run out of money halfway through next season. We wouldn't have been able to pay the players' wages. And without the 17,000 season ticket holders, we would have had to sell another player. Now we have to try and bring in sufficient players to strengthen the squad.

'Joe is a home-produced player and it is a huge shame to see him go. But the fact is, we made him a really good offer last summer, which he refused. Even if we had been in the Premiership, Joe was going to go this season – no club wants a Sol Campbell situation where you lose a big player for nothing. If we hadn't received a realistic offer, he could have stayed. But the offer was realistic, with Joe having 12 months left on his contract, and the club couldn't say no to it. Glenn is in an extremely difficult position due to the financial implications at the club. He wants as strong a team as possible but the priority was to secure the finances of the club.'

Former boss Harry Redknapp said, 'When I heard the news about Joey going, I was very disappointed. It's a sad, sad day. Joe was priceless and what they are doing at that club is a disgrace. The fans deserve better.'

Eriksson's assistant, Tord Grip, was surprised by Cole's move but he insisted, 'Joe will have to work to get into the first team but the other side of that is he'll be together with very good footballers every day in training. It's not only the games he plays but the players he plays with that will teach him about his game. He is an ambitious boy, so he will want to learn in any way possible.' Cole and Veron's arrivals took Abramovich's outlay on players to £58.6m.

Arsene Wenger, when told about the signing of Cole and Veron, joked, 'Chelsea must buy a new team coach as well, then, to get everybody on.' Another comment to be heard about the new era at the time was, 'One of the most impressive things about Chelsea this season will be the vehicles in the reserve-team car park.'

Yet, Wenger insisted he was not envious of Chelsea's new-found wealth. Of course he wasn't! He explained a touch unconvincingly, 'Either you try to make the best of what you have in your life or you always envy other people and are never happy. Ideally, I wish the club had more money. But, player-wise, I'm happy with what I have. As for Chelsea's spending, it's a good thing if it gets the market moving again but I think it has created a wrong impression. The money they have spent in recent weeks doesn't reflect the true state of the market.'

However, one could be forgiven for not believing Wenger when he continued, 'Chelsea buy one player per day and we buy no player per month, so I can understand that we look a little bit poor or out of shape. Chelsea have won the Lottery and we cannot compete financially so we try to compete in a different way. What's important is what happens on the pitch and you will say that on the pitch we are good. To write us off just because we have not spent £100 million is too easy.'

Vieira laughed at the suggestion that Chelsea would covet a player like him. 'It's quite exciting for Chelsea but the big question is: is it going to work? We know that, as individual players, they are fantastic, but it is different as a team. You need more than individual quality. When you buy these sort of players you expect to win the League, so there is big pressure on Chelsea to do well. Chelsea have made a lot of signings and, if they get the mix right, they will be very strong. They can beat anyone over one match but we'll have to see how the players are going to be together, whether they can string results together.'

Vieira was not looking further than a familiar tussle between Arsenal and United. 'Manchester United know how to win the Premiership, so I believe they will be the best team in the country. I was quite surprised Veron and Beckham went because they are influential players. But I don't think the loss of Beckham and Veron will make Manchester United less strong.

'We have so many international players. I believe we are stronger than any other team. Maybe we have fewer players who can make individual differences but, as a collective force, we are stronger than anyone. Last year, we gave the championship to Manchester United. We were the better team. This season, we are going for stability and, as the squad has not changed much, we know each other even better. We still have a step to take to reach Real Madrid but, for me, Arsenal is still the team of tomorrow. The English season will be another Arsenal–Manchester United duel while having to count, too, with Liverpool, Newcastle and Chelsea. Manchester United and Arsenal are used to winning the title. They know how it is done.'

Vieira ended months of speculation by signing a contract keeping him at Highbury until summer 2007. But he still dreams of playing for Spanish giants Real Madrid at some stage in his career. He added, 'I have made a choice and, sincerely, I think it was the best one to make. Yes, everyone dreams of Real Madrid and that is normal when you see the players that make up their side. But if they win the Champions League, it will be no surprise. If they get knocked out, they will have stones thrown at them.'

Zola was continuing to bang in the goals during pre-season training and nabbed a hat-trick within the first 15 minutes as his new side Cagliari beat Trentino Team 7-2 in a friendly. Zola scored four goals on his Cagliari début. Zola believes Terry can help Chelsea win the league and hailed Cole as the player he would have signed as his replacement. Zola said, 'It's strange, but the most important player at the club could turn out to be the one player who cost no money at all. I watched John Terry for many years and I always thought he was going to be a special player, but he has surprised me because he has developed so quickly. Chelsea can be built around John, who is a strong character. He'll become a world-class player. He is the heartbeat of the side and will be there for many years. Arsenal had a leader in Tony Adams and I hope John does the same for Chelsea.'

Zola points out similarities between himself and Cole. 'Joe Cole is very similar to me. He'd have been the player I would have bought if I were Chelsea Manager. He's a young boy with great talent. Going to Chelsea will help him make the final step. He has amazing skills and is beautiful to watch – like me.' This view of their similarities is reiterated by Ranieri, who has said of the young star, 'Joe can be my little Zola ...'

Zola thinks Abramovich's money has strengthened Chelsea, but he warned that it does not guarantee success. 'What is happening is good for the club as football's finances are bad. If you have the finances, you can buy good players and improve the team, but it is not everything. You cannot buy trophies. It is not only about money. You have to buy the right footballers, who can give something on and off the pitch. Money can be great as long as it is used wisely and in the right place. Roman Abramovich looks like he wants to do something amazing for the club, but I would offer a note of caution. Nobody can spend and expect instant success. I cannot say anything bad about him because he is spending money and so they have a chance. But Chelsea have to build team spirit and the right mentality. Our problem was a lack of consistency and they must get rid of that. '

Zola believes Ranieri can lead Chelsea to the championship, but feels he only has two seasons to achieve it. 'He has maybe two years to win the League at Chelsea and it is possible he will do so. Claudio has proved a very good coach, but I do not feel the new owner will be patient. You don't spend that money just to come second.'

15

THE CHAMPIONS LEAGUE BECKONS

CHELSEA FANS, ALREADY SHELL-SHOCKED by the speed and quantity of the signings, had finally come to realise that much of the transfer speculation reported on a daily basis in the papers was coming to fruition.

Far from running out of cash, Roman Abramovich was amassing even more. The proposed merger of two of the country's biggest oil groups, Yukos and Sibneft, was approved in Russia. Through his Swiss-based company Runicon, Sibneft joined forces, as planned, with Yukos, multiplying Abramovich's wealth. In addition, he acquired £300m in oil dividends.

The fans didn't have to wait long for Adrian Mutu with the promise of even more stars to come ... and the prospect of Champions League football was an added attraction. As far as his strategy was concerned, Abramovich explained, 'Initially, we wanted to get at least seven new players by 31 August but nothing is written in stone. Everything could change. It's fair to say that we could add at least one more quality player to the squad by the end of the month, but I will not say any more because every comment could result in an increase in prices.'

Abramovich also made a commitment to Claudio Ranieri. 'Ranieri will stay. He speaks simple English, so it's easy for us to converse.' Ranieri needed, though, to avoid another European nightmare, saying, 'There is a danger of losing because I have many new players. I lack a team.' Abramovich diplomatically suggested he believes the new team will take time to blend. 'There will be many new acquisitions playing, so it is hard to believe this season will be successful. Even if we buy the best players, we won't be a team. They need time to play together.' However, the reality is that he is expecting to see an instant challenge to Manchester United and Arsenal's supremacy.

Ranieri insisted he was not overly worried at the pressure. 'Look, every coach feels pressure. I like it and, you know what, I'm ready for it.'

But a poor start would make Ranieri's position untenable. Unable to spend a year earlier, he hoisted Chelsea back into the Champions League. Now flush with more money than any other manager, he is threatened by the club's lofty ambition. Nothing short of an immediate challenge for honours is good enough.

'I feel like the luckiest football manager in the world at the moment,' added the Blues Manager, 'but Ken Bates says the pressure is on me to be successful, and I know he's right.'

Abramovich pledged his long-term commitment to Chelsea. 'It's very long term. It's hard to talk about 10 years. Maybe 20 years, 50 years.'

Ken Bates, before departing for the first European adventure under the Abramovich regime, remarked, 'I suspect that Roman wants to see a huge return on his investment. I'm hoping, as Roman is, that we will be one of the élite clubs in Europe within two years. I know some people will say things about Roman and ask about his commitment but deeds speak far more than words. He has put in a substantial amount and I can't see any reason why we should suddenly change that. He is immensely wealthy but if he wants to indulge himself in sport, he can do so. It's a hobby, of course, but one he can spend money on. Roman's business is oil and aluminium but he wants to be as successful at Chelsea as in all the other businesses and I believe the omens are looking good.'

But Ranieri could not afford any more European banana skins after three miserable and humiliating UEFA Cup campaigns, having been knocked out by St Gallen, Hapoel Tel-Aviv and Viking. A prominent role in the Champions League was now the minimum requirement, as he went into the qualifying round against Slovakian champions MSK Zilina, who'd beaten Maccabi Tel-Aviv 2-1 on aggregate, without the strikers he wanted to sign.

Abramovich collected players the way schoolchildren collect Panini stickers and the arrival of the first striker for £15.8m brought his spending to £74.3m, but Adrian Mutu wasn't signed in time for the qualifiers. Players had to be signed by 11.00am on Thursday, 7 August, but Mutu arrived the following Monday.

The former Parma captain is a replacement for Zola. Mutu will be best remembered as one of the goal-scorers in the Romanian side that knocked Kevin Keegan's England out of Euro 2000 in the 3-2 defeat in Charleroi.

On a five-year contract, Mutu became the seventh player to sign for Chelsea, but that was far from the end of the spending. A Chelsea insider told me, 'Who's counting? Only the journalists. Roman will spend as much as it takes to make Chelsea successful.'

Parma originally denied that he would leave but the deal was confirmed by Coach Cesare Prandelli after the pre-season friendly against Southampton at St Mary's. He said, 'Mutu did not travel to England with us because of the deal that was taking place. When the offer came in, we simply could not refuse it. Mutu was voted the best player in Italy last season. He scored a lot of goals, and has all the qualities to be a big success in the Premiership. He played wide left as a striker for us and showed great potential. He is not scared of anything and has a great personality. He is also very good at taking free-kicks.' The fee doubles Parma's outlay on him after just one spectacular season in Serie A.

The police in Bucharest had investigated Mutu for allegedly assaulting his wife, Alexandra, a charge which, if proved, carries a six-month jail term. Alexandra was keen to press charges after a fight broke out outside her house when the actress and beauty queen refused to hand over the keys to the couple's car. Mutu denied hitting her, but accepted that the pair had had an argument. She later dropped the charges, but is pressing ahead with a divorce. Their 11-month-old son Mario has been placed in the custody of Alexandra. Mutu was trying to win custody of Mario to live with him in London. His lawyer, Florin Gatejan, said, 'Adrian loves his child and will personally look after him. Alexandra and her lawyer want publicity so badly. They said that Adrian is not interested in the child. On the contrary, we want to prove to them that Adrian can raise his son.' Alexandra had claimed he did not want his son with him – now she insists he is a coward. Alexandra's lawyer, Catalin Dancu, said, 'If Adrian Mutu wants custody, then he chose a cowardly way of letting us know – through his lawyer.'

Mutu was eagerly looking forward to his new-found celebrity status in London. He says, 'I am not afraid of the beautiful women in England who,

I hear, chase after footballers. I won't take the risk of losing my position as a player for the sake of a pretty women.'

Of his move to Chelsea, he said, 'This was an offer I couldn't refuse. It was far too important for my future and Parma's. Dan Petrescu had told me about Chelsea and he suggested them to me. I asked my club to consider the offer and I thank them for doing this. It was not an easy decision to leave Parma and I have a lot of feelings for everyone at the club. But now it is done and let's think of Chelsea.'

Petrescu was part of the first foreign revolution at the Bridge in the late 1990s and became so popular that the fans dubbed him 'Super-Dan'. He said, 'Chelsea are now at a major part of their history and I believe that, with Roman Abramovich in charge, the magic moment of sweet success is getting near. I know that Mr Abramovich wants to be a champion of England and to win the European Cup, and I will be the happiest man alive if I see him, my club and my friend Mutu achieving that. I believe completely in Mr Abramovich and, for Mutu, this is a huge opportunity and one I can tell him all about. In 1995, when I first came to Chelsea, it was the club's big ambition to start winning trophies again, and we did that.

'Chelsea knew they had to sign big players and they went straight for Gianfranco Zola, Ruud Gullit, Gianluca Vialli and others, plus a great coach like Glenn Hoddle. The trophies followed – but now Chelsea are at the next stage and I am so glad that Adrian Mutu will follow me at the club I still love. I just truly regret I am not younger so that we could play together at Chelsea for a few seasons. That would be unbelievable.

'It will not be easy for Adrian in the beginning because here in England it will be different in almost every way to what he is used to in Italy and Romania. English weather, the driving and especially the English football, which is more dynamic and more tough than anything he has experienced so far – they will be culture shocks. But I've told him that the referees won't be whistling all the time like they do in Serie A and the fact Mutu is joining Chelsea from Italy like Gullit, like Zola, like Vialli, is good for him. Serie A teaches you and I'm not worried for him. If he arrived at a big club like Chelsea from some small club then it might be different, but him having been at Inter and Parma means he is used to high expectations and fans who are very demanding.

'Moreover, I know that with an Italian in charge like Claudio Ranieri, Adrian will soon find his feet as they share the same language. Mutu is a winner and he will succeed, I'm sure of that. And, for the moment, he can stay in my house in London. If he likes it, he can stay for the full five seasons of his contract. It's only a five-minute journey to the stadium so it is perfect. I have a lot of Romanian friends in London and I will ask them to help Adrian and Chelsea settle in together and speed up the time it takes for him to feel at home in the city and with the English style of life.'

Mutu said, 'I am ready to start a new period of my life and I'm not afraid. It's a challenge and I like challenges and new experiences. I will play in the mother country of football, in a very strong competition with big clubs. I hope I will receive my work permit in time to be on the pitch in the opening game against Liverpool. What a big game that will be. For me, the choice wasn't anything to do with money but for the sporting opportunity to play in a great team with great ambitions and great players. There is also the sure fact they will play in the Champions League. I know that in England the emphasis is on force and the play is more free, there are not so many tactics-based moments during the game – but I'm not scared. The Coach is an Italian. That's great as it will guarantee I will have a good relationship with him and be able to produce some spectacular football. I'm also not afraid about the weather. Somebody said it is cold and always raining in England. These are only excuses. London is not Greenland and I'm sure the pitches will be better than the ones I had in Verona, for example.

'To be here is already a won bet. London is a city that I like and that I know well and Chelsea is an ambitious club with clear ideas. It is a dream to be able to join such good players as those at Chelsea. It's an incredibly exciting challenge.'

Mark Viduka wanted to partner Mutu, but he was not on the wanted list. Auxerre's Djibril Cissé and Real Mallorca's Samuel Eto'o were under review. Prising Cissé from Auxerre was difficult because Coach Guy Roux threatened to quit if a striker was sold and has an understanding with his friend Gérard Houllier that Cissé will move to Anfield in the summer of 2004.

Eto'o, once valued at around £12m, was available for £6.9m because of financial problems at Mallorca. Tentative talks with Chelsea were held after Mallorca's friendly at Bolton. Eto'o has a disruptive reputation after being involved in several verbal and physical incidents in Spain. The Cameroon ace blew his top when new boss Jaime Pacheco refused to let him swap his shorts for tracksuit trousers. Eto'o claimed he was freezing as Mallorca trained in Birmingham on the first day of their 12-day stay. He walked straight out of the training camp.

Chelsea wanted a goal-scoring match-winner to rank alongside Ruud van Nistelrooy and Thierry Henry, and a deal for Vieri in excess of £20m had been mooted, but Inter's Sports Director Marco Branca said, 'Vieri is not on the market. We have not received any official offers for Vieri. He will definitely stay at Inter Milan.'

Asked if he felt he still needed to sign a top-class striker, even if it was not Vieri, Ranieri tetchily replied, 'What I need I speak with Mr Abramovich about – not you.'

Zahavi's mission was now to sort out the midfield before moving on to the strikers.

PSV Eindhoven's Dutch international midfielder Mark van Bommel was on the standby list because the £17.5m bid for Roma's Brazilian Emerson had been turned down. Chelsea turned to van Bommel as an alternative. PSV spokesman Pedro Salazar said, 'We have heard something from an agent who said that he was acting on behalf of Chelsea. He asked us what van Bommel would cost. But the man could not show us a guarantee that he was really speaking on behalf of Chelsea.'

Van Bommel said, 'I will speak with them only after the clubs have reached an agreement. And even then I first want to look around in London and at the Chelsea stadium. But their ambitions sound good. Chelsea at last want to make a real effort to win the championship and they want to have a serious role in the Champions League too.' But he was very much a stop-gap after Mekelele, Chelsea's first choice, if they couldn't get Emerson or Patrick Vieira, who was about to sign a new contract at Arsenal.

Agent Marc Roger let it be known that Chelsea offered £7m for Makelele. Roger, speaking outside the Bernabeu, insisted that Makelele was keen to join Chelsea where his wages would double to £2m per season. 'Unless Madrid improve his salary, next Monday will be his last day at the club. Claude has not been happy for the past two seasons. David Beckham has just joined Real and he is being paid five times more. An unhappy player is not a good player.'

Mekelele was definitely not happy. 'I worked really hard in midfield last season. Now Beckham has arrived, I will have to work three times harder. If I do the work of four, I should be paid four times as much.' Once Abramovich made his move, the price was always going up as Real knew he had the money and that they could still keep the player.

Makelele refused to train with Real and was fined £100,000 and left out of a friendly at Valencia. Real Madrid Sports Director Jorge Valdano demanded confirmation in writing that Chelsea had not 'unsettled or approached' Makelele, who twice refused to train, submitting a doctor's note to excuse himself. The note claimed he was depressed and unable to train or play. Valdano said, 'Chelsea suddenly have lots of new cash and their new owner seems to believe that money solves everything. But Chelsea are not in charge of this situation and if their owner thinks that money is the answer to the problem, then he is quite wrong.' Valdano then pragmatically agreed that he expected to 'welcome directors from Chelsea' to the Bernabeu offices to talk about the Makelele situation 'because we are a courteous club and we will always open our doors to other respectful people'. Valdano indicated that Real will do business if they can find a midfield replacement for the Frenchman and, if Makelele apologises for his behaviour. Ironically, the player Chelsea wanted most was Vieri.

Makelele said, 'My head's not right just now to train or anything like that. The only thing that's for sure is that I have a brilliant and important offer and I feel it must be studied. Every year, the player who has the most offers from elsewhere is me and that means a lot. I'm not happy but I will not allow myself to be taken advantage of. I have to feel good to be able to give my all.'

Real informed FIFA that they would refuse to release Makelele for international duty against Switzerland because, if he was not able to train or play for the club, then the same conditions should apply to France.

Roger said, 'Florentino Perez said last year that he would sell Makelele for 10m euros and I am sure that Chelsea will offer a lot more than that. Perez even named a price for Claude – 10m euros in cash or 12m euros in two instalments. On Monday, the people from Chelsea are coming here; I have a great deal of respect for Florentino and I respect his word.'

Makelele's wages are a fifth of those of the club's high-profile stars like Ronaldo, Zidane, Raul and now Beckham. 'Claude knows he cannot earn the same as the top stars, but he feels badly treated,' continued Roger. 'He would be a star for Chelsea but he will never be one at Madrid.'

Makelele, who has won 24 caps for Les Bleus, was desperate to seal a move to London as quickly as possible. The former Nantes player still had three years left on his contract at the Bernabeu after moving to Madrid from Celta Vigo in 2000.

Birch hinted that the move for Makelele had broken down despite the French midfielder's decision to go on strike over his wages. Birch said, 'I don't think there will be any movement with Makelele. We want to stay out of it.'

Meanwhile, the awkward possibility of Chelsea meeting Maccabi Tel Aviv in the qualifying round for the Champions League did not appeal at all, regurgitating some painful memories. Chelsea crashed out in the second round of the UEFA Cup to Maccabi's neighbours, Hapoel Tel Aviv, two years earlier, a defeat made more embarrassing by the refusal of six players to travel because of the repercussions following the 9/11 terrorist attacks in America. Current players Desailly, Gallas, Petit and Gudjohnsen all took the decision to stay at home because of security fears. Chelsea lost the first away leg of that match 2-0. Ranieri's team were then held 1-1 at Stamford Bridge as Hapoel secured the best ever result by any Israeli team in European club football.

A successful run to the later stages of the knock out phase would earn Chelsea £15m to £20m, but it is the glory, not the money, that matters to Abramovich.

Ranieri said that he was not concerned about which of Zilina or Tel Aviv his side would have to face. 'It is important to be in the Champions League, it is not important the name of the opponent. I have watched too many matches at Highbury with Arsenal against other teams in the Champions League.'

Asked about facing an Israeli team and whether or not he was concerned that some of his players may refuse to travel, he joked, 'That's why I buy 22 players.'

UEFA announced that due to ongoing tension in the region, Israeli teams would continue to play their home matches on neutral territory until mid-August. Then UEFA would make a final decision. Had Maccabi beaten Croatians SK Zilina over two legs, their third-round qualifier against Ranieri's side would have taken place in Cyprus.

Ranieri remained impressively impervious to all of the many slights regarding his survival prospects. Once Chelsea acquired a target-man, there would be cover in every position, something even Arsenal and Manchester United couldn't boast. 'I have 22, 24 players at the moment. Too many, too many!' Ranieri said with a knowing smile. 'It is very important that my players understand the new opportunities. All the big teams have good champions, they must understand this. I picked every one of my players, everybody, and then they know I like them. But I must pick 11. If they understand this, I think we are halfway there. We have four competitions, and at the moment you play every three days. I need everybody. I like to make changes in a match, but the style, the philosophy, we keep the same.'

Marcel Desailly signed up for an extra year. The 34-year-old defender was expected to retire when his contract at Stamford Bridge runs out at the end of the 2003/04 season. But Desailly signed a new agreement that ties him to Chelsea until 2005. He explained how the rebuilding under new owner had persuaded him to stay on. 'The new people running the club have shown that they are building for the long term. This means that I will be able to finish my career in Europe at a big club. This is a new beginning for Chelsea. There is a new management team and a new generation of players at the club. I am captain and I think the new Chairman wants me involved thoroughly. I am really glad to have extended my contract. I will be able to begin the new season calmly, without the need to ask myself next April what I should do. That has been sorted out. There is no way I will regard the new deal as a thank-you for services rendered. Footballers don't get given those sort of presents.

'Our aim is to do the best we can and be consistent at the highest level. But it is certainly not to win the Premier League. I believe we have recruited very cleverly. The Chairman doesn't want to pull off an instant coup. He is thinking long term. All the new signings are aged under 30. Joe Cole has achieved great things with West Ham and Juan Sebastian Veron could become the engine of the side. He wants to build something that is long lasting and we should follow the excellent example set by Manchester United. We look very well equipped to achieve a great season, but it was a similar story with the French national team ahead of the 2002 World Cup finals and then we got knocked out in the first round. Our aim is to do the best we can and be consistent at the highest level. But it is certainly not to win the Premier League. There is a lot of pressure on the club now. Results are expected instantly, but the team needs time to gel. We will achieve results in the medium term. Chelsea have signed a lot of players and that has not gone unnoticed by other clubs because nobody besides ourselves has been buying players this summer.'

Desailly wanted to land the biggest club prizes before he retired. 'This is a really important season for Chelsea and I want to bring the biggest prizes to the club. We have to start well and hopefully we can surprise some people. It's really important that we progress in the Champions League and get to test ourselves against the big teams. We're not looking too far ahead but have to get through. We have to be careful. We need to play as a team and maintain a high level.'

Ranieri fielded almost £50m of new talent against Zilina – Bridge, Veron, Duff and Geremi. Ranieri said, 'This is the first game of our season and it is important to do well. But I am sure the players will not be nervous. If they are nervous, I will shoot myself. For everybody at Chelsea, our life has changed. This is a new Chelsea.'

Ranieri demanded that the club forget past humiliations and instead repeat their run to the last eight of the Champions League three years ago before he was in charge. He added, 'It was fantastic for Chelsea to reach the quarter-finals. But I want to taste the atmosphere myself.'

Ranieri's notorious tinkering with a much smaller squad was blamed for loss of form around Christmas 2002, but he remains adamant that he will continue to experiment. The 51-year-old, a bundle of nervous energy at the best of times, is fascinated by tactical systems and variations. Maybe it is significant that Zilina's premier tourist attraction is the Provazske Museum ... dedicated to the history of tinkering!

He said, 'I change my players because I am a 'tinker-man'. Some players can play in lots of positions and it's important to be flexible. In my opinion, the modern game is all about changing things during the match. I will not play one team for Europe and one for the Premiership. There will be one team, one Chelsea, but I have a lot of players and they must be flexible. I gathered the list of players I wanted and now I'm happy.'

Strangely, there was little interest in the game from most radio and TV outlets. The BBC eventually bought all the rights for the game for less than £50,000.

Ranieri's pampered athletes were guaranteed an inhospitable experience in the uncomfortable 12,000-capacity Pod Dubnom stadium. The Slovakian champions were also enjoying exciting times, winning their first domestic Double, although Chairman Karo Belanik sacked three managers during the season before Coach Milan Lesicky delivered the silverware. Chelsea's spending up to that point had hit £75m; in the corresponding two months, Zilina were forced to sell their captain for £500,000, the club's operating budget for the entire season is £650,000 and their record signing cost just £100,000. Veron earns more in a day than any of the Slovakians earn in a year. Although they reached the quarter-finals of the European Cup Winners' Cup in 1961, Chelsea's visit was the biggest event in the club's 95-year history.

Lesicky described his team as the 'Trabant' of the tournament, a reference to the old East German motor industry. Comparatively, they faced a veritable Rolls-Royce. Yet he believed his team had a chance. 'It's a huge game and we're very excited. We're a small town and it's the first time we've played against such a big team. Chelsea are a big European club and they hope to become the biggest. It's going to be very difficult but we have a 10 per cent chance. Even if we get one draw over the two games, it will be a great achievement. For our supporters, it will be a big day, a holiday for football fans. It's going to be a big celebration for everybody in Slovakia. I hope they have a good time. Everybody wants to see Chelsea and all their great players. It's a very big moment for the city of Zilina.'

John Terry was adamant the players would respond to Ranieri. 'We want to do very well for Claudio. There has been a lot of speculation about Sven but the Manager has done a superb job to get us where we are before he got any money. He gets the lads buzzing during training. He is the Manager who gave me my chance at Chelsea and I want him to stay. Now he has some money, has brought in new faces and is looking to take us further. It's down to us now. He has done a lot for the players here and we can reward him by qualifying. The signings we have made have raised expectations but it won't happen overnight. However, we should do well.'

Terry sees the extra competition for places as an advantage. 'We're not too sure what team he's going to play. Obviously, some of the lads have had a shorter pre-season than others and maybe that'll influence his squad. I don't know, but it'll be a strong side whoever he picks. We've clicked straight away. I thought it'd take a few months and the lads have surprised me with how quickly they've settled in. It'd be wrong for me to say that players are happy sitting on the bench because that won't be the case, but we'll have games coming thick and fast. If we have a good run in the Champions League, we could have 60 games and it's difficult to play that many. If the Manager thinks that a player needs a rest, then he can bring in a player who's just as good.'

It was time to stop being a soft touch in Europe. Terry continued, 'It's about time we put all that right and qualified for the Champions League. We are expected to beat Zilina but it depends how we play on the day. Everyone wants us to slip up, but I can assure you it won't happen this time. We have let the fans down in the past, let the club down and ourselves down over the last few years. This time we're going to put it right and have a good run.'

Terry was shocked at the speed of the Abramovich revolution. 'I have been as surprised as anyone. When I went to sign my new deal, I asked Chief Executive Trevor Birch whether there would be any new players and wanted to know if William Gallas and Eidur Gudjohnsen were staying. He said they were staying and, with a grin, said there would be new players coming. The takeover came out of nowhere but it is great for the club. Now we are all looking forward to the Champions League.'

Abramovich was regrettably still in Russia on business but he was given regular updates abroad his yacht, *Le Grand Bleu*, which was bought from Miscrosft founder Paul Allen for £50m, and at 355ft, is the fourth-largest in the world. He missed out on Chelsea's nine-hour trip to the most northerly outpost of Slovakia, which included a final 180-mile coach trip from Bucharest to Zilina. He had the game beamed round the world via a live BBC satellite feed to the dining-room table of his luxury yacht in Alaska. It was probably no surprise to him that Hasselbaink was left on the bench while young Forssell partnered Gudjohnsen up front. He had been kept informed of every move, every decision, including the team selection. Johnson and Bridge made their competitive débuts, as did Veron, but there was no starting place for Cole as Duff and Geremi joined Lampard in midfield.

Gary Lineker opened the BBC2 coverage explaining that he had not expected to be covering a qualifier in the Champions League, but Alan Hansen described events at Chelsea as 'phenomenal'. Co-commentator Mark Bright had been roaming the local streets for interviews with travelling fans who had told him how excited they were with expectations of winning the League and doing well in Europe.

MSK Zilina 0-2 Chelsea

Duff earned Hansen's praise for an exhilarating first-half display. A late own goal and a first-half strike by Gudjohnsen sealed it. With the exception of the ineligible Mutu, all six signings played. Five started, with Cole coming off the bench to replace Duff. The team in full was: Cudicini, Johnson, Bridge, Desailly, Terry, Veron, Geremi, Lampard, Duff (J Cole), Forssell (Gronkjaer) and Gudjohnsen. The substitutes not used were Ambrosio, Hasselbaink, Melchiot, Huth and C Cole.

Joe Cole played a part in the second goal on 75 minutes, releasing Gudjohnsen. Just as the Icelander was about to shoot, substitute Michal Drahno assisted by curling the ball past his own keeper and into the corner.

Ranieri was delighted with a commanding display at full-back from Johnson, impressing watching England assistant Tord Grip.

Lampard knows his place is under threat, yet missed a cracking chance for an early lead. After Dutch referee Rene Timmink had played a sensible advantage following a foul, Lampard, with only the keeper Trabalik to beat, screwed the ball wide.

Duff caused the Slovakian champions considerable problems and Chelsea took the lead in the 42nd minute with an impressive flowing move, with Duff playing a one-two with Forssell before delivering a perfect low cross from the left that Gudjohnsen guided in at the far post. From one corner of the ground, the Chelsea fans, 260 of them, started their first celebrations of the campaign.

Ranieri said, 'Wayne Bridge and Glen Johnson helped make the team compact and also pushed forward. Geremi gave good balance in midfield, Juan Veron gave a lot of quality to the team but I think Damien Duff and Joe Cole played very well. Duff was the best. Every ball he made was very dangerous. Our touch and movement was very good and it was very important to win.'

Lesicky admitted, 'Chelsea were the better team.'

Gudjohnsen lost half a stone in a bid to improve his sharpness and is feeling the benefit. He said, 'I missed out last year and was always a step behind the other players. I did a lot of extra training during the summer and am feeling a lot sharper, a yard quicker and a bit leaner. I want to play every week and just have to take my chances. It's always nice to score, especially as a forward. As a striker you thrive on goals and have to try to stake your claim. We've always had lots of strikers and, if you play in a big team, there's bound to be competition for places.'

Gudjohnsen had a fight to keep his place with the arrival of Mutu and speculation intensifying over the recruitment of a new centre-forward. The 24-year-old also urged Chelsea fans to give the side time to settle. He said, 'It's a big game on Sunday and there's a lot of expectation. Liverpool will present a greater footballing challenge. We should do well but, with new players, it always takes a while. It might sound a bit cautious but with seven new players to fit in, it will take time. I hope the fans don't expect fireworks straight away.'

Forssell made his first Chelsea appearance in 14 months raising further doubts over the future of Hasselbaink. The Dutch striker was dropped to avoid him becoming cup-tied in Europe in case he was sold, which would affect his value. Hasselbaink has attracted interest from Real Betis and Real Mallorca, but is adamant that he will stay and fight for his place. He said, 'There was talk last season about me leaving but I've always said I want to stay. I still feel I have something to give and I'm ready to play if the Manager picks me. The competition is high but that's fine. We've got five good strikers and every Premiership team would like to have the players of Chelsea. I want to stay and fight for my place, which I am going to do.'

Duff felt his new team could have played better. 'We've had five or six pre-season games. We all feel good and we were all looking forward to the game tonight. It was our first competitive game and we are glad of the win. There are a lot of top-quality players here. I did think we played well but obviously we could play better. It's always nice to set up a goal – that's my job. It was important to get a win tonight. We've got a huge game on Sunday so were all looking forward to that.'

Lampard was clearly concerned about the possibility of the signing of Makelele. He said, 'We can't lose sight of the people that are already here – we have a lot of good players that can take the club forward where the boss wants to be.

'I'd like to think I can be involved with that, along with several other players. It will be difficult to get into the team but our club is unique – we can buy pretty much anyone. We have got the players to win the League and do well in the Champions League. Now we have got to go and do it and it was good to get off to the start we did.

'It is a challenge. You try and raise your game to meet that and I am trying to do that. I've heard the rumours of Makelele and it will be a lot of competition. But I am sure he would not be guaranteed a place. That would be madness.'

Lampard was the only member of last season's midfield who started the first game. 'I thought we had a good squad last year and, if we had not beaten Liverpool in the final game of the season to get into the Champions League, maybe none of this would have happened. But I would like the players who got us here in the first place to be able to stay and play a part along with the ones who have come in. I would like to think the likes of myself, John Terry and the others who were regulars last season are the heartbeat of the team and that we are going to be given the chance to help take the club forward.'

Asked if he had explained to Hasselbaink and other squad members why they had been omitted from the starting side, the Italian boss said, 'I didn't explain the selection and I'm not going to do that. I've got 26 players, so if I had to explain my decisions to all of them I'd have to spend all my time doing that and never get on the training ground. But, of course, if they want to speak to me, I'm ready to talk.'

The biggest dilemma will be finding a way to get the best out of Veron, who started on the right and demonstrated commitment and industry allied to his natural vision, but appeared to relish more his spell in the middle. Veron was keen to come in off his flank and Lampard added, 'Seba's got licence because he's used to playing on the left or through the centre. We want to get him on the ball and he can roam to find it. It's up to us to get him the ball because if we can do that he will pick the passes out, over the back four and in behind people. I know that with him coming in then maybe I will have to hold a bit more at times, but I would like to play the game I did last season. If I have to restrain my game, I will do that, although I still think getting forward is part of the way I play. I want to play my own game and, hopefully, that will get me in the team.'

Johnson was preferred to Mario Melchiot and grasped the opportunity as he allowed Veron the freedom to wander by patrolling the right flank. Johnson said, 'It's hard to believe what's happened, but I have tried to take it all in my stride. I feel composed and calm, I always have been. That is the sort of player I am and the sort of person I am. Somebody told me Tord Grip was there. People say if I can break into this Chelsea team, I might have a chance for England, but I'm not paying any attention to that. It's good to be part of this.'

16

RAISING THE STAKES ...
AND SLASHING THE ODDS

ROMAN ABRAMOVICH ARRIVED AT the Bridge on Friday afternoon for a summit meeting with key Board members for a comprehensive update, before flying by private helicopter to Merseyside, where he would be escorted to the ground by a fleet of security cars to watch his first Premiership match in charge of Chelsea.

First to arrive was Claudio Ranieri, stopping only for a photograph with a young fan; then came Pini Zahavi, looking tanned and as youthful as ever. Eventually, Abramovich arrived flanked by four security minders; he was casually dressed in his trade mark faded jeans, a green, untucked Burberry polo shirt, and open-toed sandals. Abramovich and his advisers were analysing the most expensive experiment in the history of football ... 46 days, £75 million, nine new players.

Speaking through a trusted interpreter and with a broad smile on his face, he said, 'I can't wait for the season to start, I'm so excited, it's the most excited I've been for a long time. There is a great deal of pleasure in building something up, now we have to build something special here at Chelsea.'

Abramovich was stopped by a fan close to the Megastore, eager to show his appreciation. 'Welcome to Chelsea, Mr Abramovich, welcome to England. Thank you for all you're doing, good luck, thank you.'

The Friday summit included Manager Ranieri, Chief Executive Trevor Birch, Director Richard Creitzman and super-agent Zahavi. Having arrived at Heathrow just after lunch, he flew by private helicopter to Battersea and arrived at Stamford Bridge together with his entourage in a pair of silver 735iL BMWs.

Richard Creitzman acted as interpreter in the meeting between Abramovich and Ranieri. What did they talk about? 'He wants success, a three-nil win at Liverpool,' Creitzman jokes, before adding earnestly, 'He wants to win.'

Ranieri might advise caution to his fans, but he knows he has to deliver with the goods presented to him. 'The expectation is higher now, but I still do not think we can win the League. Maybe the stupid man could think Chelsea will win the championship and set the expectations too high, but the intelligent man cannot think this way and nor do I. There are three big, big teams who have been together for many years – Manchester United, Arsenal and Liverpool. We are starting now and there is a big difference between us and them. How many years was Alex Ferguson working with his team before Manchester United won the title? We start now. It's impossible to compare us. Of course I want to win the title, but we are outsiders at the moment and the underdog can always win, but everything has changed here in one go. We are not favourites because lots of new players are coming and it started a few weeks ago.

'The other thing is we have brought young players like Glen Johnson, Joe Cole and Damien Duff. If you want to win the title immediately, you should be buying players who are 28 or 29 and who have that experience. Then you can try to win. We are trying to build, but we are as ambitious as Arsenal and United. I would love to have the responsibility of being the favourite but I'm not now.'

On the eve of the new season, a total of £172m had been spent in player transfers among the Premiership clubs – £75m of it by Chelsea.

But that figure would have been even lower because so much was spent in England – £54m – which has filtered through initiating other deals in a knock-on effect. The £7m paid for Wayne Bridge, for example, enabled Southampton to bring in seven players, including £3m striker Kevin Phillips. Chelsea's contribution was 44 per cent of the total spent by all 20 clubs and only £20m less than the other 19 combined, but there was still time.

Manchester United Chief Executive Peter Kenyon enthused, 'It hasn't changed our strategy because we play our own game, but there is no doubt the activities of Chelsea have ignited what was otherwise a pretty stagnant market. In most, or even all, cases, we've never been head to head with them on players, so we've never felt any direct influence. But the one positive factor is that a lot of money has been circulated in the English game, which is the first time that has happened in a long time, and that is what has stimulated the other moves.'

Eddie Barnett, box-office manager, was calculating the increase in income. He said, 'The whole place is just electric with excitement, whether you be an employee or a supporter. I think the fact that we've sold a record number of season tickets is a reflection of that. We did stop selling season tickets at one time after reaching our original capping point but, with the signing of Damien Duff, our Chief Executive, Trevor Birch, decided to reintroduce sales because of the demand. Now we've discontinued non-corporate season-ticket sales because we've reached our increased maximum of 20,508, the figure set by the Board to be fair to our members and people who can't afford season tickets. That's worth a monetary income of more than £13m, which is a record and a magnificent performance. I think it shows the dedication of Chelsea supporters as they see the quality of players being signed. I will be very disappointed now, with the quality of the team we have got, if we do not sell out for every home Premier League match. Of the 19 league games at Stamford Bridge last season, six sold out totally, which means corporate and non-corporate. We want that to be the case for home matches this season. The team are setting high objectives so everybody at the club is doing the same.'

For all their expenditure on famous players over the generations, the only time Chelsea have ever won the League championship, in the 1954/55 season, it was largely with a job lot of footballers in a predominantly Third Division-inspired forward line under Manager Ted Drake. The Championship-winning team had two inside-forwards bought from the Third Division South – John McNichol, signed from Brighton in August 1952 for £15,000, and Les Stubbs from Southend United, who also cost five figures in the following December. The most inspired acquisition of all was the 18-year-old left-winger Frank Blunstone, from Crewe Alexandra of the Third Division North, who in no time at all would be playing for England. He arrived in February, 1953, the same year Derek Saunders, red-haired and reliable, a quietly effective left-half and captain, came from amateurs Walthamstow Avenue for nothing. He didn't miss a league game in the championship season. The same club provided the British Olympic international winger, Jim Lewis Jnr. Seamus O'Connell, a blond inside-left, like Lewis, still an amateur, had played for Bishop Auckland. There were veterans such as Ron Greenwood, the future West Ham and England Manager, who had 21 league games that season at centre-half, and John Harris, now a right-back, who had been the centre-half before him. Ken Armstrong, a Yorkshire-born right-half, had once filled in at centre-forward. But now the position was splendidly taken by Roy Bentley, the one outstanding talent in the team, and England's striker in the ill-fated 1950 World Cup Finals, scorer of 22 of Chelsea's 81 league goals in that celebrated season. He came in 1948 from Newcastle United for £11,000.

They took the title with 52 points, four ahead of Wolves, Portsmouth and Sunderland. They should have gone on to contest the first ever European Cup, but their Chairman Joe Mears, also President of the Football League, was bullied out of it by the League's Secretary Alan Hardaker.

The 2003/04 season kicked off with 15 shopping days before the 31 August transfer deadline and Chelsea were chasing at least two more players.

As well as Vieri there were discussions about Hernan Crespo, while Makelele was still very much 'on'. Birch said, 'Will we see more signings this month? I can't really comment. There is a possibility because there are areas we are looking at. Christian Vieri and Hernan Crespo are on the list that Claudio's looking at but it's a long list. Buying this many players is unusual and that's where the skill of the Manager comes in, blending things and getting the balance right. From what I have seen out there in training, there's a great spirit within the club and the new boys seem to have settled in really well.'

Neil Barnett, Chelsea TV presenter and programme editor, said, 'I do three live phone-ins a week and sense from the fans who are calling up that, more than trophies or championships, they're looking forward to entertainment. There's a lot of celebration at Chelsea at the moment as a place of high entertainment after the signing of players like Veron, Cole and Duff. I've interviewed all the players who have been bought this summer and the best was probably Joe Cole because we were live on air when he signed. He was filmed signing and then whipped into the studio. A lot of Joe's family are lifelong Chelsea supporters and people aren't generally aware that Joe went to our 1994 and 1997 FA Cup Finals. In '94 he played for Chelsea schoolboys that morning against Tottenham because we were trying to sign him. We won 4-2 and he scored a goal that's still remembered, flicking the ball over his head and then turning round and cracking it.

'In training, Veron has been unbelievable. His touches are beyond belief. I would say he's made the biggest impact on the first day of training since Gianfranco Zola. The only other person I've seen have an impact anything like that was Hoddle on his first day as player–manager.'

Parma received the first instalment of the £15.8m fee and, although Mutu received his work permit, he was not granted his international clearance because of a public holiday in Italy on Friday. Mutu flew into England on Thursday and trained with his new team-mates after their return from Slovakia. Mutu, handed the number 7 shirt, hoped to play in the opening match against Liverpool after spending three weeks in summer training with Parma, playing in three matches, but he would have to wait a little longer for his début.

Ranieri said, 'Mutu will be the second striker. He is young and scored many goals in Italy, which shows he is dangerous and he is clever and strong. I have said Jimmy is a shark and Carlton Cole a lion. Mutu is another predator – I have a zoo!' Starting out as a professional in 1996 with small Romanian side Arges Pitesti, Mutu's wages were just £75 a week, and rose to £6,000 a year when he joined Dinamo in 1999. In his first season at Dinamo Bucharest he scored a goal a game, and netted a further 18 goals in Serie A over the next two years.

Gallas could only make the bench, having sustained a knee injury in training. He said, 'I have only just begun training again and I do not think I will play against Liverpool. I expect John Terry and Marcel Desailly to play in the centre of defence. The injury was caused because I started training later than everyone else after I was in the Confederations Cup and I was trying to be ready for the Champions League. But I am not worried. I need to take things slowly and must be given the time to find my rhythm, but I know I will find my form very quickly.'

That ensured a start for Glen Johnson and the kid was aiming high in his ambitions for the team this season. 'It has to be the title. No one goes out to finish second, do they?'

Geremi is still struggling to find his bearings since making his move to the capital a month ago. He ended up on the outskirts of Oxford as he tried to find Chelsea's Harlington training HQ near Heathrow Airport. Geremi was travelling round the M25 after leaving his Chelsea hotel, but missed the turn-off for the M4 and took one for the M40 instead. Damien Duff sympathised. 'I haven't a clue where I'm driving at the moment. London's streets can be a nightmare.'

Geremi prefers the defensive role in the middle of the park, but can also play as a containing right-midfielder or right-winger. And he knows all about Makelele because the Frenchman kept him out of the Real side for three years, forcing him to try his luck elsewhere – and Makelele's shadow may well loom again at Stamford Bridge. 'Last year went so well for me [on a year-long loan] at Middlesbrough,' Geremi says, 'and I got such a kick from playing in England that I was really keen to stay in the Premiership. The game really suits me and I am just pleased I went to Boro last season. They are nowhere near as big as Real, but they gave me a wonderful opportunity to get a taste of the Premiership. Boro gave me the chance to show managers what I could do. I played in most matches and did pretty well, so I guess it served as a launchpad for my career on these shores.'

Geremi freely admits that his move to SW6 is a dream come true. 'To be at one of the biggest clubs in the country, if not Europe, where there is clearly lots of ambition and competition, is unbelievable for me. The new owner wants to turn Chelsea into one of the superpowers, and we know it is up to us to help him achieve his ambition. We've been given all the help we can hope for to challenge for the biggest honours, so there can be no excuses. I came here to be a winner.'

Just how quickly success will come? 'It's difficult to say because there are so many new players. That's just a reality, so we have to make sure we get off to a good start. Looking at it now, I would say we have a better chance of winning the Champions League. The Premiership is a tricky competition that requires more experience to win, but we are perfectly set up for Europe.'

Houllier was under his own pressure at Anfield. He said, 'Everyone would like to have that sort of thing – every manager in the country would be happy to have it. But you can live a very unhappy life if you spend your time pushing the curtains and watching people outside with better food, better clothes or better pay than you. I think I have great players, with a great mentality, and I have great belief in them – and they know that. Sometimes we have a tendency to think that the grass is greener in other places but I have no sentiment of jealousy or envy. We are all excited about the prospect of having a new, extremely strong competitor in the Premiership.

'In fairness, Claudio Ranieri has done a good job, and he has consistently done well. Sometimes, it does not take long for players to gel. The team itself can be achieved very quickly depending on the quality of players you have.

'It is an exciting season for all of us, made even more so by Chelsea rebuilding themselves. It's good that sometimes things change and they have changed the whole market for the good of some clubs. Chelsea will be as big a threat as Manchester United or Arsenal, because they had a good base beforehand.'

Houllier worried that the clash came too early in the season for the Kop after the Londoners' incredible summer shopping spree. 'The fixtures are not under my control but, in an ideal world, I'd like to play them five or six games into the season. You don't have Arsenal against Manchester United on the first day of the season. I would prefer to play them with my full team.' He was without midfield dynamos Steven Gerrard and Dietmar Hamann.

Houllier insists he wouldn't do anything differently – even if he had Abramovich's buying power. 'I would have made some signings if I had that kind of money, but I wouldn't have made all of them. I would have waited. It doesn't take long to build a team, but it takes a lot longer to build a club. The whole culture and philosophy of the place cannot be built overnight.

'Father Christmas has arrived at Chelsea and I don't think they expected that to happen. Abramovich has changed the face of the club. It will make things more exciting, but we work a little bit differently here. We may not be able to buy everyone but we have qualities some teams can't buy. I'm sure Chelsea will challenge for the title, but time will tell if they can last.'

Owen was concerned about Chelsea's potential to stay ahead of Liverpool. He said, 'Before they have even kicked a ball in the League, I can see them finishing between first and fourth place. I would put them behind Manchester United and Arsenal at the moment because they are such an unknown quantity. They had a good team before the spending started and I felt their defence was one of the best in the Premiership, and the addition of Johnson and Bridge will make them even stronger in that department. It all depends on how quickly they fit together as a unit because it does take time for new players to adapt. But if they hit it off straight away and get on a roll, they will take some stopping.'

Houllier remains convinced he can improve last year's disappointing fifth-place finish. 'No manager, even Alex Ferguson or Arsene Wenger, can say they are going to win it, but we will fight for our lives to do so. This team is gradually getting near to it. These two or three coming seasons will be very exciting for the club.'

Chelsea had won just once at Anfield since December 1935, and the big question was whether a new group of players who'd been thrown together could become a team overnight.

Ranieri observed, 'I am sure the puzzle is good, but only the matches can say if it is or not. What we achieved last season was from unity. What everybody expects this season is the maximum. Mr Abramovich asks me, "What, Claudio, what do you want? What do you need?" I give him a long, long list, and one by one they come. It is like having a new Ferrari a day. I am not afraid of the responsibility. I came to be a manager because I like this responsibility. It is the best job in the world!

'No player is guaranteed a shirt. Take Veron. I am a "tinker-man", but I am not stupid. For me, Veron can be everything he wants in my team. I have good ambience with Argentinian players, with South Americans. With Veron, he must be in the middle. Why did I start with him on the right in Zilina? Simple ... he had been with us only a few days. He is intelligent, very intelligent. I ask him to play this role, he understands. But I believe he is a better player than you saw in Manchester. You will see, but don't ask me to say in how many matches. We have many new players, I have to make the blend and it would be stupid to say we will be better this season than Manchester, than Arsenal, than Liverpool.'

'Look,' he says earnestly, 'I spoke to all my players and told them, "If everybody thinks they are first eleven, there is a problem. If you can think you are second eleven, we can bond very well." If a player is happy to do his job within the group – fantastic. But if a player suffers too much, I will try to help him in every way, and if it is impossible, I'll help them to find another team. I want loyalty. If you are not happy to fight for a place, don't come here. Intelligent players can create a good group feeling – and this group could win everything. But if your first opponents are your team-mates, you win nothing.'

Ranieri won't rotate one team domestically and one in Europe. 'No, no,' he says, 'I prefer to be a "tinker-man". There isn't a first or second Chelsea, there is one Chelsea.'

But whatever is said, it would be the actions on the pitch, and the results, that would define the manager's future and that of the players. 'Everywhere,' muses Ranieri, 'even under the sea, they are talking about Chelsea.'

How long it will take him to turn the profusion of new players into a winning unit is the one question he cannot answer. 'I don't even know for how long I will have the chance,' he says. 'With time, we can do everything. It's like a building. At the moment we have bought a good area in the middle of Chelsea and the project is fantastic. But Manchester is a castle! Liverpool is a castle! We need time. How much, I don't know. You know when you build something, and you have a problem because it rains, then you need iron and it doesn't arrive ... Of course, I'm ambitious for a roof garden, but the foundations and the lower floors are what matter now. If we put that down, I'm telling you, the building will be fantastic.'

Ranieri planned to achieve what Sir Alex failed to do with Veron. 'I've always had good links with South American players. Only Ariel Ortega was a little difficult at Valencia, but all the rest, Careca [Brazil] at Napoli, Enzo Francescoli [Uruguay] at Cagliari, Daniel Fonseca [Uruguay] at Cagliari and Napoli, Gabriel Batistuta [Argentina] at Fiorentina and Claudio Lopez [Argentina] at Valencia, I had a good relationship with. Veron is very intelligent, he doesn't need to always be saying, "I'm the best." He's a fantastic man.'

He thinks his 'Little Witch' will flourish. Ranieri said, 'Do I believe I will get more out of Veron? Yes. It's difficult to say why he didn't do it at Manchester United, but I think I have a very good link with Argentinian players and if I link well with Veron he will be a different player. I think I can get more out of him, it's a feeling.'

And Veron's best position? 'In the middle.' So why play him on the right in Slovakia? 'It was the first match. I cannot change too much. I may be the "tinker-man" but I'm not stupid.'

Since the Second World War, Chelsea have won only twice at Anfield. The most recent victory occurred in the season before the Premiership began and the goal-scorers were Vinnie Jones and Dennis Wise ... it would be some start, then, if the new Chelsea could win at Liverpool.

17

THE REDS GET THE BLUES

ROMAN ABRAMOVICH'S PERSONAL BOEING 737 touched down from Moscow at the John Lennon Airport in Speke moments after 2.00pm, as a posse of his friends and close associates had just arrived from the same destination on the Global Express business jet. A private helicopter ferried in his security contingent from London. A convoy of sleek silver Mercedes completed the journey to Anfield together with the security team.

The Abramovich party of 14 arrived with Roman in a smart suit but without a tie. He stopped briefly at the entrance to Anfield to sign a few autographs. A brief appearance on the touchline with Richard Creitzman, Trevor Birch and his minders, brought him closer to the Chelsea fans than ever before and, when they spotted him, the travelling army of supporters gave him a warm welcome. He gave them an embarassed-looking wave.

The Russian delegation breezed past a stunned-looking Boardroom steward as the Tsar of the Bridge and his entourage took his seat a quarter of an hour before kick-off to soak up the atmosphere ... with a tie. One of the edicts governing the directors' boxes at Anfield states that ties are mandatory, so Roman was duly supplied with one.

In the directors' box, Abramovich was flanked by his wife Irina, and accompanied by ten-year-old son Arkady, the eldest of his five children. This time, the strict 'no children' rule was waived. Irina was sporting the glittering £10,000 diamond-encrusted and gold Chelsea pin, and so, too, was Arkady. They were presents from Bates who had them made the day after Abramovich bought the club – one for Roman and one for his wife. As Roman had difficulty pinning it on his suit, his boy wore it proudly instead.

The story behind the badges is that there are only ten in existence. Bates had the first six made by a bespoke, indepedent jeweller, for his former Chief Executive Colin Hutchinson and his wife Linda, one for his ever-loyal fellow director Evonne Todd, one for Ruth Harding, one for himself and one for his partner Suzannah. Bates decided to commission them after Matthew Harding and Glenn Hoddle had been sporting their own versions of a Chelsea badge.

As the atmosphere built around Anfield, the England Coach arrived, and as Sven-Goran Eriksson walked through the doors, he bumped into a group of football reporters, one of whom caught his eye and asked, 'Come to watch your team, then?'

Only the new owner and his closest aides in the Anfield directors' box knew just how long Ranieri would remain manager. Seated beside Abramovich were business associates Eugene Shvidler and Richard Creitzman, the men whose advice the Russian relies on the most, with Suzannah and Bates on the outside.

It was a dream start. The supposedly private, almost reclusive and unemotional Russian looked intoxicated by the whole occasion. His body language throughout signalled unequivocally that yes, indeed, he was enjoying himself, so much so that after the match he stayed in the car park signing autographs for ten minutes.

Ranieri had spoken to Abramovich only three times prior to this game; he now had an opportunity to speak with him both before and after the match. Abramovich wished him good luck before the game, and congratulated him afterwards. The Manager recalled, 'All he said to me was "Good luck" before the game. I saw him afterwards and he was very happy.'

He sure was ... leaping up and down, high fives and yelling with delight at Seba Veron's opener, burying his head in his hands and then politely clapping when Michael Owen eventually scored from the penalty spot at the second attempt, and cheering with sheer delight at Hasselbaink's winner. The final whistle brought smiles, punching the air, clapping on the back and congratulatory handshakes from his entire entourage, who all went into overdrive. It was the first time Liverpool had lost their opening game at home since 1962, before the Beatles' first single, in fact, and it was only Chelsea's third victory at Anfield in the last 50 years, and their first victory at Anfield in the Premiership.

Abramovich, who had spent £75m on players so far, said, 'It was so exciting and an incredible experience. I'm very pleased with the performance and the result. I felt it with my heart and loved every moment. It was worth all the money I've put into this club and I'm so very, very happy.'

Despite the unprecedented spectacle of Chelsea's new Board and old Board sitting side by side in the directors' box, all eyes were fixed on the field. After the strains of 'You'll Never Walk Alone', it was to be a roller-coaster of emotions for the new owner as he watched his side make a perfect start. It was all the more remarkable that such an expensively assembled team was capable of producing such a display in just six weeks. But it was the new that fascinated the Chelsea travelling fans as they soon sang out 'there's only one Abramovich'. One of his fellow directors suggested to Abramovich that he acknowledge the fans with a clap. Looking a touch sheepish, he declined. But he didn't hold back as the goals and near misses punctuated an intense, if not classic, encounter.

Abramovich was poised to get the cheque book out again but Ranieri said, 'I don't know anything about more transfers, I am focused only on the Liverpool game, maybe tomorrow, but not now.'

Hasselbaink secured Chelsea the points with a late winner after Liverpool equalised through Owen's twice-taken penalty after Veron's opener – the new and old Chelsea blending perfectly when no one thought they would. Ranieri insisted Hasselbaink, who came on as a substitute at half-time for Gudjohnson, still has a future at Chelsea even though new striker Mutu had already been signed and the club wanted either Crespo or Vieri to lead the attack. Ranieri confirmed, 'I never said Jimmy was out of the club, others have said that, others brought it up. I have never said that Jimmy's out. I said I wanted to have 22 champions because, when you have some problems, you then have another champion to bring in. For me, this doesn't change anything. I made the change at half-time because we played in Zilina three days ago and I was sure Jimmy was very powerful before the match, and I said now you can play and do everything.'

The way the Dutchman celebrated, tearing his shirt off his back and twirling it over his head, suggested that he was making a statement of intent, aimed particularly at his Manager. He explained, 'It is exciting to try and get into the Chelsea team now. We have got 24 very good players at the club and everyone is fighting for their place. We all want to be part of this great squad and I am no different. I have already said that I am going to stay, nothing has changed.' No doubt, Jimmy also feels that he ought to be part of Chelsea's long-term future. We shall all see soon enough.

No one could quite understand why the Coach started with his wingers on the flanks opposed to their playing strengths. The 'tinker-man' quickly resolved the dilemma. Ranieri made his customary tactical changes throughout the match, with the first bringing a goal within seconds as Jesper Gronkjaer switched wings and pulled the ball back for Veron to score. 'I spoke to the players before the game and told them to be careful because I am the "tinker-man". I can switch everything.'

Ranieri had an ominous warning when he insisted they have only begun to scratch the surface of what they can achieve. He said, 'The new and the old players showed the same character – they showed they have heart and soul. It is a great start to the season. But we'll continue to work hard because the team is not a team yet. We will build slowly because there are a lot of players who have arrived. The new players as well as the old players showed their spirit and their heart, and that is a good sign.'

Veron revelled in the role as his team's anchor-man and playmaker in a five-man midfield that afforded him the protection he was never given at Old Trafford, and it was one up on Alex Ferguson. In just two games inside four days, he was looking like the player who tempted Fergie to splash out £28.1m two years ago.

Almost everything Chelsea conjured up stemmed from Veron, like the cunning first-time pass which should have seen Gudjohnsen put the match beyond Liverpool before half-time. There certainly seemed plenty of elation when he whacked home the opener as he arrived late to pounce on Jesper Gronkjaer's cross. The world already knew about his passing ability, but he proved what Phil Neville had been saying about his work-rate. Veron was chasing back and harrying defenders or sliding in with well-timed tackles, or defending bravely by heading clear from corners. 'I prefer to judge on a season rather than one game, but Veron showed what he can do today,' said Ranieri.

Veron felt that he was already beginning to settle down in London. He said, 'I believe that this could be the last team I play for in Europe, then after I leave here I could return home to Argentina. I can't believe Chelsea paid quite so much money as they did for me. I know the boss described me as the world's best midfielder. For me that is very flattering, because I'd never had the chance to work with him, and when your own coach says that, it puts a lot of responsibility on your shoulders, more than anything for the duty to correspond my play with what he said.'

Cole said, 'Veron is definitely the best player I have ever played with – better than anyone I can think of. He did very, very well. He was a great player at Manchester United and I am sure he will be at Chelsea, too. He is just quality and he could end up helping the England midfield as well in a way – I certainly hope so.'

Cole is convinced his new club can mount a serious challenge despite so many acquisitions. 'It will take time for us to gel totally as a team because there will be lots of different players used at different times. But good players can play well together anywhere. We've got off to a great one, but it is a long, hard season so we'll just keep it going.'

Cole started on the bench before replacing Duff. 'Every player coming to Chelsea knows the score. They know there will be times when they have to wait for their chance.'

Johnson and Bridge showed just why they could establish themselves as an international pairing for England, let alone their club. Both are assured at the back, although Bridge's challenge for the Liverpool penalty was rash, and both have the essential pace. Duff will cause even more problems, while Geremi provides the calm, steadying assurance of a rock-solid holding midfielder.

The Liverpool line-up comprised: Dudek, Carragher, Henchoz (Finnan), Hyypia, Riise, Kewell, Murphy, Biscan (Baros), Cheyrou (Diouf), Owen and Heskey.

Chelsea's team for the opening Premiership fixture included: Cudicini, Johnson (Gallas), Terry, Desailly, Bridge, Gronkjaer, Geremi, Veron, Lampard, Duff (J Cole) and Gudjohnsen (Hasselbaink).

Houllier was convinced his side should have earned a point but he was forced to concede that the new Chelsea are genuine contenders. The Frenchman said, 'I feel sorry for the players because they did really well. We had at least half a dozen chances in the first half. They had two – one was a save by Dudek and they scored with the other. Maybe our finishing is a problem – but Chelsea had a bit of luck at times. It's just a shame that, after getting the equaliser, the strikers didn't realise we were short in midfield or stay compact enough for their winner.'

Match officials have been told to keep an eye on the movement of goalkeepers at penalties this season. 'I thought the turning point would be the equaliser but it didn't prove to be the case,' Liverpool Manager Gérard Houllier said. 'We had a lot of chances but at the moment they aren't going our way. We had a good Liverpool performance in terms of effort and running. We had a lot of the ball but, once the first goal was scored, we knew it would be difficult.'

Even assistant referee Dave Babski's decision to give Owen a second chance from the penalty spot after Carlo Cudicini strayed off his line only served to heighten Hasselbaink's moment of glory. The replays showed that initially the linesman got it wrong as Veron had claimed at the time and Chelsea should have had a throw-in; and it was harsh on Cudicini having the penalty retaken as the Italian keeper only moved minimally as a reaction to Owen taking the kick.

One win only postponed discussions over Ranieri's future, yet the display of Veron in particular suggested that the Italian may retain his keys to his office at the Bridge for a while yet.

After the match, Ranieri asked Chelsea's fans to give his expensively assembled team time to blend. 'The team isn't a team yet and that's OK. It will be slowly, slowly for us. I have told my players they must work hard because they are not a team yet. But that is normal ... when you change a lot of players and they arrive all at once, it is not easy.

'Playing your first match at Liverpool isn't easy, but this win is important and it gives us a lot of confidence. We made mistakes because, for my players, everything is new. But I was very pleased because the old players showed the same character as the new players.'

For Ranieri, the most encouraging aspect was the early signs that his old guard may really have been inspired rather than cowed by the new competition. As Terry put it, 'Everyone wants to play well – and they know they can't afford not to.' Lampard had admitted that the sheer scale of the new influx had been a little unsettling, but the Romford-born midfield player reacted to the competition in exactly the right way, by raising his game. He had a hand in both goals and his performance suggested a player determined to hang on to his place.

Terry, originally living down the road from Lampard at Barking, turned in another awesome display at the back in front of Eriksson before joining up with Lampard for England duty. Terry revels in the competition for places at Chelsea. 'I know there could be another couple of new faces before the transfer window closes, but I don't mind the competition. If the

Manager buys another defender, then so be it. To be honest, there's been competition at Chelsea in my position for a couple of years so it will be nothing new. All you can do, if you get the opportunity, is take it. If you're in the team then it's down to you to stay in it and no one else. There is a real buzz about the club these days and the players are just as excited about what has happened as everybody else.

'We knew that Mr Abramovich was coming to see the match against Liverpool but, quite honestly, it made no difference who was in the grandstand. I thought we were the better team and deserved to win. The timing of their equaliser was a problem but we showed the spirit to come back. Even though there wasn't a lot of time left, I was shouting, "Come on, we can still win this," and we did. If we go on showing that kind of character, then anything can happen this season. Anything is possible.'

Ranieri said, 'John Terry got Man of the Match and I agree, but it's hard to single out any one player.' Clearly there were many men of the match! Cudicini won the Sky verdict, Terry another, while many thought it should go to Veron.

As he disappeared in a silver Merc, Abramovich was left speculating that, after the expected signing of his fellow Russian Alexei Smertin and a top-rate centre-forward, this was going to be an exhilarating first season in football.

Abramovich asked Veron for his shirt as a lasting memento of Chelsea's opening-day victory. 'He congratulated me and he asked me for my shirt after the game,' Veron revealed. 'I have a very good relationship with him.'

Veron's move to will allow him to prove he can be a Premiership star. 'I had good games in Manchester but I believe I will have better games at Chelsea because of the way we play. The Coach gives me more freedom and Ranieri and his praise is very important to me. It fills me with pride.'

Hansen, in his *Daily Telegraph* column, made some pertinent observations. He said, 'The players assembled by Roman Abramovich will have learnt one thing at least by now: that they have instantly become a team who everyone wants to beat and that the real tests lie ahead. For now, the signs are good. I have watched them come to Liverpool over the past two seasons and put in better performances than that, but lose. They have underachieved in previous seasons, but the strength in depth they have now is phenomenal and they showed the character to come back from a bizarre penalty decision. The £74.4 million worth of new players are no closer to evoking the hunger and desire that comes so easily at Old Trafford, but they have made a good start. I have already said that the kind of spirit that wins Premiership titles is not available to buy, however much money you have. But if this Chelsea team are not still in contention for the title at the end of the season, then the fans will have the right to ask why.'

Chelsea have so much available in their transfer kitty they have signed player number eight for £4.2m, more than most Premiership clubs can afford for a star acquisition, and immediately loaned him out to Portsmouth. Bordeaux's Russian midfielder Alexei Smertin will learn to adapt to life in the Premiership on the south coast before Ranieri decides whether he can break into his star studded new squad. The 28-year-old midfielder, who can also play in defence, was looking to return home to Torpedo Moscow until Abramovich's personal involvement. The big Italian clubs often sign players and then farm them out to gain experience and Chelsea are the first club to sign a player and loan him out before he kicks a ball for the club that now owns him!

Terry started his first match for his country at centre-half, with Eriksson saying, 'Terry's improved as a player very much over the last year, he's much more mature and quicker than he was 18 months ago. He is a big, big talent and still very young. Hopefully, he's going to be in there for a long time now.'

Terry said, 'I got on against Serbia and Montenegro but to start a game for my country is the fulfilment of a lifetime ambition.' Terry had plenty of familiar faces around him – Lampard, Bridge and Cole were all in the squad. 'It always helps to have players you know around you. It's great to have all those Chelsea players in the squad. If you think back a few years, Dennis Wise was the only Englishman playing for Chelsea but now there are quite a few of us. You have to give Claudio Ranieri credit for that. When he came in he said he wanted to get more English players and that's exactly what he's done.' It was a sweet moment coming almost a year since he walked away from court having been found not guilty of affray following an incident in a Knightsbridge club.

When Duff turned out for the Republic of Ireland, he played his third game in seven days in a third different country. Having appeared for Chelsea in Slovakia and at Anfield, Duff was back in his homeland for a friendly against Australia as Ireland's most expensive player.

Duff's international team-mates were thrilled by what has happened to him. 'I was excited for him when I saw him linked with Chelsea,' said the Ireland captain Kenny Cunningham. 'To sign for Chelsea at this moment will prove to be a great transfer for Damien. I think he will grow as a player in that environment, playing alongside some world-class players. He's mentioned to me already the quality of the day-to-day training and that can only help his development and his confidence. Hopefully, we will see the benefit of that over the next couple of years.' Duff was marked by Lucas Neill, who describes his former Blackburn team-mate as 'a special, exciting player'.

18

HELLO TO TWO MORE GOOD BUYS

CLAUDIO RANIERI FELT HE needed a proven goal-scorer and a Roy Keane-type midfield dynamo to win the title and to make a significant foray into the Champions League.

Hernan Crespo is younger than Christian Vieri, while boasting an impressive scoring record, and the Blues were confident that they could entice him with guaranteed Champions League group action following their third qualifying round, first-leg win over MSK Zilina. A source close to the club said, 'We rate Crespo the best pound-for-pound striker in the world at the moment. He has all the attributes you could wish for in a centre-forward, but has only just turned 28. Vieri is 30.'

Crespo shares agent Fernando Hidalgo with Juan Veron. Crespo, who in July 2000 moved from Parma to Lazio for £35m as the world's most expensive player, certainly has the speed, aerial ability and nose for goal that would suit Chelsea – and potential new strike partner Adrian Mutu. He has already scored well over 100 goals in Serie A, won the UEFA Cup with Parma in 1999 and has hit 19 goals in 36 matches for his country.

Inter Director General Massimo Moratti confirmed that there had been an enquiry. He said, 'One month ago in our meeting with Roman

Abramovich in Italy, he asked us for several Internazionale players, including Crespo. However, we replied that our players were not for sale. Since then, we have not had any contact with the English club.' Marco Branca, the club's Director of Sport, said, 'Crespo will remain at Inter, we are not willing to sell the player, he is an important player in our team.'

In the 2000/01 season, Crespo finished 'capocannoniere' – top scorer in Serie A – with 24 goals in 32 games for Sven-Goran Eriksson's Lazio. He told the club website, 'Inter represents the icing on the cake, the dream of any player, one of the most important clubs in the world.' The Buenos Aires-born goal-scorer who took a pay cut in June in order to remain with the Nerazzurri, had a contract with Inter until June 2006 and was clearly reluctant, initially, to leave, as well as Inter refusing to sell.

But it illustrates the new power of the euro at the Bridge that both views were overturned as Chelsea pursued a striker who had averaged almost a goal every other game in his six seasons in Serie A, although he has been overshadowed by Gabriel Batistuta for most of his international career. Inter had bought Crespo from Lazio for a cut-price £12m a year ago, and Chelsea were offering a substantial profit. Injury interrupted Crespo's last campaign. Eriksson says of the Argentinian striker, 'I took him to Rome and one year later he was the top scorer in Serie A. He is a fantastic natural goal-scorer and a wonderful player.'

Chelsea also monitored events at Real, where Makelele was on strike and seeking either a pay rise or a move to London. Crespo was with the Argentina squad in Florence for a match against Uruguay, but he had already agreed personal terms and Inter officials were in London putting the finishing touches to the move. His agent Fernando Hidalgo confirmed, 'Talks with Chelsea have moved forward.' Moratti said, 'First and foremost, we look out for the interests of our players and of the club. If there is an offer, we are willing to evaluate it.'

Crespo did little to quieten speculation. 'Everyone knows what sort of life a footballer leads. Last summer I was sure that I would be staying at Lazio. Ten minutes later I was on my way to Inter. You never know what can happen next in this game.'

Ranieri spoke to Crespo first to gauge whether he was prepared to move. When those talks were successful, haggling over the fee began.

Crespo was reluctant to swap Serie A for the Premiership, but Ranieri asked Veron to persuade him while the pair were on international duty. Veron's influence proved vital. Veron said, 'The team is looking for Crespo, who is one of the greatest strikers in the world. It will be very hard, but not impossible.'

Ranieri compared Crespo to Ruud van Nistelrooy and Henry and expects the Argentinian to make a similar impact in the Premiership. Eriksson adds, 'You can expect goals from Crespo, always. He was top scorer in Italy and Argentina before that. He is a very gifted player and he is very clever in the box which, of course, is his great strength.'

'I am happy with these words,' smiled Crespo, whose own favourite players, he said, were Marco van Basten and Gary Lineker. Crespo's £16.8m took his personal total in the transfer market to more than £70m after moves between Parma, Lazio and Internazionale.

Crespo has played in front of Veron since they were teenagers in Argentina. Crespo said, 'I always talk to Seba and he spoke very highly of Chelsea. That is why I am here. It is always easier for me when Seba is in the team. I have played most of my best football with him in Italy and for Argentina. Manchester United and Arsenal have dominated the Premiership for many years but we intend to break that up and make sure we challenge for the Premiership.

'The world of football has been shocked by what has been happening at Chelsea. We might not have the prestige of Real Madrid and others yet, but that will come. Here we can write our own history. I met Mr Abramovich only briefly but I have seen from the way he watches games that he is passionate about football and with a businessman like him behind us anything is possible. Playing in the Champions League is always stimulating. Inter Milan reached the semi-finals last year and to get that far you need a lot of quality and a little bit of luck.'

English football has not had a high profile in Argentina since the days of Ardiles and Villa. Crespo did have an English idol as a kid – Gary Lineker, responsible for the Golden Boot heroics in the 1986 World Cup when Diego Maradona broke English hearts with his Hand of God goal and the feet of an angel. Crespo said, 'Lineker was such a big player in the area, someone who scored many goals. His movement was excellent and he always made the most of his opportunities. I remember him at the 1986 World Cup but I remember even better Maradona's second goal in the quarter-final. English football has not been so popular in Argentina since Ardiles and Villa were at Tottenham, but I hope we can revive that interest. At the moment, there is only Spanish and Italian football on the TV at home but I hope that Seba and me at Chelsea will put a stop to that.'

How long had it taken him to decide? 'Not too long because the two clubs had made an agreement,' Crespo said. He also denied there had been a falling out at Inter, where Christian Vieiri, a Chelsea target before him, has raged at allowing his strike partner to leave. The 'economic crisis' in Italian football had meant that his move was 'simple', he said. It also offered an opportunity to British teams who, he claimed, were 'not so far behind Italian football'. 'Three years ago there were no Italian teams in the quarter-final of any European competition,' he said when asked about last season's Italian domination of the Champions League. 'So it is all relative.'

Chelsea can now be challengers, he was sure. 'Real Madrid, Juventus and Inter have been building their history for a long time. Now we'll try and write our history for the future,' Crespo explained. 'To get to that stage, you need a lot of quality and a little bit of luck. Hopefully, we'll have a bit of luck because I'm convinced we have the quality. It's all about the growth of the team – and if we achieve union in the team, we'll go far. I'm a very positive and optimistic person and I'm convinced things will go in the best possible way. I'll do everything I can to make sure they do.'

Meanwhile, a fee was agreed for Smertin, Abramovich's compatriot. 'In principle, we have agreed everything and Alexei will sign a four-year deal with Chelsea,' Paulo Barbosa, the player's agent, said. Smertin, who was with Russia in Moscow for the friendly against Israel, would be immediately loaned to Portsmouth. Smertin had to accept the arrangement as he said, 'It's probably the best possible solution for me right now. I need to get accustomed to life in England and to the Premiership, and I need to learn English. Playing for Portsmouth will mean that I have a smoother transition.'

Chelsea also moved a step closer to signing Makelele. 'On Thursday I will be training,' said Makelele. 'If I have not been training, it is because I have not been feeling well. At no point did my non-attendance constitute part of some sort of strategy or a way of putting pressure on the bosses at Real Madrid. I wasn't training because I couldn't.'

As Chelsea waited for Makelele, complex negotiations with Inter, the Inter President and his emissaries taxed Abramovich's aides. Moratti called the deal off in the morning and then it was back on again by midday, after he was faced with a violent revolt from Vieri and from thousands of disgruntled fans. Finally, Moratti sanctioned the deal, even though Vieri threatened to walk out and strike the club's directors!

Moratti finally decided to sell as he had given his word to Crespo, and the player told him his mind and heart were already with Chelsea. The Inter owner also wanted to keep faith with Abramovich, as both men are in the oil business.

The £25m fee was much less than Inter asked for originally, but it is also much more than Chelsea offered to start with – £14m. Over two dinner dates with Inter representatives in London, the price was thrashed out. Inter's Sporting Director Marco Branca and Technical Director Gabriele Oriali dined with Zahavi and Chelsea officials. Branca, speaking from the airport departure lounge, gave nothing away when he said, 'We will have to wait a couple of days to see if it's everything or nothing.' But back in Milan, Moratti confirmed the move.

Ranieri, when asked if more players would arrive, said, 'Wait ... but don't worry about it.' Ranieri indicated that the transfers will not stop there, adding, 'I don't have a spending limit.'

Crespo admitted the move is the biggest challenge of his career. 'Few Argentines get the opportunity to play in the Premiership and I want people to talk about my spell there when I retire. I'm excited by the challenge and the opportunity to play for Chelsea in the Premier League. I have always looked for challenges wherever I have gone in my career and this is one of the biggest challenges I have undertaken. I have heard great things about Chelsea and what they hope to achieve. It's easy to want to be part of that if you have ambition and you want success in your career. Life is about challenges and I have never run away from a challenge in my life.

'I know Premiership football is fast and furious but if you have confidence, you can play anywhere in the world. Of course, there is always pressure when you join a club for a big fee but I can live with that ... I have lived with the burden of huge transfer fees wherever I have gone in my career. That is a fact of life.

'I know that if I start to score goals straight away, everyone will be happy and they will all say I'm worth the money. On the other hand, if I don't find the net, they'll all say exactly the opposite. I'm used to such behaviour, it's part of the game even if you don't necessarily agree with it.

'I'm not involved in the transfer fee nor have I been in the past. Football has evolved and you never know how much someone is going to pay for you the way the transfer market is these days. The game has changed very fast, what with sponsorship, television rights and the stock market ... it's hard to predict how much a player is worth until someone agrees to pay a fee and buys you.

'I have always said that you need to work hard in order to improve and every day I look to improve as a player. Every day I work, I train and I focus all my energy on the job and that way I know I will progress. I've never considered myself to be a truly great player. Other players have extraordinary power, formidable determination and amazing speed – but can you honestly say that I have any of these qualities in abundance? These things cannot be easily achieved. In fact, some of them are simply innate. But I can work very hard, tirelessly, every day ... I always have done, it's my way of life. What I don't have I make up for in commitment and sheer hard work. Nobody can ever criticise me for not trying.'

Crespo will earn £20m plus signing-on fees and bonuses over a four-year contract. 'I'm joining Chelsea because of the prospects rather than the money. There's been a lot of intrigue about Chelsea this summer, but I never thought I would end up there. It's good people like Abramovich are putting money into football, but I know you don't always achieve things with cash. The fan is the one who ends up the winner.'

Inter's players said their farewells to Crespo. Fellow countryman Javier Zanetti said, 'I am sorry Hernan is leaving because, as well as a good footballer, he is a good friend and comrade who is leaving Inter. But those are the rules of football and the choices made by the club. I am sure he will do well because he has the qualities to achieve great things. We say goodbye with a big "good luck" from all of us.'

Veron and Crespo played at Lazio briefly during Eriksson's reign and Crespo indicated that it helped to persuade him. 'I know in my country anything which smells English is not very well looked upon, but between Juan Veron and myself we're going to try and turn Chelsea into a club which has supporters out there. Of course, it's an interesting prospect to link up with Juan, we are great friends.

'We first got to know each other in 1996 at the Atlanta Olympics. Before that, we'd always been opponents. I was with River Plate and he was with Estudiantes, and then Boca Juniors. When we both found ourselves in Italy, he was on his own at Sampdoria and I was in the same situation at Parma. We used to encourage each other if we were feeling low. It was the first time we had left our home country, and we had left behind the way of life that we knew so well. So that's how our friendship started and it has remained strong ever since. He says that, with a bit of luck, we can turn English football upside down. Argentina wear light blue, Chelsea royal blue and next to me there will be Veron. If I shut my eyes, I'm going to think that I'm in Buenos Aires.'

Ardiles believes the striker will make a huge impact in English football as he is as good as Raul and Ruud van Nistelrooy. Ardiles was the first Argentinian to play in England 25 years ago when he and Villa joined Tottenham. He said, 'I rate Crespo very, very highly. He is one of the best strikers, right up there with Van Nistelrooy, Henry, Raul and Ronaldo.

Chelsea will be quite a force with him this season and have such a strong squad now. Can they win the Premiership? Certainly. They will be fighting Manchester United and Arsenal all the way.'

Ardiles, enjoying a second spell managing in Japan in charge of Tokyo Verdy, tracked the career of Crespo ever since he burst on to the scene playing for River Plate. He added, 'By the time he left Argentina for Italy, he was already a big, big star. He is a big, strong guy and he is a winner. He is aggressive, quick, good in the air and has a very nice touch. He scored a lot of goals in Italy in a difficult league. In England, the game is more open so I think he will score even more goals. I think he will be a great success. He is the number-one striker for Argentina right now. The others, like Saviola and Aimar, play around him – that's how good he is.'

By scoring 106 goals in 186 Serie A appearances for Parma, Lazio and Inter, Crespo has established himself as one of his country's most successful exports and will not have to face the same problems Ardiles had to contend with. 'The biggest problem was the language and other stuff that will no longer be a worry for him because of globalisation and developments in communication systems,' he explained. 'Crespo will be able to bring as many friends and family over from Argentina and Italy as he wants. He'll settle well.'

Crespo declared, 'The advantage of having an Italian coach who speaks Spanish is sensational. I won't suffer any handicap because of the language. Ranieri has a very good reputation in Italy. I know he's been following me and that he asked Abramovich to buy me.'

Ranieri admits, 'This is my biggest test as a manager. People want to put me under pressure but I will work in the same way. I want to see a team with the new players linked together. My philosophy is to get them all helping each other. It's a challenge whenever new players arrive as the Manager is under pressure to get them all playing together.'

Vieri, the original Chelsea target, launched a scathing attack on Inter. 'You have to buy the players – not sell them. If Inter sell Crespo it means there is a big difference between my way of thinking and the club's. If they sell Crespo, I'd rather they sell me, it will be better that they sell me. What do I stay here for, another second place, or third or fourth place? What are we doing? Instead of strengthening the squad, we are weakening it. Inter have already sold Ronaldo and got Crespo in his place, and now they sell him. They had better sell me, seriously, once and for all. I'm fed up giving them advice because, in the end, nobody listens to me. I have recommended Veron. I said that in my judgement Inter should buy Veron because you can only win trophies with great players like him, but Veron hasn't come, has he? The executives have to stay very well away from me because in the mood I'm in, I'm going to push them against the wall.' Vieri is a big guy and his violent threat should ensure that Inter's directors steer clear of him!

Moratti gave a press conference at the HQ of his family oil company Saras. 'It was not our initiative, it was Crespo's plan to push for this outcome. Chelsea's offer was quite interesting, and at Inter we have many good strikers, all fighting for a place in the starting eleven, maybe Crespo demanded to be a certain starter but at Inter Milan only Christian Vieri can expect such guarantees.'

As for Vieri's reaction, he said, 'I haven't yet managed to speak with him, but normally we understand each other even without talking, because there is a mutual respect. I've spoken to other players and the situation is completely calm. Vieri's reaction was an emotional one but it was also courageous and, in the end, it didn't upset me; it means that Vieri has character; he has accustomed us to this sort of outburst, but he is a good friend of Crespo, so we can understand it.' Moratti is unlikely to fine Crespo, although he said, 'It depends on those executives that he wants to attack to the wall!' Crespo's move does not seem to have blunted his skills – he scored three goals in his final training session.

Ranieri was also buoyed when Mutu was given international clearance. Mutu celebrated by scoring both goals in Romania's 2-0 win over Luxembourg. The Blues' striker scored a goal in each half to stun the 30,000-strong home support at the Shakhtar stadium. Mutu's first came from the penalty spot in the 28th minute and he doubled his tally after 58 minutes. Gronkjaer put Denmark ahead in their 1-1 draw with Finland, while Gudjohnsen took just five minutes to find the target for Iceland in their 2-1 win over the Faroe Islands which took them to the top of Group 5.

Terry led his country against Croatia for the final ten minutes. 'I was only captain because David Beckham had been substituted but I'm still very proud, especially as all my family were there. One day, I would love to be skipper on a full-time basis. But I know I'm a long way off and Becks is doing a fantastic job.' His long-term ambition is to take over from David Beckham as England captain. As the only England player to stay on the pitch for the entire match, he was given the captain's armband. 'I'm going to have it framed.'

Cole did not impress when he was introduced as a second-half substitute. Eriksson said, 'We were 2-0 up and then 3-1, and Cole leaves his position and tries to take on people. It is nice to see but when there are five minutes to play, I think the most important thing is don't give the opponents one opportunity to have a shot. He must learn in a qualifying game or World Cup game with five minutes to play we don't need to make it 4-1; 3-1 is OK. It is a friendly and I understand Joe and a lot of the others want to show me how much they want to play. I said when I first came to England that Cole is one of the greatest talents. He is a diamond you have to polish because tactically he is not the best. You could see that in this game.'

Lampard hammered in a scorcher to finish off Croatia and could have had another. Eriksson added, 'Frank Lampard is growing as a footballer. He is getting better and better, stronger and stronger and scored a marvellous goal.' Lampard, who came on as a first-half substitute for the injured Nicky Butt, capped another fine performance with his goal.

Wayne Bridge's biggest problem has been coming to terms with London traffic during the 60-mile drive from his home in Winchester to Chelsea's Harlington training ground. After less than a month of commuting, he is fully behind Ken Livingstone's congestion charge. Bridge said, 'I'd only been up to London a few times before signing for Chelsea and it's a bit hectic. Driving around can be hard work but I'm sure I'll get used to it. I'm looking to buy a house up here so that should make things better.'

Bridge began the arduous process of house-hunting around Cobham, where Chelsea will build a new training ground if they receive planning permission, but his footballing move has been completely stress free. He said, 'There's a good chance that I might not play every game and I'm prepared for that. It'll be difficult after playing every week for Southampton but it's something I've thought about. If I want to move on then I'll have to put up with it. There's going to be a fight for my place but I'll keep my head down and train hard. If Chelsea go far in a lot of competitions then no one's going to play in every game. I'll just do the best I can. The main reason to come here was that it's clearly a step up. It was a once-in-a-lifetime chance and may not come again.'

Leicester Manager Micky Adams, the only Premiership boss to recruit more players than Abramovich but for far, far less, spotted Bridge while he was still a player. Adams took his side to Stamford Bridge after signing 11 men for a total of just £250,000. Adams wanted a crack at top-flight management ever since his playing days – he coached youth teams while at Coventry, Leeds and Southampton and also ran a Sunday pub team in Wakefield while an Elland Road player. Adams explained, 'I was coaching the Under-13s for Southampton and one Sunday I went out to a park in

Winchester to see the son of a mate. But I noticed this brilliant little left-winger, who was talented and rapid. It was Wayne Bridge. I spoke to his parents and the next night he came along to Southampton's academy and they soon signed him up. He was the first player I spotted and not a bad one. Now he's worth £7m and playing for England.

'Of course, there are many people who have played big roles in his development but it does give you a sense of pride to see what he's achieved. It's a good thing that Chelsea have bought most of their players from English clubs. That can only have a domino effect on the lower leagues and the game has been missing that for a while. All the money has been going out of the country but Chelsea have bought the best of the English bunch. I might have made even more signings than Chelsea but, with respect to them, the players I've got are mainly at the wrong end of their careers. I couldn't have signed Les Ferdinand when he was 24.'

Adams knows about the pressures a manager feels at the arrival of a big-spending owner. After securing promotion from Division Three at Fulham, the club was taken over by Harrod's boss Mohammed Al-Fayed – and Adams was sacked just ten games into the following season. 'When we lost games at Fulham, there were top people linked with the job on a daily basis. That will possibly happen to Claudio. It won't be a nice feeling for him. I don't know what relationship Claudio has got with the new owner. I had very little dialogue with Mr Fayed and you need a dialogue with a Chairman, even if it's just to put his arm around you when you've lost a game.'

Leicester were only six months out of administration and two months out of the First Division. Adams said, 'I can't imagine what the expectation is like for Claudio Ranieri; I can't know because I have never had any money to spend. I am not envious because I am here at Leicester City and I understand how my cloth has been cut so I get on with it.'

For the first time since he left the Blues eight years ago, midfielder Muzzy Izzet fancied his old club's chances. Izzet said, 'It's an old cliché – but it's 11 against 11. I fancy Chelsea to do well this season. I watched them against Liverpool on Sunday and thought they looked strong all over the pitch. They've bought some terrific players and it must be fantastic being a Chelsea supporter at the moment. But the way I look at it is that all the pressure will be on Chelsea to win. It's their first home game of the season and the expectation level at Stamford Bridge has never been as high. On the other hand, we have already been written off as no-hopers by everyone. No one gives us a chance and the way some people are talking you'd think it was lambs to the slaughter.' Micky Adams joked he was 'frightened to death' watching Chelsea at Anfield. He quipped, 'I'm thinking of going scouting this weekend, instead – and leaving it all to Alan Cork!'

Izzet remained upbeat. 'We all know there have been far bigger upsets in football than us getting a result against Chelsea. Sometimes you can make being underdogs work to your advantage – simply because you have nothing to lose and all to gain. So what have we got to worry about? If we lose, everyone will be right. And if we were to win or draw, people would still say it was because Chelsea didn't play very well, rather than give Leicester any real credit for it. But Chelsea won't be any fitter than us. And I doubt whether their players will work any harder than us. They have some great players and it's going to be difficult for us to close them down and prevent them creating chances. But we'll give it our best shot and see what happens. As professionals, these are the games you want to get a result out of. And it's not as if we haven't beaten good Chelsea teams at Stamford Bridge before. But all the pressure will be on their players to deliver – and the longer we're still in the game, the greater that pressure will get.'

Adams would not tolerate his players getting star-struck. He banned any souvenir hunting. He said, 'There are going to be world-class internationals all over the pitch but I don't want my players getting star-struck. I don't want them in the tunnel deciding whose shirt they are going to get at the end of the game. No one expects us to get anything there and it would probably be best if we don't turn up. I'm not sure that Claudio Ranieri will be quaking in his boots at the thought of us playing them.'

Mutu looked forward to his début. He said, 'Abramovich is a bit crazy as a President but I like such crazy people a lot. It's not important that he has a lot of money, the most important thing is that he invests in football. With that kind of guy in charge of our club, everything is possible. Abramovich has turned me into his number-one fan since he informed all the Chelsea players how crazy he is about our game. When he spoke to the squad last week, he told us he was once sitting in his house in Siberia excited about a vital game from the Russian championship. Suddenly, his satellite connection wouldn't work and it became impossible for him either to see the game or get the system fixed in time. It was incredible what he did next. He took his personal jet and flew for nine hours.

'I already adore my team-mates. Some of them have immediately shown what good guys they are – and also that they are really funny. I was bitterly disappointed that my clearance did not arrive in time to play against Liverpool. But, after the game, Jimmy Floyd Hasselbaink burst into the dressing room, jumped straight into my arms and shouted, "Adrian, next time it will be you who scores the winner."

'Our stadium is absolutely sensational. Everybody tells me it is easily the best stadium in London. And, as I'm looking forward to my first game for my new club, I have to praise what I saw of the pitch. It is very impressive, like a snooker table and I think it's going to be a pleasure to play on. Victory at Anfield has given us massive self-belief. We have a team which has big chances to win important trophies. I would say this team is definitely good enough to battle Manchester United and Arsenal for the title. I heard that Claudio Ranieri said anyone who thinks we will win the title is crazy. But I think the boss had it on his mind that it is tough to make a smooth-running team with so many newcomers.

'I also like the fans in England. Our relationship with them is much calmer than in Italy. There, you could never avoid them – they were always pestering you. In England, they seem to stay politely behind the gates and stare at you.

'I will bring some fantasy, some Latin spirit and passion. I am also here to learn and the players around me are very competitive. Chelsea is a big club and I want to win things. We have a very powerful team and a lot of champion material.'

Ranieri said, 'Mutu can start. The night before the match I think about everything and will choose my first eleven. We want to show the same commitment we managed against Liverpool.

'I once said Jimmy Floyd Hasselbaink is like a shark and Carlton Cole like a lion. Well, Adrian Mutu is another born predator. In fact, Mutu is like a snake.

'When I was coach at Valencia, it was me who nicknamed another great Romanian player 'The Cobra'. That was Adrian Ilie – and the nickname stuck. Like Ilie, Mutu is so clever, so cunning and stays hidden until it is necessary to apply the killer finish. No matter the size of our squad, I bought Mutu to play in the first team. The position of left-sided striker is made for him. He can ghost in from behind the main striker and, when he does, the goalkeeper will be a dead man. This is why I have dreamed of signing Mutu for such a very long time. Adrian scored 18 goals in Italy last season. He is intelligent and will also help the team with a lot of assists. Immediately Mr Abramovich asked me to draw up a list of the players I wanted, I put Mutu right at the top. The first name. He is a champion, a strong character – and I demand champions and strong characters in this side.'

Ranieri believes Mutu has the steel which has been missing when they have beaten the best only to wilt against the weakest. Ranieri smiled as he said, 'Mutu has impressed me with his winner's mentality. He is really strong. I've never seen him crying when he gets hit. He's too hard for that. He also always plays with his head up, which is why he reads the game perfectly and can smell out the goal. I've watched him play for Verona, Inter Milan and Parma. What he did at Parma last season was incredible. If Mutu brings even half that brilliance to Chelsea, he will have a great year.'

Ranieri replied to Mutu's fears that the Italian was being too conservative in claiming it was foolish to predict Chelsea could win the Premiership. 'I could easily say about this season that I want to win everything. That would not be a lie. Yet I know very well that even though we have bought a lot of top players, we are not favourites. There are more experienced teams than ourselves, like Arsenal, Manchester United and even Liverpool, despite them losing to us last week. The difference is they have all played together for a long time.'

Ranieri can hardly come to terms with the vast array of talent he now has at his disposal. 'I feel like a child in a sweet shop. I have so many talented players to choose from. And yes, I like this problem. I'm not working to a budget. There has not been a limit put on spending. But you will have to wait to see if more players come in. To build a team is always difficult. Maybe with the money available you can choose better, but then it is only about what happens on the pitch.

'Leicester also have many new players, so their Manager Micky Adams has the same problem I have – to get them playing together as a team. When the sides line up, it is still 11 versus 11. It is not, say, £100m versus £2m. The big problem is leaving out players who are so rich in talent. But it is important everyone understands the new philosophy. I want it to be like Real Madrid, Inter Milan and Juventus. You might not play, but you are still important to the team.'

Ranieri pointed out to Chelsea fans that megastar footballers do not guarantee success. 'I am from Rome and you have a saying here, "Rome was not built in a day". That is how it will be with Chelsea. Alex Ferguson only started to win things after seven years in charge and I won't know if Chelsea have closed the gap on Manchester United or Arsenal until the end of the season. When things were not going right for Chelsea in previous seasons, some wanted to kill the Manager. Now I have a little money, I can chase good players. Yet it is still very important to win. If I don't, you can kill the Manager again!'

Ranieri demanded the same mean streak against the Foxes that his team showed at Anfield. 'It's important to carry on where we left off, though that result was not so important as wanting to see my team play away with confidence, play good football, link well and help each other. This is my philosophy.'

Previous Romanian imports to England, such as Florin Raducioiu and Ilie Dimitrescu, were failures. Mutu, however, has bags of confidence. 'I will succeed where other Romanians have failed because I am Adrian Mutu. If you doubt that, then wait until you see me on the pitch. The rules of football are the same wherever you play. I have confidence in myself to play well. I'm told that it is maybe more physical in England but I know I'm quick enough to get away from my opponents and do things for the rest of the team. Since the very moment when I found out that Mr Abramovich was interested in the club and wanted to pursue a number of well-known names in European football, I realised he was a president who wanted to put a very competitive team together. Chelsea want to make a name for themselves and I want to be part of that. This is the most important thing I've done in my career. I decided the day I heard about Chelsea wanting me that I would come. I look at the squad and see a powerful team with a lot of championship material. If we can make a team out of all this talent, we will certainly do well.'

Ranieri said, 'If a striker can score 18 goals in Italy, he can score anywhere in the world and that is why Adrian will be very important for us. He is a different player to Gianfranco but I hope the fans will take him to their hearts in the same way.

'We have to be consistent and show that we are linking together more and more. I understand that people want to put me under pressure. Last season, when I could only bring in Quique De Lucas, you all wanted to kill me. Now I have the money to bring in the players I want for us to win. I know it might be a problem with so many players now. It is important that everybody understands our philosophy has changed. We must be like Real Madrid, Juventus, Inter and AC Milan. Whether the players play or don't, they must realise they are all important for the team.'

Mutu added, 'I hope that I won't disappoint the fans and I want to help the team win. If Crespo comes, it will be a problem for the Manager how to play us together. Now I just have to do my job against Leicester.'

19

ABRAMOVICH COMES HOME

ROMAN ABRAMOVICH WAS GIVEN a standing ovation at Stamford Bridge with the latest and most expensive signing, Hernan Crespo, there to watch. In his programme notes, he pledged that his spending in the transfer market is designed to transform Chelsea into one of Europe's élite clubs.

Abramovich toured the perimeter of the pitch during the warm-up to his first home match in charge, shaking hands with fans and signing autographs. It was symbolic that so many fans turned up with a variety of T-shirts and flags with variations of the hammer and sickle. Given the phenomenal investment and magical impact that he has made, transforming the side into genuine title contenders, the warmth of his reception was hardly surprising, neither were the songs referring to the depth of their new owner's pockets! His welcome was completed by a melody of songs, a Russian waltz and even 'Fiddler on the Roof' played over the PA system as he took his seat in his Millennium Box where he could entertain his guests. They included the President of Iceland and his wife, whom he'd flown to the game on his private jet before dropping them back home after they had spent some time on an unofficial visit to Chukotka.

Abramovich could relax, tie-less, of course, in the box that was on sale for £10m for a ten-year lease, directly over the halfway line in Chelsea's East Stand.

Ken Bates joined in the pre-match festivities. When the DJ aired a traditional Russian tune, 'Kalinka', Bates tried to Cossack dance in the directors' box.

It certainly belied any hint of fears for Abramovich's safety, as there had been a dramatic report that morning suggesting there would have to be an increase in security because of renewed warnings of an assassination attempt, after an acquaintance of his, Igor Farkhutdinov, died in a helicopter crash in Siberia. Three Siberian governors had been either murdered or died in suspicious circumstances in the previous 18 months.

Instead, Abramovich looked relaxed and was enjoying himself. With Crespo in the main stand along with his girlfriend, it was clear that Abramovich's spending was not over yet, with a big-money move from Inter wrapped up.

Writing in the match-day programme, Chelsea's new owner told fans, 'You have been so warm since I arrived at Chelsea and I want to thank everyone for making me, my family and my colleagues so welcome. I especially want to thank the shareholders who enthusiastically took up the offer to sell their shares so that we could move quickly in helping Chelsea Football Club become one of the élite clubs in Europe.

'It was only earlier this year that I decided to become involved in the Premiership and when my team looked into clubs with the best possible fundamentals and prospects, Chelsea really did come first. The ground, the location, the Champions League qualification, the staff and players and the fan support were, and remain, a wonderful foundation. I don't want to change what works. I just want to help take what we have at Stamford Bridge to the next level. And I want us all to work hard and have a lot of fun doing it.

'The atmosphere and electricity when we beat Liverpool last week was amazing. I believe the English Premier League offers the best atmosphere and level of competition in the world, with Chelsea clearly among the top clubs in the League. I look forward to a long and fruitful partnership, and to sharing the excitement, future successes and fun of Chelsea Football Club with fans old and new. I wish you all a thoroughly enjoyable season.'

Ticket touts were doing brisk business charging £120 a seat. If the anticipation outside the ground was something, the scenes before kick-off were equally remarkable. No club can ever have devoted eight pages in its club programme to their summer signings and introducing each to a thrilled audience took a good 15 minutes.

One of Abramovich's expensive new recruits, Mutu, put in a swashbuckling début display to inspire a 2-1 win. At times rather showy, perhaps even over elaborate, he displayed his full range of trickery and struck a thunderbolt from 20 yards to clinch victory just before half-time and left to a standing ovation.

There were still several nervous moments for Chelsea, especially in a feisty second half when Geremi was dismissed with 23 minutes left. However, Leicester then had two players – Rogers and Scimeca – sent off in the closing stages of what was hardly a bad-tempered game, and the Blues held on.

They were still indebted to Mutu, who had lived up not only to the pre-match billing of Ranieri, who called him a 'snake', but also to his own promise to bring 'fantasy' to the club. That used to be the preserve of Zola, whose name is still chanted in reverence by the fans, much like that of Cantona at Manchester United.

Chelsea's team on the day: Cudicini, Melchiot, Terry, Desailly, Bridge, Duff (Cole), Geremi, Lampard, Veron, Hasselbaink (Gudjohnsen) and Mutu (Gronkjaer). Chelsea enjoyed some good fortune, handed an early lead through an own goal by Nalis, only for Scowcroft to equalise when Izzet's long-range free-kick hung in the air inside the Chelsea area five minutes before half-time, and Scowcroft managed to out-jump Terry to power a header into the far corner. The cameras zoomed in on the directors' box. Abramovich managed only a shake of the head, shrug of the shoulders, and a wry smile. Leicester fans were quick to rub it in with a chorus of, 'Roman, what's the score?'

When Mutu's free-kick flew straight into the wall and rebounded to him, the Rumanian let fly with a follow-up effort that rocketed into the far corner on the stroke of half-time.

Four years ago, Leicester derailed Chelsea's title bid late in the season by hauling their way back from 2-0 down to draw 2-2. Not this time. Hasselbaink struck the near post from a tight angle after racing past Walker. Geremi was sent off with 23 minutes left for a two-footed tackle on Scimeca. It was a harsh decision from referee Rob Styles, especially as Geremi won the ball, but he still went in studs-first and the official felt bound to act. Chelsea's task eased when Rogers was dismissed for kicking Gronkjaer on the ground after pushing the Danish international over with six minutes left.

Deane still burst straight through the centre of Chelsea's defence only to plant his header against the bar. But that was it for Leicester, who had Scimeca dismissed with two minutes left for his second bookable offence, a tackle from behind on Cole, who then rattled the bar himself. Cole's stunning effort in injury time deserved more as he twisted and turned on the edge of the box before crashing a shot against the bar. He deserved to cap the day in style, but Ranieri was happy nonetheless. 'It was a special day for so many reasons, but the most important thing was we won the game and, in the end, we were very relieved to do that because Leicester showed a lot of fight and gave us some difficult moments. This was a normal performance for us. Liverpool last week was a big surprise because it will take time with so many new players, but I don't know how long. It will be all right in the end. At least we are winning games as we learn. We can play better. When you change a lot of players, sometimes you play well, sometimes not.'

Ranieri added, 'Mutu was very good. It was a special goal with his left foot and I am very happy with the three points.' A montage of the magical Zola was played on the giant screens, but there was a new master of tricks and skills in Mutu. Adams observed, 'That's what you pay £15.8m for ... not that I would know!'

Suddenly, there was a profusion of dead-ball specialists. Ranieri is happy to let his superstars scrap it out but admitted, 'Maybe we have too many players wanting to take the set-pieces – Veron, Hasselbaink, Mutu, Duff, Geremi, Joe Cole and Eidur Gudjohnsen. They all want to take them. It's up to them to decide. There is no pecking order. They must see how the wall is positioned, how far out the ball is and then sort it out among themselves. Whoever feels good should take it.'

Mutu said, 'Usually, I strike the ball with my right foot, but my left one is not just a form and a shape. I use it quite frequently but the right is stronger. I play on the left-hand side but aim to penetrate in the middle so I can use both feet. When I was young I only played with my left foot because I was a great admirer of Gheorghe Hagi. He set a great example and I wanted to follow him. When I was 10 or 12 years old, I did everything with my left leg to try to make it stronger.'

Mutu was pleased to get through the game after a hectic week when he had to catch five planes to reach Donetsk for Romania's 2-0 win over Ukraine, in which he scored both goals.

He also had a nasty gash on his right hand for which he required nine stitches. He said, 'My goal was a great start but that's not the most important thing. The style is not important and I'm just pleased it went in. My father is a mathematician so I obviously inherited his sense of angles! The style and beauty of the goal is not as important as the weight of the three points. If it hits the back of the net, it's good enough. I hope it's a good omen and I want to carry on in this way. I was delighted that the crowd took to me straight away. I was running on empty but they gave me wings!

'I love my tricks and flicks and like to entertain the crowd. Fans in England appreciate these fine touches as there are not many players around who can play like that. My arm was quite badly gashed but the Premiership's not bad if you can take the knocks. I was pleasantly surprised at the amount of space I found. In the future, I may be marked more closely, but I should still be able to create gaps for others and allow them to play.

'Zola was a great player for Chelsea and cannot really be replaced. He was a unique personality and I can only try and raise my game to his level. I don't see myself purely as a forward. I like to operate as a second striker, linking play from the midfield. I bring something different. Many English strikers are all about power, but my game is based on speed and fantasy. I am a Latin player and love to have the ball at my feet so I can go past defenders.'

Mutu hopes that, like Zola, his career will come to be defined by his achievements at Chelsea. After Inter, Verona and Parma, he believes Chelsea can help him become recognised as one of the world's top strikers. 'For a player who wants to make a name for himself in the international arena, this is the only club.'

But who will be taking free-kicks? Mutu said, 'We decide who takes them on the field when it comes to it. We're all mature and accomplished professionals and make an ad-hoc decision. Whoever feels best suited takes it.'

Veron was ostensibly on the left of a four-man midfield but he rarely stuck to that position. That kind of flexible, free role is the one Veron craves, but it will take time to develop. Adams didn't even think Veron would play, based on his 'spy' at the Friday training session. He said, 'My information was that Juan Sebastian Veron wasn't going to play. I thought he might rest him for the Champions League and play 4-4-2. So we set up our game plan on that basis. Then the Chelsea team sheet comes in and his name is on it.'

A smiling Ranieri replied, 'Obviously, the spy was not very good. I think they should change him. I was playing young players against experienced ones in training.'

Leicester's new away strip, a copy of the Leicester Fosse outfit used back in 1884, was even more baffling! And as the game progressed, the letters fell off the players' backs.

But the name game was going well enough for Chelsea – played three, won three – but this performance posed more questions than answers over their hopes for the campaign. Yet Ranieri acknowledges that, in spite of two league wins on the trot, it will be a while before we see the best of his new-look side. 'Everyone was nervous before this game because expectations were so high. We didn't play very well. That is when it becomes important that champions like Mutu create something special like he did here.'

Adams made the point, 'It was not a game that justified three red cards and we are very disappointed by the decision to send off our two lads, but I am not going to criticise Mr Styles for the sake of it. In the end, we could have nicked a point and, while we rode our luck at times, I felt we got the tactics just right against a side with so much talent. In the end, despite that late chance, we just fell short, but I really enjoyed the occasion. It was a memorable day. We're going to need a lot more of that because we have to learn how to compete with clubs like Chelsea ... even though they are on a different financial planet to us. When Mr Abramovich took over at Chelsea, I wondered why he didn't fly to East Midlands Airport instead of Heathrow. He could have bought us for £5m. But that doesn't mean we don't turn up.'

Asked about Geremi's dismissal, Ranieri said, 'If I was to get upset about this, I would get upset about everything.'

That new-found fortune makes Chelsea the team every other club in Europe wants to beat. Terry said, 'Leicester's players said after our game on Saturday they were desperate to come to the Bridge and upset everyone involved at Chelsea. Every team now wants to turn us over. We're like Manchester United. Everyone will raise their game against us.'

Far from worrying about the extra demands, Terry said, 'The atmosphere at the club has completely changed this season. The financial pressure isn't there any more, but because we've signed so many players we're now expected to win things as a team. Last year, the players were reading things about our financial problems and obviously that wasn't nice. Mr Abramovich has removed that. We definitely want to pay him back. When he came to meet the players he told us he wants Chelsea to win the Premiership. The players don't want anything less. This is the start of a big adventure and there is a real buzz about the place. When you're training every day with the likes of Veron, Mutu and now Crespo, you just can't wait to get out there and try new things.'

Terry was only a spectator when Chelsea reached the Champions League quarter-finals four years ago. 'I got a small taste of it in Slovakia the other week. They played the Champions League music before the game and Marcel Desailly was telling us 'This is what it's all about.' If we get past Zilina, there's a good chance we could find ourselves in the same group as Real Madrid, Juventus or Milan. That's the sort of game the fans want to see at Stamford Bridge.' Terry believes the club are now ready to challenge at the peak of European soccer. 'We've got the players now and we want to win the Champions League. That's what the players here want'

Terry discussed the club's European prospects with Desailly, who won the trophy twice with AC Milan in the 1990s. He said, 'Marcel's won the European Cup twice and it'd be great for him to lift it again. I think it's possible. We've got a good enough squad.'

But will that 'good enough' squad see any more high-profile signings? Ranieri is in no rush to put away Abramovich's chequebook. 'Is the spending over? Maybe. Perhaps there will be more. If I want others, I will speak with Mr Abramovich.'

Ranieri struggled to hide the fact that Crespo would be the next superstar arrival. 'I don't know what will happen there,' he said trying to keep a straight face, while making a gesture to suggest his nose was growing. 'Once I am told Crespo has signed, I will tell you.'

Mutu had signed too late to play in the final qualifier. As changes were anticipated, Cole said, 'One of the biggest attractions of coming here was the chance to play in Europe. Every time I watch a Champions League game, I want to be out there playing. It's a great celebration of football. The closest I've been to the Champions League is on my PlayStation. This is the nearest thing you can get to the World Cup. It's such a great celebration of football and so many different styles. Every game I watch on telly, I think, "I'd love to be out there." Everyone who comes to Chelsea knows the score. You're fighting for your place.

'It's easy to see with players like Marcel Desailly and Juan Sebastian Veron the standard has gone up. But I could do with a day off. There are no days off at Chelsea. It's really hard work.'

Ranieri has every faith in Cole, despite Eriksson's comments after his last England run-out. 'Joe is a fantastic player. He's young but coming here and playing with big champions will be good for him. If Joe follows me, he will arrive at the highest level, right at the top, not only in England but in Europe and the world.'

Cole accepts that his style is ideally suited to the role of a game-winning substitute, but he is yearning for the opportunity to start. He says, 'If I keep doing well as a substitute, then I'm sure I'll get the chance to show what I can do.'

Ranieri will not be tempted to pick players just to keep them happy. 'My first priority is to win. I will pick my first XI to win. I won't be giving opportunities in order to keep happy players.'

Smertin signed and Chelsea's outlay soared past the £100m mark with Crespo. With so many big names jostling for places, egos may well be dented over the next few months, but Ranieri said his squad would not become a cohesive unit for some time. 'I cannot say whether it will be ready tomorrow. I don't know when it will be ready. All I ask is that we play with concentration and a big heart – like we did against Leicester.'

He also accepts he is living in the shadow of Eriksson. 'There is a total feeling between Abramovich and myself. But it is obvious that feeling can only be kept or bought with victories. I wasn't born yesterday. I know how things go in football. I'm not worried. I realise I must live with this soap opera. There's nothing I can do if Eriksson comes out at every corner. I just try to do my best and then it will all come to account.'

How important it was to qualify for the group stages of the Champions League was summed up by Desailly. 'We must just think about how it is going to be beautiful if we get into the proper Champions League, how beautiful it will be going and playing against Milan, Real Madrid, Inter, Juventus, and teams like that.'

Chelsea 3-0 Zilina (Chelsea win 5-0 on aggregate)

Icelandic Prime Minister Olaf Gunnar Grimsson and his new wife Dorrit joined Abramovich and his friends in the Millennium Box and eye-witnesses told me just how much he enjoyed himself.

Abramovich had one concern – the Bridge was far from full. Perhaps the £35 tickets deterred many supporters for an unglamorous opponent. Abramovich would have preferred the prices to have been £20 to encourage more support. No doubt, the pricing strategy for similar games will be reviewed.

More than 19,000 empty seats, including the entire upper tier of the West Stand, was a sad indictment of an argument as to whether Chelsea fans were merely fickle or more selective because of the cost. Admittedly, the tie was effectively over, Chelsea having won the first leg. In addition, Mutu was ineligible, Crespo was still to sign, and the resting of star attractions like Veron and Duff had been widely publicised. Yet so had the home début of Cole. The 23,408 gate was not a one-off. Chelsea's crowds have consistently fluctuated more than their main rivals. Chelsea's ticket prices, which go up to £67, are obviously a factor, but significantly cheaper prices were also available ... but maybe they weren't cheap enough.

Crespo, dressed in all black, completed his move and was paraded at half-time. He received the biggest cheer of the night. The announcer built up his arrival before the start by suggesting, 'Stay in your seats,' because 'something very special' would be happening at half-time. Cue more Russian music. Abramovich introduced Crespo to the Icelandic Prime Minister and his wife, who is the daughter of a famous London jeweller.

Crespo signed a four-year deal and Ranieri said, 'You can play the greatest football in the world, but it's no good if you don't put the ball in the net. And it's my neck that is on the block! Crespo is a fantastic striker who scores a lot of goals. That is what can decide tight games for your side. He was the second top scorer in the Champions League for Inter Milan last season. That is very important. He's very fast, good in the air and I am delighted to have him. He attacks space superbly and is strong and clever.

'It is more difficult to score in Italy because they have a defensive culture. England is different but he'll adapt. Crespo's characteristics are good for English football. I now have five strikers and can pick two every week. In September and October, we will have games every three days, so it's important to give the players a rest. He is another champion who wants to fight and never gives up. He is my new little lion ... and I like lions!'

Ranieri maintained that Crespo had been his number-one target. He said, 'I expect him to score goals. His impact on this league will be the same as Ruud van Nistelrooy. He is a different kind of player but he is a tremendous goal-scorer. He has scored goals consistently in Italy where the culture is all based around defence. If he can score there, he will score in the Premiership too. I am sure he will be a huge success for us.'

Crespo told Chelsea TV how much he enjoyed the 'wonderful welcome'. 'It was very satisfying; it was great to be in front of our home fans.' He added, 'I played together with Seba at Parma, Lazio and the national side. We had a lot of chances to win things with the teams we were at and we hope to do things at Chelsea together. This move is very important to me because it's a great sporting chance and a great social chance with a great group of players. Mario Stanic, he was at Parma with me, and I played against Desailly. I also know all the other players but I've never played against them. I've come here to win things, not just to participate. We will do everything we can to win things. I see myself as the first striker but I have no problem if the Manager wants me to be the second striker.'

Veron's reaction was ultra-positive to Crespo's arrival and he felt that the club was now in a position to challenge Manchester United's supremacy. Veron said, 'The two teams are obviously very different; however, Chelsea's activities in pre-season show they can also make it to the level United are at. There are very few clubs in the world like Manchester United, but I think Chelsea can also become as big, if not bigger, than they are.'

Veron insists the duo will be even more successful at Stamford Bridge than countrymen Ardiles and Villa were during their glittering spell at Tottenham. Ardiles and Villa were the last two Argentinians to link up at an English club and both starred when Spurs won the FA Cup in 1981. Veron said, 'I think Hernan and I are going to surpass the achievements of Villa and Ardiles.'

'Veron's early displays suggested he will finally do himself justice in English football as he hinted Sir Alex was to blame for what went wrong at Old Trafford. Veron said, 'Italian and English football is very different, and perhaps that is what caused the change in my form over the last few seasons. But I feel I can make it in the English game too. What I aspire to do is to leave the same image of myself in England as I did in Italy. I want to be seen as a champion – as a professional and a person. I didn't have my flow for United. One of the problems could be that I played out of position, but what I lacked was the continuity more than the actual position. I did speak to the Manager about it, but in a big club like United you have to take advantage of the time and the places that you can play. Last season, I felt I was in some of my best form before I got injured against Leeds – so maybe Mark Viduka was to blame for injuring me. It was unfortunate I could not show my all at Old Trafford but I don't regret anything and all I am doing now is looking forward to playing for Chelsea. What I have to show now is only to the people of Chelsea – the Manager, the players and the fans. I will play in whatever position and that comes down to the Manager. But my favourite is central midfield where I can attack.'

The £10m Chelsea will earn from qualifying for Europe's biggest club competition was not the issue; getting to the group stages would attract even bigger names in the future.

Ranieri refused to rule out one more signing before the transfer window closed. 'I think it might be the end of my spending, but I've left the door open a little. If I get all the right players in now, maybe we won't have to buy any more the next time round.'

Ranieri is banking on Veron to bring the best out of Crespo. 'Veron and Crespo have known each other since they played together for Argentina's Under-21 team. They have a good link together and Veron will be able to explain to him all about English football. Veron can help explain English football to him! Crespo is a good leader on the pitch. He's a new champion for us. He is a fantastic striker and could be very important to the team. I will try and speak to the Italian FA about whether he can play on Saturday.'

Glen Johnson said, 'Crespo could really make the difference for us this season and win us the Champions League. I've seen Crespo play and everyone knows a lot about him. He's a different class. I can't wait until he gets settled in and starts banging in the goals for us.'

Despite the latest superstar arrival, teenage defenders Johnson and Huth both scored their first senior goals in the win over Zilina to confirm Chelsea's place among the European superpowers. Chelsea's team on the night was: Cudicini, Johnson, Terry, Desailly (Huth), Babayaro, Gronkjaer (Stanic), Lampard (Petit), Geremi, Cole, Hasselbaink and Gudjohnsen. Johnson had only celebrated his nineteenth birthday the previous Saturday, while Huth is also 19. Ranieri observed, 'I was delighted to see them both score. It was good for everybody to see that.'

Ranieri could rest Veron, Duff and Bridge, while Mutu was ineligible, so it underlined just how comfortable the Chelsea boss was feeling coming into this match with a 2-0 lead. Ranieri made five changes to the team that beat Leicester, but few of the incoming players seized their opportunity with any real vigour. Cole again looked isolated on the left-hand side of midfield and Gudjohnsen, despite shedding several pounds, played as if he had a considerable weight on his mind.

Lampard's free-kick was only partially cleared and Johnson, lurking with intent just inside the box, was unchallenged as he steered a header inside the far post. Huth, a 64th-minute sub for Desailly, scored within three minutes of his arrival. The German rose to powerfully head in from fellow sub Petit's corner. He even shoved Hasselbaink aside to smash a 30-yard free-kick against the bar with such astonishing power that Cole could be forgiven for missing a simple tap-in from the rebound.

Hasselbaink, who had earlier been guilty of a horrendous miss from two yards, refused to be denied in the 78th minute. He raced on to Geremi's precise through ball and steered his angled shot beyond the reach of the advancing keeper Branislav Rzeszoto. As Chelsea's top scorer, it wasn't a bad display for a striker supposedly on his way out. It was a statement of intent from the Dutchman, just as Ranieri's decision to select him signalled that he will not be leaving, especially as he is now cup-tied for European purposes.

Chelsea claimed their place among Europe's élite for only the second time in their history. Ranieri added, 'It was important to win, and we've done that. Now we have achieved qualification for the Champions League group stage, and that was important for the new Chelsea. Our target is to reach the same level as Real Madrid, Manchester United and Arsenal, although the first thing is to build a team, and hopefully do that winning games. They have had good squads for a long time and will not be worried about us. I'm sure these clubs will not think about Chelsea at the moment but if they don't take us seriously, it could be to our advantage. I hope it is.'

Mutu, Crespo, Hasselbaink, Veron, Geremi, Cole and Gudjohnsen all fancy themselves as free-kick experts, but there was a new kid on the block, the one they call 'The Wall'. Huth's awesome late free-kick has really captured Ranieri's imagination. Huth almost shattered the crossbar with a 30-yard piledriver which flew back into play so quickly the match officials did not spot that the ball had already crossed the goal-line. Ranieri said, 'He has more power in his free-kicks than anyone I have ever seen. Not even Roberto Carlos strikes them so well. We have a lot of big-name champions at the club but they all respect this young man because he almost breaks the goals with his shots in training.

'Huth was fantastic when he replaced Marcel Desailly. He scored one goal and should have had another when that free-kick landed over the goal-line. When he was preparing to go on, I said, "Hey, if there is a free-kick, get up there and shoot." No matter who else was lining up for the kick, I wanted Robert to take it. I said that if there was a problem, he should speak to me on the bench about it, because I made it clear he was going to shoot before anyone else.'

Berlin-born Huth has now been at the club for nearly five years after being spotted by Chelsea's scouts playing in a youth tournament during Gianluca Vialli's reign as Manager. The 6ft 3in defender only turned professional in February last year and made his Premiership début against Aston Villa in the final game of the 2001/02 season. Terry has no doubts about Huth's pedigree and said, 'Robert is going to become a Chelsea legend. There is absolutely no doubt about that.'

Chelsea were among the second seeds at the draw in Monte Carlo. Eriksson tipped Real Madrid to be European Champions for a record tenth time. 'I see a battle between Italian, Spanish and English teams. I see AC Milan, Juve and Inter, as well as Manchester United, as contenders. But for me the favourites are Real Madrid. It's hard to see them exiting the Champions League before the semi-final stages. They have the mentality and the strength to tackle the European games at their peak.' No mention of Chelsea, then?

Johnson is confident they can beat anyone. 'It'd be nice to play Real Madrid. It'd be fantastic to come up against some of their world-class players. They're the biggest team in the world and it'd be great to knock them out in the next round. I'm confident we could do that. Everyone's got a chance haven't they? I was talking to Joe Cole today and we're both enjoying every minute of it.'

Bates and Birch represented the Blues at the ceremony in Monte Carlo, as Abramovich anchored his yacht in the harbour but chose to stay away. Spokesman John Mann explained, 'Roman is a very private individual and would not have liked the attention his appearance at the draw would have undoubtedly caused. His style is to appoint people to work for him and then let them get on with the job. Trevor Birch would have been representing Roman's interests. Roman doesn't have to be at the draw himself to know exactly what is going on.' But he was kept fully informed in between a shopping expedition with his wife.

The final on 26 May 2004 will be indoors for the first time at the home of German club Schalke. Chelsea drew Lazio, Turkish side Besiktas and Czech outfit Sparta Prague in Group G. Bates said, 'It's a tough draw but we are confident of coming through. They [Lazio] are the only team that have won in Europe at Stamford Bridge, so we owe them one. I was hoping we were going to get Dynamo Kiev and Lokomotiv Moscow but, unfortunately, Arsenal got those. It would have been rather ironic given our new ownership. Moscow would have been fun. As for Veron and Crespo, they might feel they have a point to prove against Lazio. Will we win the European Cup? Who knows, but we have 1 chance in 32.'

The Rome club paid £35.4m for Crespo in 2000, while Veron was also a star in the Olympic Stadium when they won the Italian championship during Eriksson's spell as Manager. Like Chelsea, Lazio finished fourth in their domestic league last season and had to win through the qualifying round. They beat Benfica 4-1 on aggregate.

Terry did not play in Rome four years ago but walked away with Veron's shirt after watching Chelsea hold the Italians to a 0-0 draw. Terry recalled, 'I travelled with the squad and was really in awe of the whole experience. I'd always admired Veron greatly. I knew it was a long shot but I was determined to come away with a souvenir from the game, especially as Chelsea had done so well. Because I was wearing a Chelsea tracksuit, I managed to talk my way into the home dressing room. You can imagine I wasn't the most popular person in there. The Lazio players even started booing me and trying to get me thrown out. But I'd got so far, I wasn't leaving without a trophy and finally succeeded in getting Veron's shirt.'

Lazio got their revenge with a 2-1 victory at Stamford Bridge later, the only team to beat Chelsea at home in the Champions League. The clubs met again in a pre-season friendly, which Lazio won 2-0. That was six weeks before the arrival of all the big names, including Veron.

Terry added, 'Lazio outplayed us in the summer and were very dangerous at set-pieces. Jaap Stam looked very strong at the heart of defence, and that's a position I always watch closely, for obvious reasons. Claudio Lopez was also very dangerous and they looked a great side even then. But I believe that was Glen Johnson's first game for us following his transfer from West Ham. In just a few short weeks, look at how Chelsea has transformed. There is virtually a whole new team in place. We are probably one of the teams everyone is keeping a close eye on in the Champions League. That is a big honour, but also a reminder of the challenge we face and the pressure is on us to deliver. Lazio are probably the toughest team we will face in the group. They have the tradition, reputation and big-name players. But all teams that get to the Champions League command respect – that includes Chelsea.'

Lazio Director Giuseppe Faballi said, 'Our old friends Veron and Crespo will make it hard for us. It will be a great pleasure for us to met them both in Rome again.'

Ranieri said, 'You are asking me about whether these players can win the Champions League already, but give me time. I am trying to build a house and put some tiles on the roof but the house is not built properly yet. One of my problems is keeping so many champions happy. I know that and I have talked to them all about it.'

Birch met Madrid officials and Makelele's agents after the draw. Makelele would become Chelsea's tenth star signing of the summer in the biggest spending spree in football history, at just over £110m. Makelele said, 'Real do not want me to leave and I would not go if I considered it a backwards step for my career. But Chelsea are a very big club and it is flattering to know a club that wants to become the biggest in the world wants you to help out with that. I had some great times at Real Madrid but now we must see what happens. I am still fiercely ambitious and I want to carry on winning things for many years yet.'

Makelele was persuaded to join after Abramovich spoke directly to him and he was convinced that they 'really wanted me'. He added, 'A breach opened up between me and Real and, when I spoke to Mr Abramovich, I really got the impression that here were people who really wanted me. That was the difference and that is what convinced me at all costs I had to move to Chelsea. I hope I can bring the experience I've just had with Real Madrid, in the Champions League, the Inter-Continental Cup and the Super Cup. If I can bring all this experience I've had to Chelsea, it will make the Manager happy, it will make me happy and that's what I'm aiming for.'

As usual, Madrid were saying little about the possible deal, a sure sign that something was afoot. 'I have no news regarding the matter,' Emilio Butragueno, the club's Technical Director, said. 'That is the only thing I can say.' Florentino Pérez, the Madrid President, said, 'Claude is a Real Madrid player unless a club buys out his contract, which would cost an enormous amount of money. He remains our player and retains our friendship.' Bates was trying to be funny as well as elusive when he remarked, 'Who does he play for? I've only ever heard of his brother, Ukelele.' Deal done, then?

Pérez cheekily offered to reduce the £16.6m fee if Chelsea would also take Steve McManaman, the former Liverpool midfield player, off their hands on a free transfer. With McManaman and his £3m-a-year wages gone, Madrid could afford a £15m offer for Roberto Ayala, the Valencia central defender. However, Chelsea were not enamoured by the suggestion, so the former England player was free eventually to be reunited with fellow Scouser Robbie Foiwler at Manchester City.

Makelele missed Madrid's 3-0 victory against Real Mallorca because of 'illness' but, afterwards, trained with his team-mates. Ranieri said little. 'All I am focused on is our game against Blackburn Rovers on Saturday,' he said. Makelele, though, was always on Ranieri's hit list. 'It is not a piece of paper that I have,' Ranieri said, 'it is in my mind, my head. I say that we will go in this direction or go in that direction. It is important to get players who will link with our other players. When they are on the pitch together, we will see.'

Ranieri finally disclosed that the deal would beat the summer transfer deadline which had been extended from Sunday night to 5.00pm on Monday. Ranieri said, 'We're talking to Makelele and you'll know everything in two days. Wait until then.'

Tottenham goalkeeper Neil Sullivan's transfer was virtually finalised. 'Sullivan is also very close,' he said. Ranieri needed the £500,000, 33-year-old Scot as cover for his first-choice keeper Carlo Cudicini. Summer signing Jurgen Macho has a serious knee injury, leaving Marco Ambrosio as the only other senior keeper.

Eriksson was due at the Bridge for the first time since the infamous meeting with Abramovich for the match with Blackburn. FA Chairman Geoff Thompson said, 'I think Sven explained the situation about that meeting. I believe him and trust him. Sven has a contract, and that means he will honour his commitment to England. We have three Euro qualification games to go and we are all concentrating on those. I'm very pleased with the job Sven is doing.'

Duff was up against his old club so soon after his big move he could hardly take in the players who signed up after him. He said, 'It's unbelievable. At times you have to laugh about it all. We've got so many amazing players, it's frightening, and you don't know who's going to turn up next. We could probably put out two different teams. At Blackburn, we had a squad of about 16 or 17 but here there must be 24 or 25 people capable of playing in the first team. I've no regrets about my moving here. It was a big decision for me because I had a great time at Rovers. But I love it here.'

Souness was not entirely convinced of the validity of the media speculation about one of Abramovich's acquaintances, banker Alexander Mamut, who failed to buy a club in his own country, turning his attention to Rovers. In any case, Souness hinted that such a Chelsea-style takeover would not be welcome. He said, 'Every manager would like more money to spend, but we have a solid set-up club thanks to Jack Walker. I don't believe anybody here would be happy to hand over power, thank you very much.'

Chelsea 2-2 Blackburn

Abramovich once again received the appreciation of his adoring public as he took his seat ten minutes before the start. Crespo made his first appearance as a late substitute, but Blackburn spoiled his welcome party with a deserved point. It spelt the end of Chelsea's 100 per cent start.

The strains of 'Kalinka', Chelsea's new Russian anthem, were still fading when Blackburn stunned the crowd by taking the lead. Blackburn shocked their high-profile hosts after 19 seconds, lifted by the occasion as all Chelsea's opponents will be. Chelsea kicked off, Veron gave their third pass away cheaply, Jansen harassed Desailly, who kept the ball from crossing the line, then slipped to allow Jansen a free cross for Cole to volley home from 12 yards into the left-hand corner of Cudicini's net.

The travelling fans couldn't resist the obvious taunt of 'What a waste of money ...'

Chelsea had not beaten Blackburn at home since 1988, but their bench reflected their new prosperity, with Crespo, Joe Cole, Gallas and Petit among the substitutes, so it seemed this was as good a time as any to end the sequence. The full team against Blackburn was: Cudicini, Johnson, Terry, Desailly, Bridge (Cole), Veron, Lampard, Geremi, Duff (Petit), Mutu (Crespo) and Hasselbaink.

After a quarter of an hour, Ranieri switched Duff from the right to his preferred left flank with encouraging results.

Mutu slid the ball in the net after 29 minutes but his celebrations were curtailed by a contentious offside decision. Mutu was not offside when he turned in Geremi's right-wing cross, but Hasselbaink had been earlier in the build-up. The timing of the flag, however, suggested that the referee's assistant was penalising the final touch.

Mutu, who scored on his début, struck again in first-half stoppage time. Veron swept a ball forward to Hasselbaink, who laid it off to Lampard, and his through-pass sent Mutu racing through the middle, past the statuesque Amoruso. In rounding Friedel, the Romanian seemed to have taken the ball too far out to the right, but he met the challenge like a natural finisher, scoring from a testing angle.

No Makelele to parade at half-time, but at least there was the new keeper Sullivan, who managed to inspire only lukewarm applause.

Ranieri made a baffling substitution at half-time, sending on Petit, who is hardly a match-winner these days, in place of Duff, who can be. In the consequent reshuffle, Geremi found himself switched to the left. Tinkering again.

Petit, bloodied, claimed Flitcroft had elbowed him in the face. Ranieri volubly supported his contention in animated conversation with the fourth official, Paul Durkin, and when Souness joined in, there was a tense situation before sense prevailed.

'Everybody knows Flitcroft,' Ranieri explained. 'He did the same to Sinclair of Manchester City on Monday. Petit was very angry.'

A ghastly gaffe by Cudicini presented Cole with his second, and Blackburn were ahead again in the 58th minute. Thompson's effort was denied by a great save from Cudicini, who tipped over his 25-yard free-kick for a corner which was never cleared. The busy Thompson fastened on to possession again and crossed from the left, and Cudicini's ineffective flap at the ball left Cole to stab in his second from four yards.

Again, Blackburn were unable to hold on to their lead. Within five minutes, Geremi's cross was handled at close-range by Neill and Hasselbaink made short work of the penalty, dispatched low inside Friedel's left-hand post in the 63rd minute to gain a hard-earned point.

Mutu gave way to Crespo, in black and white boots, and Cole managed another brief cameo.

'In 20 years, we have not beaten them at home in the League,' mused Ranieri. 'Why is this? It is always difficult against our bogey team, Middlesbrough ... sorry, Blackburn. Slowly, slowly, everybody played for the team, but we must learn to kill the opponent.'

Lampard admitted, 'We gave away a couple of terrible goals which we wouldn't normally concede but showed a lot of character to twice come back. The Manager likes to change things and was searching for a formation to win the game. Sometimes it works for us but this time it didn't quite come off.

'Manchester United have built up their championship-winning side over a number of years. The pressure is on us to build it in a couple of months.'

Cole, a five-time title winner with Manchester United, said, 'I don't think Chelsea can win the League this season. It's too much of a tall order with so many new players against two such quality teams as Arsenal and Manchester United. I think they will have more games like this, where they drop points they don't expect to.

'Opposing teams will raise their game when they play Chelsea because they've spent a few bob. Everyone wants to beat the big boys and they'll have to learn to deal with that as United, Arsenal and Liverpool have done over the years.'

Ranieri concluded, 'We are still working to make a group,' but Souness didn't subscibe to the view that top-class stars needed to settle in. He explained, 'If you're a proper player you don't need any time to settle in, you can play – end of story. Chelsea have bought some of the best in the world and at Christmas, if it's not happening, Mr Abramovich will spend again. To win the league you've got to have good players and Chelsea have. The league is not beyond them this year.'

Cudincini was realistic. 'We've got a lot of work to do. You can see the team is not playing fluently. We've got great champions in the team but the Manager needs time to work with them. We haven't gelled completely yet.'

Makelele passed up a place alongside Beckham, Zidane and Figo in Real Madrid's all-star midfield to complete the £110m spree. But Lampard is adamant the £16.6m star will not be taking his place. 'I'm here to fight because I want to play week in, week out, and it doesn't bother me who the Manager signs.' Lampard is the only member of last season's midfield to have survived despite the arrival of Veron, Duff, Geremi, Cole and Smertin.

Makelele poses the greatest threat. Lampard added, 'Where does this signing leave me? Hopefully, still in the midfield. I played 50 games last year and I want to do that again. I'm not planning to go back on the bench at this stage of my career and I won't let that happen. If there comes a time when I don't play, I'll train hard, fight and I'll get back in the team. There is a lot of competition now but I can play on either side of the pitch either as a defensive or attacking player. My all-round game has really come on over the last year and I've got more confidence about my own ability. I've got a good relationship with the fans and the Manager and want to keep playing.'

Geremi's impending three-match ban spared Ranieri any immediate decisions. Geremi started in the middle, moved to the right wing, the left wing and then left-back. Solid everywhere. But it was Lampard's superb first-time pass which opened up Blackburn's defence for Mutu to score.

There was a last-minute hitch. Makelele's agent claimed the transfer was 'very unlikely' even though the clubs and the player agreed terms in a $24m (£16.6million) transfer deal. Real refused to give him his slice of the transfer fee. And with the Spanish deadline at midnight on Friday, Roger feared the deal could fall through. 'It is very unlikely that this situation will be cleared, it is very, very difficult,' Roger told Spanish radio station Marca. Roger criticised the Primera Liga champions for being disrespectful to Mekelele, and insists his client is owed 15 per cent of the agreed fee, $3.5m (£2.1million). 'Real Madrid does not want to pay the percentage that every player has for every transfer. The player feels that he is being disrespected,' said Roger.

Real's Sporting Director Jorge Valdano insisted the deal would be finalised when Real received the necessary guarantees from Chelsea's bank. 'All is agreed. Some guarantees have to arrive by noon on Monday at the latest, but otherwise the contracts have been signed,' Valdano told the French newspaper *L'Equipe*.

Makelele finally became a Chelsea player after backing down over demands. Valdano said on Spanish radio, 'The fax is going now, with Makelele's signature on it; Chelsea have accepted all of the conditions.'

Valdano insisted Madrid were not prepared to allow him to rake in £2.4m on top of £70,000-a-week wages at Chelsea.

Makelele was in London after holding talks with Chelsea and has undergone a medical. He made no secret of his desire to leave Madrid. He said, 'My work there was not properly valued. I gave my all but I was ignored when I asked for my contract to be revised. My stance had nothing to do with jealousy and envy, I only asked for what I was due.

'I know I am wanted at Chelsea and a player would go to China to enjoy that feeling. I came to Chelsea because my time at Real Madrid had come to an end and this is an ambitious club. The timing was perfect.

'Some say I'm going to be the Roy Keane or the Patrick Vieira of Chelsea but comparisons don't worry me. I've known Patrick for a long time and know how to get the better of him. I would also remind the Irishman that the Real team I was in defeated Manchester United in the Champions League. Chelsea have a more balanced team than Arsenal and United, especially in midfield.'

He also felt Chelsea can be superior to Real Madrid as he trebled his wages with a four-year, £40,000-a-week deal.

He insisted, 'I didn't just opt for this project because of the money. I reckon Chelsea may dominate European football in the coming years. I have already enjoyed that experience in Spain and it would be marvellous to repeat it here. The squad Chelsea have put together is one of the best in the world, nobody can doubt that. They are in the hunt for everything in England and in Europe. Football is a squad game now and it is important to have competition for places. It can only help the club progress and I am going to fight for my place like everybody else.

'I am used to that as I had to do it at Real Madrid. I just hope that I can bring something to Chelsea to make the directors and supporters happy. My first job is to try and get into the team. I hope to bring my experience from playing in the Champions League to help them.'

Privately, the power-brokers at the Bridge concede they paid over the odds for Makelele, and as he once trained as an accountant he can be excused his belief that he came at a reasonable price. Add the £8m the 30-year-old pockets from a four-year contract and it is clear Makelele is not coming cheap. Yet the Congo-born ball-winner, who moved to France from Kinshasa aged four, said, 'I run and I battle and I would love to see the day when contracts are signed on distance covered ... that would make me into a multi-millionnaire! I am one of the best midfield players in the world because I have mental strength and good technical qualities. Moving to the Bernabeu gave me complete confidence in myself. If you get there, it's because you are a great player. That might sound pretentious but getting to Real through my qualities alone and not because of my trophies or reputation did me enormous good.

'I have missed the train at international level. My generation won the 1998 World Cup and Euro 2000, but I was not part of those teams. I got lost along the way and by the time I turned up, the train had gone. Thinking how I should have been a part of those successes has left a great pain in my heart.'

Makelele never scored in 93 Spanish League appearances for Real, and netted just one goal in 38 Champions League ties.

'That's it. No more. We've finished,' declared Birch, who only tied up the Makelele deal 30 minutes before the Spanish transfer deadline, much to the consternation of his former team-mates in Madrid. French team-mate Zinedine Zidane moaned, 'Claude allowed me the freedom to play further forward where I can do more damage. It would have been ideal if we had kept him because now I will have to change the job I do for the team. Without Claude, we would be a much weaker side, unable to function in the way Real Madrid expect and want us to.'

Defender Ivan Helguera, who may be moved back to midfield to cover Makelele's absence, argued, 'Claude was indispensable. The club can try and replace him but they won't find anyone as good for us as he was. When Makelele didn't play in important games last year, we definitely missed him.' He was credited with forming the solid base that allowed Real to play their free-flowing, attacking football.

Crespo hailed Makelele's arrival at the club. He said, 'I have seen Claude on TV and know what a great player he is.' Turning his attention to his own personal ambitions, Crespo added, 'The thing that has been missing most from my career is a league title. I did win one in Argentina but in Italy I never had the opportunity. I had a chance to win at European level, but not in Serie A. I want to put that right and try again at Chelsea. It means a lot to me, more than scoring goals. In Italy, I scored a lot of goals and I hope I can score at Chelsea. The most important thing for me now is to win the Premiership.'

Desailly said, 'I'm in a bit of shock when I hear people saying we're going to win the League. That makes me scared because there is too much confidence. There's a lot of belief and a lot of hope, but let's wait and see. We've seen Chelsea winning against Liverpool, Leicester and get to the Chamions League. It means we're focused this year and something beautiful is starting. There's a lot of belief and hope.'

The feeling of optimism was running through the dressing room as Hasselbaink would love to add to his solitary Portuguese Cup-winner's medal. 'It's not that we can win something, it's that we have to win something.' As for the fear of losing his place, he put it succinctly. 'I know every time I play I have to produce. I have to give my best, that's the challenge. Buying Adrian and Hernan is fantastic for the club and for the fans, but it is for me as well. It will make the club better. We will play better and will have more options. I can live with that. I just have to produce.'

Sir Bobby Robson, the 70-year-old Manager of Newcastle United, commented, 'This is my 53rd season in football. I'd never seen a club sign nine big purchases in one go.' The nearest comparison, he said, was Sunderland back in the '50s, when it was nicknamed the 'Bank of England' club. Robson, known as someone who likes to spend, has been remarkably quiet, with just the arrival of Lee Bowyer on a free transfer. His inactivity is typical.

The transfer window opened with a bang with the sale of David Beckham to Real Madrid for a fee that could rise to £25m. But of the other 34 deals registered that day – including the Football League and in Scotland – only one other involved cash being declared. That fee was just £100,000. In all, 308 deals took place in July 2003, quite a high volume of activity, although that included 120 free transfers, 17 loan deals and a very large number of players who were out of contract. The total amount of money changing hands was £101.365m with the vast bulk of that, of course, involving Chelsea and Manchester United.

The pattern was repeated in August, when 265 deals were registered in the English and Scottish leagues. The proportion of loans rose to 75 per cent and declared free transfers to 83, but because of the same two clubs, the amount changing hands was £89.065m.

Virtually all the money spent in the transfer window has been by six clubs, of whom only one really registers at all: Chelsea, with an outlay of just over £110m. The others are Manchester United (£26m), Blackburn (£13m), Tottenham (£12m), Liverpool (£8.5m) and Birmingham (£8m). Chelsea's spending spree accounted for more than half of the money spent on transfers across Europe in the summer.

Makelele brought an end to the biggest summer spending spree in history, taking the club's expenditure on players since the takeover by Abramovich on 1 July to £111.25m. How Ranieri will fit all of his star signings into one team and keep them all happy will be an extraordinary balancing act.

20

SIGNING OFF CHELSEA'S FUTURE ... AND ANOTHER SIGNING ON

CLAUDE MAKELELE'S £16.6M MOVE from Real Madrid hours ahead of the closure of the transfer window brought Roman Abramovich's spending to £111.25m on ten star recruits in 62 days – £1.79m a day. World football, let alone the English game, has never seen anything like it.

The purchase of Makelele, an impressive piece of the jigsaw, attracted worldwide attention. Over valued, most definitely, but a key signing as Arsene Wenger observed, 'Makelele's signing shows Chelsea are now on a different planet. Real Madrid didn't want to sell but Chelsea can buy when they want and that makes them a world force. None of us can compete financially with Chelsea at this moment.'

Makelele was relieved his transfer had finally been completed. 'I am happy to be at Chelsea, it's a relief for me. The saga between Real Madrid and Chelsea was long but turned out well and I've ended up at a big club. My goal is to be physically ready as soon as possible. I will not have much time to adapt because of the price that was paid for me. Real Madrid is in the past, now my life is with Chelsea. I knew that if I left Real Madrid it would be for a club outside Spain. I have thought about playing in England for a while as it is a competitive league with good teams.'

Makelele believes Madrid's decision not to pay him 15 per cent of the fee was perhaps precipitated by the club's lavish spending. 'Real acted strangely with me,' said Makelele. 'I was astonished by Real because, if they're capable of cutting that back, it's because they really have got money problems. But if they needed money, they might have told me beforehand – I would have let them keep my commission. I was upset and surprised, as I believed that I'd behaved impeccably throughout the last three years.'

Madrid discarded ten players in the summer of 2003, including the captain Fernando Hierro, and recruited only David Beckham. 'Several players have left the club precipitately,' Makelele added in the French sports newspaper *L'Equipe*. 'That can't just be the players' fault. The truth will out one day.'

Certainly, the truth of Chelsea's audacious bids began to emerge. Franco Sensi, the Roma President, announced that he had rejected a bid of £24.6m for Emerson.

'Roman Abramovich offered me 40 million euros and I said "no",' Sensi said. 'I told the player that I would never have sold him and I have assured him that we will extend his contract – he will get what he deserves.' Chelsea also tried to buy Edgar Davids, Juventus's Dutch international, before they settled on Makelele.

Didier Deschamps, now Coach at Monaco, concurred. 'To have a winning side you must always have a balance. Of course, you need players with fantasy and flair but you also require ones with strong spirit and a willingness to work for the team. Makelele is just that sort of player.'

Veron, Crespo, Mutu, Geremi and Duff are all potentially brilliant signings, but Makelele is the steel Ranieri needs to make Chelsea serious contenders. Makelele says, 'Chelsea can be superior to Real Madrid in this campaign – we can be a better team than them. Chelsea will play more as a unit. Madrid base their team around certain players. Everybody is talking about Chelsea. Real Madrid is no different to anyone. There's lots of interest.

As the window closed, it was not the end of the spending, only a halt to it until the window reopens in January 2004 and Abramovich and his team of advisers assess the progress and how far the team have progressed in the Champions League and where they are in the title race.

Although, of course, that's not exactly true. We are talking about the new Chelski, after all. And despite the closing of the transfer window, another extraordinary signing was made, which will have massive implications for the club and its performance off the pitch, as well as on it.

Pini Zahavi was behind yet another coup with the appointment of Peter Kenyon as Chief Executive, poaching a member of Manchester United's Board with the style and panache of signing a star player. In fact, he could turn out to be more important a signing, I was told.

Abramovich's brief was, 'Find the best man there is,' and Zahavi turned to someone who three times in his three-year tenure as Ferguson's immediate boss had signed cheques that broke the British transfer record.

Just 24 hours after the Abramovich takeover, in Les Ambassadeurs, the upmarket Park Lane casino-restaurant, Kenyon was deep in conversation with Zahavi. That was not unusual, as Zahavi and Kenyon had completed many transfers together and were attempting to secure Ronaldinho's services for Manchester United. The then Manchester United Chief Executive made a quick exit when spotted by a couple of city journalists he knew. Normally, he wouldn't be so jumpy. Les Ambassedeurs, ironically, was the venue for the first meeting between Zahavi, Barnett and Birch when the discussion moved from shifting players out of the Bridge to the precarious finances and the need for a new investor.

Was this the moment that Zahavi made the first mention to Kenyon that he would recommend him to Abramovich? That scenario would certainly fit in with the amazing events that had transpired at the Bridge almost on a daily basis. To fulfil Abramovich's long-term strategy to develop Chelsea into a worldwide brand, Zahavi told him there was no one better than 'my friend Peter'.

Seven weeks and £111m worth of signings later, Kenyon called an unscheduled meeting in London with Sir Roy Gardner, Chairman of United's Plc, to tell him he was resigning to go to Chelsea. At about the same time, two of Abramovich's right-hand men, financier Eugene Tenenbaum and lawyer Bruce Buck, called in Birch to tell him they were hiring Kenyon but they still wanted him to stay.

United's directors, as well as Ferguson, were unaware of Kenyon's proposed move; Bates and Birch were also kept in the dark as talks were conducted in the kind of secrecy that were a hallmark of Kenyon's bid to bring the England Coach to old Trafford. 'Within football circles, it was more unexpected than any of the Russian billionaire's dressing-room signings,' was an observation in *The Times*.

Birch, the Chief Executive who had skilfully guided the club through a turbulent 18 months, was left to find himself another post, and might be regretting not pushing for the Chief Executive position at the FA when it was vacant, prior to the appointment of Palios. Bates had heard the whispers that Birch would have been considered at Soho Square but made it known he would not countenance an approach.

Birch performed an efficient job supervising the purchases of players for Abramovich, but his expertise is taking care of companies in financial difficulties. This has meant that he was crucial to Chelsea's strategic thinking since his appointment by Bates, but there has been financial stability since the takeover.

Birch was 'devastated', and although he was asked to stay at the club in a senior role, he knew that with his responsibilities severely reduced, his job was untenable. Birch's departure was cushioned by a £2.9m pay-off, far more generous by Abramovich than he needed to be as the severance settlement was written into his contract at £2.25m. But Abramovich was determined to show his recognition and appreciation for Birch's efforts in working so hard in his role acquiring so many players in such a short space of time.

Birch, who was in the Liverpool squad for their European Cup Final triumph over FC Brugge in 1978, spent the first eight months at Chelsea with his wife and three children based in the hotel at the stadium. Now he was on the move again.

Kenyon was a United employee for six years who became a fan when he was taken to the 1968 European Cup final as a 13-year-old. Kenyon trained as an accountant after attending the local grammar school and gained a reputation for turning around troubled companies. In 1986, he joined Umbro International, the loss-making sports retailer, and helped to sell it to an American group before joining United in 1997 where he became football's highest-paid administrator. He joined as Deputy Chief Executive at Old Trafford before succeeding Martin Edwards as Chief Executive three years later. Since then, Kenyon has secured Nike as sponsor, bringing in £303m over 13 years, and has been instrumental in numerous other deals with the likes of Vodafone, netting the club more than £100m a year, and a ground-breaking agreement with the New York Yankees.

Kenyon's record on major transfers is less convincing. He failed to convince Ronaldinho to join, drew criticism over Beckham's transfer and suffered accusations that United paid over the odds for Veron and Rio Ferdinand. One of the few clubs with no debt, United have turned in an operating profit of £14m–£19m in each of the past four years. In that time, they have won three Premiership titles, the FA Cup once and the European Cup once.

After Edwards's lucrative decision to float United as a public company, Kenyon has turned the club into the world's biggest football brand, with an estimated 53 million fans. Kenyon recognised the needed to expand Old Trafford, which now has 15,000 more seats than the next largest stadium in the country, bringing in £1.5m per match. He earned £625,000 in 2002, including bonuses, and he doubled his salary to join Abramovich in his quest for global domination, in an effort to eclipse both Manchester United and Real Madrid. Walking out on United was simply an offer that he could not refuse, as well as a new challenge.

Kenyon encouraged United's development as a global brand and made Sir Alex one of the best-paid managers in the world. When Ferguson was intent on retiring, he offered the job to Eriksson. Kenyon's move heightened speculation that the England Head Coach will follow him to Chelsea, particularly given that Zahavi, the powerful fixer who famously took Eriksson to tea at Abramovich's London home, has also been instrumental in recruiting Kenyon.

Yet, ironically, when Abramovich launched his remarkable takeover, Kenyon questioned whether all the investment could guarantee success. 'We are not worried,' he said from a United perspective. 'Why should we be? Having money is not necessarily a route to automatic success. In some ways, a "buy everything" policy can create problems.'

Kenyon's departure from Old Trafford was felt by Ferguson, who could always rely on Kenyon for support, and it was Kenyon who orchestrated the £28.1m purchase of Veron and the £30m transfer of Rio Ferdinand. Again, Zahavi was instrumental in both transactions. However, relations between the two are believed to have become a little strained this summer over the collapse of the Ronaldinho deal. Yet, his resignation is said to have left Sir Alex 'intensely disappointed'.

Kenyon's decision was strongly criticised by Oliver Houston, a spokesman for Shareholders United, an influential lobby group, who accused him of turning his back on the club for money. 'Whenever it came to fans having a pop at the Plc, Peter Kenyon would always come out with speeches about being a United fan,' Houston said. 'He is going to Chelsea, one of our major rivals. We can only speculate on the remuneration package which would be needed to take him from one of the world's biggest clubs to one with very little international reach and profile. He has always made great play of his loyalty to the club and his alleged dyed-in-the-wool support for United. How sad that his loyalty appears to have been so easily bought.'

Manchester United's Board held an emergency meeting to discuss the defection. Kenyon's solicitors issued a statement saying that he had accepted 'the job of Chief Executive Officer of the Chelsea group of companies ... the new opportunity represents a challenge that Mr Kenyon feels is right to take at this stage in his career.'

United moved swiftly to replace Kenyon, announcing they were installing their Group Managing Director David Gill in his place 'with immediate effect'. Gill remarked that Kenyon's departure had been 'like a bolt from the blue'. Maybe that should have been, literally, a bolt from the Blues!

Gill wished Kenyon good luck in his new job but warned him against trying to 'poach' key personnel from United, such as Peter Draper, the highly regarded Marketing Director. 'I know there are concerns about Peter returning to allegedly poach people,' Gill said. 'All we can do is make sure we recognise them. Besides, Peter is precluded from his contract against deliberate poaching, but, knowing the man as I do, there will be a lot of that.'

Gill was also dismissive of suggestions of a shift of power, pointing out that Kenyon may find it difficult to repeat the commercial success he enjoyed with United. 'Peter is an able businessman and he will have ideas to take Chelsea forward,' Gill said. 'But we have 54 million fans around the globe, 11 million in the UK, and these fans are with us from cradle to grave. With all due respect to Chelsea, they won't change. Some are fickle and some youngsters might choose Chelsea if they are much, much more successful, but the majority are here for life.

'I am sure Peter will do a very good job at Chelsea. I am sure they will be competitive on and off the field but we have so many strengths they can't replicate.'

Gill believes he can succeed in his first aim which is to build a good working relationship with Ferguson. He said, 'I know Alex and we have worked together over the years, but it would be wrong to say I have had the close working relationship with him that Peter had. That is something we will work on. He will get to know my style and I will get to know his and we'll work closely together. We are very pleased to have Alex as Manager and we want it to continue. It is early days regarding the Manager's contract. All I will say, as Peter had said and he was speaking on behalf of the Board, we are positive about it and we won't get into a situation like last time. That will move ahead soon.'

The fall-out at the Bridge was immense. The question of Bates's future arose again, but he said defiantly, 'Am I staying as Chairman? There have been no discussions to the contrary.' Yet it was obvious that Bates and Kenyon would be tough as a working relationship. After all, asked at a Manchester United shareholders' meeting recently about Chelsea's new owner, Kenyon laughed off Banks' concerns that Abramovich wasn't a fit person to own the club. 'They're ironic comments when you consider the case of Ken Bates...' Little wonder Bates was suspicious of Kenyon's appointment and role.

Birch, who had been summoned by Board members Tenenbaum and Buck to learn of his fate, seemed undecided whether to accept a lesser role or take up his compensation package. He met up with his close friend, FA Chief Executive Mark Palios, at Old Trafford for the England international as several players phoned him to say they were 'gutted', notably Terry. Duff's agent also called, as Birch was instrumental in convincing the club's record signing about London's qualities.

Birch has recently moved his young family from Liverpool into a house in the capital, and two of his children started new schools before he was dumped. Sympathy abounded for Birch, although an insider disclosed that he was acting 'irrationally' in the days immediately after the Abramovich takeover and some of his inflammatory remarks did not go down too well. And although he settled down to work efficiently and speedily in the amazing recruitment drive for new players, the decision on his future had long since been taken, as it was decided instantly to find his replacement. Certainly the approach was made well in advance of the rift that developed between Zahavi and Bates over the agent's claim for commission in bringing in Abramovich.

Kenyon was hired on a three-year £1.5m-a-year plus bonuses and incentives package worth £7.5m plus, to include a one-off £2m 'golden hello', more than most 'signing on' fees agreed by the world's top footballers, but I can reveal that £500,000 was to compensate Kenyon for giving up benefits worth £500,000 that included highly lucrative share options at Old Trafford worth £222,262, plus £150,000 bonuses for even more profits for Manchester United. No commission was sought by Zahavi as he is a close friend of both Kenyon and Abramovich and was delighted to bring the two together. His motives were not to bring revenge on Birch because of the commission feud with Bates.

Kenyon spent some time on gardening leave while lawyers sorted out when he could join Chelsea. In the meantime, one of Kenyon's appointees Paul Smith moved in at the Bridge.

At Chelsea, Kenyon will be moving from a Plc with shareholders to satisfy to a newly formed private company under Abramovich, where it is clear that more money will be available than at Old Trafford. 'They have brought him in to try to surpass United as part of the "new Chelsea",' said former Chief Executive Colin Hutchinson. 'He is a very good businessman. If you look globally at their financial situation –compared to Real, who have assembled a superb squad but also piled up a load of debt – they are on a sound footing. And he will be a big loss to United. What he has done commercially has made them streets ahead in England as far as resources are concerned. It is a shock and is out of the blue, concerning the rivalry down the years between United and Chelsea.

'I think the interesting thing is, Chelsea, in recent times, has got its soul back and it is back to a football club. There has been a feeling among supporters over the last couple of years that perhaps the priority was not football and there was a distraction from the Plc. I think obviously Peter will be involved throughout, but it won't make that much difference on a day-to-day basis to Claudio Ranieri. The football side has got its own structures.' Hutchinson's reference to the club 'getting its soul back' had Bates spitting blood at his one-time close confidant and chief executive whom he blames for the over-generous player wages and inflated transfer fees.

Peter Ridsdale, the former Leeds United Chairman, said, 'Peter spent a lot of money when he bought Rio Ferdinand from me at Leeds so he is obviously used to writing big cheques and that is what probably attracted Roman Abramovich.'

His tendency to refer to fans as customers raised hackles among traditional United followers. He also incurred the wrath of fans when he said that the number of professional clubs should be reduced from 92 to 40. His comments were labelled arrogant and patronising. But Kenyon is a powerful figure in football politics, leading opinion at the G-14, the collective of Europe's biggest clubs. His experience at this level of football will be useful to Chelsea, who have ambitions to become an international force. His task may be to turn the club into as big a household name in Asia and the United States as United are now.

United's shares have been rising on the back of renewed takeover speculation, but the club is worth £423m, compared with the £1bn it was valued at three years ago. Furthermore, the club remains vulnerable to predators because its shares are spread widely and Kenyon's decision to leave may spark unrest among investors, particularly JP McManus and John Magnier, the biggest individual shareholders. The rumour was that Kenyon found himself caught in the row between Magnier and Ferguson, when they fell out over the ownership of the racehorse Rock of Gibraltar, a matter which could still lead to litigation. Magnier is a shareholder of Manchester United with around 4.5 per cent of the equity and immediately prior to his departure, Kenyon was Magnier's guest of at the York races. But the rumours were quickly denied.

First Veron, then Kenyon ... who next from Old Trafford? Perhaps Sir Alex as Manager rather than Sven?

The alternative to Kenyon might have been David Dein, the Arsenal vice-chairman, with rumours of a board room split involving Dein and managing director Keith Edleman. Maybe Dein, with Arsene Wenger in tow, would be of interest to Abramovich. Soundings were taken through the usual intermediaries but Dein tells me the possibility was a non-starter. Yet, how intriguing would it have been if Deis had turned up at the Bridge, to be 'welcomed' by his old foe Bates, instead of Kenyon?

Didier Deschamps at Monaco was quick to emphasise the global interest the events at Chelsea has stimulated. 'Everybody is talking about Chelsea and the players at Madrid are no different. They were talking about the number of great signings Chelsea have made and how interesting it is. Everyone is talking about the ambition of this club.'

Eric Cantona dubbed Deschamps the 'water carrier', but having captained his country to the World Cup, Deschamps added, 'Chelsea are now a very strong team with a lot of experience; they have a great chance to qualify for the quarter-finals of the Champions League and, if they get to the last eight, they will be capable of making it all the way to the final. Everybody in Europe is now taking Chelsea very seriously. Chelsea have not had a really big name but now, everywhere you go, when people are talking about football they are talking about what is happening at Chelsea. It's incredible.

'If they can win the Champions League then it will be perfect. I hope they do because I once wore the Chelsea shirt. They can because the club has now got only international players in every position. It would be hard for them to have a better squad than the one they have at the moment. If they can all gel then the club have fantastic opportunities. Claudio Ranieri is a good coach and it is always better to work with players from the top level. But what is impressive is that he hasn't just gone and signed glamour players. He has shown, by going for a player like Makelele, that he knows what is required for a winning team. I look at the names now – Desailly, Veron, Crespo, Hasselbaink and now Makelele – phew! These players have big experience of European football and if you can afford to leave Mutu and Petit on the bench, or even consider selling him to fit other players in, you can say that is a really strong team. Yes, it is a challenge to fit the team into the right shape, and keep everyone happy, but when you have so many choices, that is a dream for any coach.'

Patrick Vieira fears Chelsea are capable of doing great things this season. He said, 'It is very good for Makelele. They are one of the contenders for the title, we will see on the pitch. If Makelele settles in well, then they they are a team capable of winning the title.

'Chelsea are one of the favourites of the League, at least on paper. They have signed several top-notch players like Juan Sebastian Veron, Hernan Crespo and Claude Makelele and they look like one of the big sides in Europe. But so far, it's just on paper. They will have a big problem keeping everyone happy. They have got great players with strong characters, and they will want to play all the time. But the Premiership won't just be about Manchester United, Arsenal and Chelsea. Liverpool and Newcastle will have a say as well, despite the poor starts they have made. Teams also need to go to places like Leicester and win – those are the sorts of games where titles are won and lost.

'I am not worried by Manchester United and Chelsea making all those signings. The club's bosses have instead opted for stability in giving contract extensions to Titi (Henry), Robert and myself. We have got some good people at the club – just look at our bench with Dennis Bergkamp and Kanu.'

Henry adds, 'They are contenders, but like any other side. I couldn't care less about the recruitment they made. It's not my problem.'

And as for the choice of Chelsea's 'champion' signings, Ranieri insists Abramovich never doubted his judgement. The Italian said, 'Last June, if a genie had come out of a bottle and told me what would happen at Chelsea in the next few months, I would not have believed him. Never in a million years. At the time, I was mainly concerned with finding a way to keep Gianfranco Zola at Stamford Bridge and worrying about how to strengthen the squad for the Champions League with little money available. The last thing I imagined is that someone like Mr Abramovich would materialise out of thin air. And when he arrived and invested so heavily in the team, I quickly realised I was in a unique position. Very few managers have been in this situation, with an owner who can and will buy them just about any player they request. Arrigo Sacchi at AC Milan in the late 1980s was one, and Vicente Del Bosque at Real Madrid over the past few seasons was another. Plus, of course, Sven-Goran Eriksson at Lazio in the late 1990s. He was able to go out and get whomever he desired.

'Mr Abramovich asked me questions about certain players. I would reply that if I could get this particular player, he would be especially useful to the team because he could do this or that or something extra besides. For example, I explained to Mr Abramovich we needed a new striker with a particular set of characteristics, as we didn't have that type of striker before. He is interested in this type of thing and seemed very happy with my explanations. He never once tried to change my mind about any of the players we have brought in. Never. The only thing he wanted to know above all was whether I was convinced in my own mind that this would be the right man to buy. He would say, "Are you sure?" and I would say, "Yes." And that was it.

'I believe he is genuinely happy to have given me the players I wanted. But he will be even happier if we win something. I believe he has fallen in love with football and now he wants to know everything about it. He has asked me questions that show he is already very competent in his knowledge. So it would be wrong to suggest I am teaching and he is learning, because it isn't like that. Our conversations are just natural exchanges.

'I was always able to concentrate on the football. Once I decided who we needed to buy, it was over to the club to try to get him. I was never involved in the financial negotiations and I must thank Chelsea for the truly professional way they went about their business. When you consider that all the new Chelsea players have already found homes, you start to understand just how quickly and efficiently the club has been working. It is important for players to feel peace of mind in their private lives, even if we in football are all citizens of the world and used to moving around. Yet I don't feel any relief that the transfer window has closed. It won't change my routine because I have been coaching out on the training ground through all of this.

'Admittedly, there won't be any more calls from cousins in Italy telling me who I'm supposed to have signed from over there. Otherwise, though, it will be the same and I'll still be concentrating on trying to win just like the players.'

The hard work is keeping everyone happy, as Sir Alex pointed out. 'It's going to take great deal of management to keep everyone happy. At the moment, it's exciting for everyone down there, but as the season goes on, I wonder how it's going to work out. They have a lot of quality and a big squad, it must be around 27 players, which is far above all the rest of us, and it's important if you get injuries. But sometimes when you have all those players, and half a dozen are not getting a game very week, when it comes to the point when you need them, maybe they will have missed out not playing regular football.'

Ranieri asserts, 'Sacchi, Del Bosque and Eriksson already had successful teams at their disposal. It was just a question of adding to the squad, which they did little by little, integrating the newcomers into the existing framework. In my case, I have effectively to create a whole new team. Or rather, I have to merge two teams – my starting eleven from last season and this summer's new arrivals, 12, 13 players who could form a competitive team on their own.'

How do you do that? 'I have a plan. Everyone knows we have a big squad with two alternatives for each position and, in some cases, three. When you have so many players, at some point you must decide. You either have a hierarchy, a first-choice eleven and a group of squad players able to back them up and come in when needed, or you continually rotate your squad. After all, with two domestic cups, the Champions League and a long Premiership campaign, there are plenty of matches.

'Most successful clubs go for the first option. Real Madrid, for example, had many superstars, but there was very much a first eleven and a second eleven. This was made possible by the fact that those who weren't part of the first eleven were intelligent enough to accept their role. This is crucial because I really believe that you win championships with 22 players, not 11. The men on the bench are often just as vital to the success of the club.

'At Chelsea, I am under no illusions – we won't be able to have a hierarchy right away. Right now, it's a learning process. I'm learning how certain players work together; they are learning how to fit into this team. At some point, perhaps by the middle of the season, we will have a clearer picture and some players will find themselves playing fewer matches. That is inevitable. But it doesn't take away from the fact that the squad as a whole will have to work together and that those who are left out will be just as important.

'I like to tell my players, "I make the team, you make the group." In other words, I decide who starts, but they have to create a strong, united group which includes those who don't play regularly. I accept that not everyone will be able to handle this. There are so many great players, so many internationals here, that it may well be that someone decides that they suffer too much when they are left out. And if it happens and they tell me they want to go elsewhere so that they can play regularly, I'll deal with it accordingly.'

The arrival of Makelele puts extra pressure on Lampard, but Ranieri says of the £11m signing from West Ham, 'I signed him to replace Gus Poyet, to be that goal-scoring midfield player. He has the innate ability to time his runs into the box perfectly, a rare quality he shares with players such as Paul Scholes and Michael Ballack. But he's also a fighter, a man who will run for 90 minutes. In fact, sometimes I need to tell him to slow down. As a footballer, you must learn to budget your energy to ensure that you are still fresh late in the game. Of course, being an Italian manager, I'm also going to be concerned with the defensive side of things and I will confess there are times when I worry when he comes forward. But Lampard is continually improving in that department and, with his tremendous work ethic, I'm sure he will do well.'

When Abramovich swept out of Chukotka and into Chelsea, the repercussions have shaken rival Boardrooms across Europe. Whether Abramovich's spectacular move into English football will act as a template for others is the topic that now rustles the game's grapevine and even its corridors of power. There are other Russian billionaires interested in buying Manchester United, but the diversity of the share ownership makes it rather more complex, and one of the reasons Abramovich didn't pursue it. Spurs, the original target, West Ham and Portsmouth are more realistic targets.

Mel Goldberg, a sports lawyer who attempted to pull off a deal with Bates with some South American investors, insists, 'It will happen but it's not going to take five minutes. Abramovich at Chelsea was exceptional. Life doesn't usually work like that.'

Whoever might be thinking of upstaging Arbamovich and taking over Manchester United won't find it as easy or the fans as accommodating and grateful. United Shareholders spokesman Oliver Houston is unequivocal. 'Whether the bid came from Florence Nightingale, Alex Ferguson or a Russian oligarch, we would not be in favour of a takeover. We gave Rupert Murdoch a bloody nose, and we're stronger and wiser now.'

Goldberg knows there are far easier targets than Manchester Untied, as he added, 'It has not been hard to find sellers. Lots of clubs have approached me.' Pulling off a deal has proved much harder. Apart from Manchester United and Chelsea, the rest have proved not to be so attractive. That's why Abramovich's purchase has been all the more spectacular.'

Surprising, too, because the City had lost faith in football club shares, the banks were no longer so accommodating, and chairmen and directors worried over the potential diminishing returns from television rights. In fact, the game was generally in recession, tightening its belt, contemplating controls on spiralling players' salaries after English clubs splashed out £4bn on transfers and wages from 1996–2002. Although the Premier League has consolidated its position as the wealthiest in the world, the 2001/02 season was the end of an era in football according to the annual review of football finance published by consultants Deloitte and Touche. Clubs spent £407m on transfers in that season – Premier League clubs accounting for £323m.

Despite the recession, Abramovich could see that the Premier League continues to pull away from its rivals in Italy, Spain, Germany and France in terms of global interest as well as finances. Total revenue was up 21 per cent to £1.132bn – more than France and Germany put together – and even more encouraging is the fact that English top-flight clubs are not so reliant on broadcast money as leagues in Italy, Spain and France because they raise more from sponsorship, licensing and merchandising, and that balance means they will be able to keep attracting top-quality players. England's total income rose by 21 per cent, comfortably the largest of any of the other leagues. In the last two year's, the Premier League has clearly moved into a 'league of its own'. A Premier League spokesman said, 'The review has crowned the Premier League the financial champions of Europe. The increase in revenue, profits, attendances and investment in stadium facilities is good news for the game. The decrease in transfer activity shows an increased level of financial prudence, while many clubs, the report suggests, are developing wage structures which can adjust to the prospect of relegation ensuring greater stability.'

So, while there was the usual pessimism, notably after the collapse of ITV Digital which left the Nationwide League adrift more than ever before, there was still room for optimism at the highest level.

The review shows that Manchester United and Arsenal were the biggest spenders on wages in 2001/02, forking out £69.9m and £61.4m respectively. United also topped the table in transfer spending in the six seasons up to 2002 with £99m. Leeds were next (£91m) and then Chelsea (£84m), Liverpool (£81m) and Tottenham (£53m). Arsenal's net spending on transfers was £24m, less than Manchester City's (£32m).

Abramovich's spending spree ensured that Chelsea took over a the biggest wage bill in English football, but there were contingency plans to increase revenues to enhance further his vision of creating one of Europe's élite, such as rebuilding the Shed End stand to give it an extra 10,000 seats. At the moment, the club's Village Hotel is attached to the back of the stand which holds just 6,000.

Bates poured cold water on such a development scheme when he said, 'We would have to knock down the hotel, all the resturants and the apartments. It would take three years to complete. The other problem is our safety certificate depends on how many people we can evacuate in an emergency and we are only 300 below our limit. I don't know how the other 10,000 will get out.'

Director Richard Creitzman said, 'Stamford Bridge is one of the best grounds in Europe, it is fantastic. But it's not the biggest at the moment. If we can increase the capacity then we will. The problem is the access out to the Fulham Road. There is a rail track down one side of the ground, houses on the other side and housing at the back. So while other grounds have exits and access all around, we don't, we only have the Fulham Road. At the moment, there is just the main entrance, a side entrance and a little alleyway and, if something happens, you have got to get 40,000 people out, just like that. That's the problem. But if we can find extra points, we will probably do it.'

Chelsea make an average £42 a seat which brings in £1.76m per game. They estimate that with Premiership games and success in European and domestic cup competitions, they stand to make an extra £15m a season from an additional 10,000 seats. In contrast, the hotel complex doesn't break even and has become more of a hindrance than a profit-making project. 'Manchester United have more seats but I know we make more money per seat than they do,' added Creitzman. 'It's the add-ons like catering, the food and the beverages. It was one of the reasons we chose Chelsea and why we would be eager to expand the capacity if it's possible.'

Abramovich extended his stake to 93 per cent buying out the club's other major stakeholders, Ruth Harding and BSkyB, and then took Chelsea Village private after buying most of the remaining shares. After a seven-year flirtation with the stock market, Chelsea was under the control of one man. On the day of delisting from the AIM, shares closed at 35 ½ p, a 57 per cent discount on the 1996 flotation price of 55p. Abramovich offered all the shareholders who sold to him a 'limited edition commemorative share certificate' which included facsimile signatures of the players and coaching staff, as well as returning existing certificates once the deal was completed. It was a way of enticing the final 12,000 small shareholders to sell up. There was little point in holding on to a handful of shares, as the club would no longer pay a dividend and it would be virtually impossible to sell any shares retained. While the transition from stock exchange to private ownership was ongoing, Chelsea said the probe by the FSA would have no impact on the timetable of its share offer, which closed on 26 August 2003.

Spurs became the first club in Britain to join the London stock market in the 1980s. Soccer shares have performed poorly on the stock exchange in recent years as clubs, under pressure from soaring player wages, have struggled to be profitable. Manchester United is the only English club that regularly makes a profit. Last year, 14 of the Premiership's 20 clubs were public companies trading their shares on the stock market. This year the number is down to 10.

What other pursuits for Abramovich? He has been taking polo lessons, according to the specialist polo press. His mansion in West Sussex, which has its own stables, used to belong to the Australian polo enthusiast and media mogul Kerry Packer.

It was also rumoured that he would expand his investments into Formula One after he attended the European Grand Prix at the Nürburgring as a guest of Bernie Ecclestone, the Formula One commercial rights holder, and his willingness to get involved in the sport was unexpectedly brought to the public attention by Sven-Goran Eriksson. 'It was a big surprise to me when he bought Chelsea,' said the England Manager. 'What I knew was that he was going into football and maybe Formula One.'

Abramovich visited the Minardi pit at Nürburgring, where his son was photographed sitting in one of the cars. 'He popped into the garage and posed for some photographs,' an eye-witness said.

Aussie Paul Stoddart said, 'We need someone who can put proper funding into the team. Minardi may be at the back of the grid at the moment but the only thing which has ever stopped us progressing is the lack of cash. I met Abramovich at the European Grand Prix and found him a charming person. He spent a lot of time in our garage and we arranged for his young son to sit in the cockpit of our car while mechanics did a practise pit-stop. We spoke about F1 and he appeared to have a real interest in the sport.'

Ecclestone dismissed the idea when he said, 'Roman will not be a team-owner in Formula One in 2004, or the foreseeable future. He likes football too much. We speak all the time, he is a nice guy and full of enthusiasm for what he is doing. But the truth is he has decided Formula One is not for him. I've become a Chelsea supporter, though.'

Abramovich continues to stockpile money and lots of it, so he must be looking at ways of reinvesting it. Sibneft makes its money by regularly purchasing smaller crude oil traders operating through Russian tax havens, aiming to lower its tax burden and boost profits. In October 2003, the company merged with bigger rival Yukos to become Russia's largest and the world's fourth-biggest private oil producer, with a market capitalisation of $36bn and daily oil output of just over 2 million barrels. The next stage in the merger will occur when a new board of directors is elected, with Eugene Shvidler as chairman, and the holding company is renamed as YukosSibneft. At some stage, the merged company will make an offer to buy out Sibneft minority shareholders who still own eight per cent of the company.

BP has been linked to Abramovich as part of the tie-up between the UK oil giant and Russia's TNK. BP said it was spending $1.35bn (£856m) to enlarge its previously announced deal with TNK to include a 50 per cent stake in Slavneft. Slavneft is a joint venture between TNK and Sibneft, the energy group which is majority-owned by Abramovich. Abramovich, or another Sibneft representative, is unlikely to sit on the Board of TNK-BP, the result of the blockbuster merger which has had to clear a raft of regulatory hurdles in Russia. BP said in a statement it was not including in the deal its interests in Sakhalin, an island off the Siberian coast near Japan, 'for the moment'.

TNK-BP will be Russia's third-largest oil and gas company, employing about 113,000 people and producing about 1.2m barrels a day from its main fields in West Siberia and the Volga Urals. It will be based in the British Virgin Islands.

In 2005, Chelsea Football Club celebrates its centenary. By then it will be one of Europe's élite. As Hernan Crespo put it at his unveiling, 'Here there is everything to win. The prestige will come. The history can be written. This is the challenge that I put upon myself.' Crespo said the £100m-plus spending spree had 'surprised the world', never mind Serie A.

Already the targets for the future are being lined up. Abramovich hasn't given up on Henry, Vieira, Owen or Gerrard, while Rooney remains firmly on the wanted list.

Owen and Gerrard both have two years left on their contracts; talks are planned for new deals but the England pair have made it plain that without the chance of Champions League football they would have to review their futures.

Gerrard dropped a strong hint that he could leave if his home town club don't show any prospects of finishing in the top four this season to provide him with coveted Champions League football to sharpen his game for England. He explained, 'I'm happy to stay here – for the time being. But I want to get back into the Champions League and play Champions League football. That's where I feel my career belongs. I've had a good taste of it for two years at Liverpool and I want more of that. So I need me and the boys to get us back in it. That's the main thing for me personally, and the club. Next season I don't want to be playing in the UEFA Cup.'

The Reds missed out on a Champions League berth when they lost to Chelsea on the final day of last season. Gerrard added, 'I've supported Liverpool all my life and I'll be driving myself over the coming months to ensure we get back in. As far as my contract goes, things haven't moved further forward. In fact, talks haven't started yet.'

At the end of this campaign, Gerrard will have only one year left on his current deal – and Liverpool will not let him leave on a Bosman free. It might prove difficult for Houllier to resist Abramovich's billions. Gerrard says he is still committed to the club and that 'the title is still the main aim. But the Premiership is a very tough league to win and if we fall short, the target becomes the Champions League.'

Owen left the door wide open. 'This is all hypothetical because I am under contract with Liverpool and I am happy with that situation. But if another club came in for me and agreed a fee with Liverpool, I would have talks with them first. The first thing I would discuss would not be the money. That has never been, or ever will be, a motivation for me. I'd need to know straight from the start whether I would be first choice on a regular basis. If I wasn't given that assurance, I would not be interested. Playing first-team football every week will always be my priority. There are players who would be happy to sit out most of the season as long as they ended up with a medal at the end of it. Personally, I would rather end my career with over 500 games under my belt, and if I am going to be greedy, I want a sackful of medals as well.'

Owen had been intrigued by the players Abramovich had acquired so quickly and, on the eve of the opening-day clash at Anfield, he said, 'The situation at Chelsea intrigues me, like it does the rest of the football world, because they have spent so much money so quickly. Clubs like Liverpool, Arsenal and Manchester United have invested just as heavily over the years but Chelsea have done it all in a few months. It is fascinating what has happened there because hardly a day goes by without them singing some top player or being linked with another one. Their own fans are going to be very excited by the season ahead and I guess a lot of neutrals will be as well. I think they have bought well, a good blend of top-quality foreigners like Juan Sebastian Veron and outstanding English players such as Glen Johnson, Wayne Bridge and Joe Cole.

'But my only doubt is where they are going to fit them all in and how they will keep everyone happy. That's why I would need to seek assurances about my first-team place before joining a club like Chelsea because there are so many good players challenging for the same spot in the team.'

Chelsea have already made some 'preliminary enquiries' about £19m Swedish star Zlatan Ibrahimovic at Ajax. Lyon offered £10m while Roma beat that by £2m. But Ajax have now indicated they are only willing to sell for £19m. Ibrahimovic, 21, has a reputation for pulling off outrageous stunts and saying exactly what he thinks about players. When playing for home town club Malmo, he drove into a red-light district pretending to be a cop. He 'arrested' a middle-aged man and took him back to his car for 'questioning' before allowing him to go. On another occasion, he took a massive pop at Norwegian beanpole striker John Carew, who plays in Spain for Valencia.

Pouring scorn on Carew's ability, Ibrahimovic insisted, 'What he does with a football, I do with an orange!'

Ajax defender Christian Chivu is another potential transfer target; so too is Real Madrid's full back Michel Salgado, the 27-year-old Spaniard who is out of contract next summer and who could leave on a 'free' in January. Croatia star Ivica Olic, who impressed during the 3-1 defeat to England in the friendly at Portman Road, claims a deal has already been agreed. The striker, 23, is Russia's highest-earning player after completing a £6m transfer from Dinamo Zagreb to CSKA Moscow. But Olic has set his sights on Chelsea. He said, 'There were various attractions for joining CSKA – they were in the Champions League and are challenging for the domestic title. And I'll be honest and say there were other reasons. I have every hope that Mr Abramovich will organise my transfer to Chelsea next year.' Abramovich – who owns a stake in the Russian League leaders – wanted to take over CSKA before buying Chelsea.

Although linked with Lazio's central defender, the Serb Dejan Stankovic, the number-one player still in their sights is Brazil's captain Emerson, irrespective of all the midfield stars that have already arrived. Stankovic was linked as an Eriksson recommendation, but to emphasise Ranieri was calling the shots, it was Emerson who topped the January 'wanted' lists.

Whatever it costs – £200m, £300m, £400m – on new players, Abramovich will spend it – albeit within reason and intelligently – to build a team to secure Chelsea's place as the supreme club in the Premiership and Europe.

21

EPILOGUE

MORE HAS been packed into the first season under the Russian Regime at Stamford Bridge than most clubs can expect to experience in their entire histories. Chelsea reached the semi-finals of the Champions League for the first time and finished higher in the league than for any time since they won the championship in 1955. If it wasn't for the Invisibles of Arsenal, who also broke records going through an entire Premiership season unbeaten, Claudio Ranieri would have amassed sufficient points to have won the title in most other seasons. Sir Alex Ferguson and Arsene Wenger both declared Chelsea's season a success, but it wasn't good enough for new chief executive Peter Kenyon who said that finishing without a trophy was a failure.

Changes have been sweeping, the transfer funds virtually unlimited and the transfer speculation staggering. This has been an historic season in every possible way, with Chelsea totally transformed from 'potential' champions to realistic contenders. Now Roman Abramovich wants the silverware as well, and to that end he has recruited new coach Jose Mourinho, after his Champions League triumph and, of course, after Sven Goran Eriksson's infamous U-turn to remain at Soho Square.

On reflection, Chelsea enjoyed an exhilarating European campaign. They had their first win over Arsenal in 17 attempts, and none sweeter than in the Champions League quarter-finals itself. They finished above Manchester United in the Premiership, with a larger points haul than even the 1955 championship side. Chelsea are now part of English football's elite alongside Arsenal and Manchester United, and clearly one of the powerhouses of European football.

For all his endearing qualities, his quaint use of English and the tears in finally beating Arsenal, it was the end for Claudio. For all the hype surrounding the torturous axing of Ranieri, the glaring errors by The Tinkerman in Monte Carlo vindicated the decisions of the Abramovich inner circle to dispense with the Italian coach. With increased gate receipts and match day income, the Champions League cash flowed, £19.8m for Chelsea compared to £19.4m for Arsenal and £19.15m for Manchester United. Ranieri concludes: 'The owner Mr Abramovich did not ask me to win a trophy for him but I was one hour away from getting the chance to do exactly that. I can hold my head high because myself and this special group of players have done a very good job for Chelsea. My way is to try to improve every year. This season we have done that so next season there must be improvement again.'

In four years, Ranieri has failed to deliver any silverware, but he says: 'I think second place in the Premiership and the Champions League semi-final is a fair return for the investment made in players. If you had said we'd achieve that at the beginning of the season, then everybody at Stamford Bridge would have been happy.'

Eriksson, the man courted as his replacement, praised the Italian for his club's performance and the way he has handled all the speculation over his future. The England coach said: 'It has been a difficult season but I must say he has done a great job. Second in the league and reaching the semis in the Champions League – it has been a great season. But I think he is used to this [speculation]. He is Italian and every day in Italy there are rumours. I think he is handling it very well.'

Even Sir Alex Ferguson conceded it was a successful season as he also put up a staunch defence of Ranieri. 'The man has shown great integrity and nerve and he has made his team play. I believe they have had a successful season. I felt for them the other night against Monaco because they could easily have been 4-0 up at half-time.'

Kenyon thanked the players and staff for their efforts but did not praise the manager. 'I'm on record on this and you should look at what John Terry